The Upper End of In Between

DIANN SHOPE

The Upper End of In Between
Copyright 2015 by Diann Shope

All rights reserved. Published in the United States of America. No part of this book may be used or reproduced in any manner whatsoever without written permission except in the case of brief quotations embodied in critical articles and reviews.

This is a work of fiction. Names, characters, businesses, places, events and incidents are either the products of the author's imagination or used in a fictitious manner. Any resemblance to actual persons, living or dead, or actual events is purely coincidental.

For information contact
diannshope@gmail.com

ISBN 978-0-9968988-1-2

Fiction–Older People, Fiction–Retired women.
Fiction–Widows, Fiction–Seattle,
Fiction–Love and Aging.

DEDICATION

This novel is dedicated to Jerry Hanna,
without whose inspiration and encouragement
I would not have begun writing.

Table of Contents

Acknowledgments vi
Chapter 1 Este Dia 1
Chapter 2 Some Enchanted Evening 35
Chapter 3 Only Connect 71
Chapter 4 A Better Version 103
Chapter 5 Unpacking 141
Chapter 6 Commencement 183
Chapter 7 Soccer Dad 219
Chapter 8 Winning and Losing 237
Chapter 9 The Borders of Reality 279
More Susannah Stories 297
About the Author 298

Acknowledgments

I'm sitting at my PC at 5:00AM, watching the rising sun turn the wispy clouds pink and trying to think how to thank all the individuals who helped me create this novel – there were so many who participated and I can't mention all the names for fear of leaving someone out.

Over the years my meditation group members have listened to stories I've written and several of them read this manuscript and gave me valuable input. More important has been their encouragement and enthusiasm. Thank you, all.

Among my very special friends and neighbors are English majors and teachers, writers, voracious readers, and people with specialized expertise who have shared their knowledge and time to help me with my writing. I've been in critique groups and writing classes whose members' and teachers' comments have been very valuable.

Thanks to Michael Kischner, author of "Sonnet 10," which was quoted at Susannah's birthday party. I have used those beautiful lines for toasts at so many weddings.

My editor, Elizabeth Johnson, has been a great help. She is highly competent, professional, tactful, and very supportive. And she has a great sense of humor.

The cover design is by Bob Lanphear, whose work I have admired for years. www.lanpheardesign.com/work/books

There are a million websites and blogs for authors, but I only read two on a regular basis. I have learned an enormous amount from Jane Friedman's newsletters and website: www.janefriedman.com. She is a goldmine of information on writing and publishing. And Dan Blank is great on the marketing end–his head's in the right place: www.wegrowmedia.com

Finally, my family has been cheering me on for several years. Special thanks to my husband Ed for his comments, proofreading and loving encouragement.

With gratitude to all of you,

Diann

CHAPTER ONE

Este Dia

Susannah Emory sat in her breakfast nook, finishing her morning cup of green tea and appreciating her kitchen. Though the decor was a little dated, it was uncluttered, homey, the epitome of cooking functionality. No one was leaving hand towels and dirty knives on the countertop or littering the island with three-day-old junk mail. Did that compensate for eating alone most of the time and sleeping alone all the time?

She gathered up her keys, grocery list, and cloth bags and locked the door behind her, pausing to see if the stairs were frosty, and to soak up the special quality of Seattle's autumn sunlight that always made her euphoric. Something about the way the sunlight slanted in at this time of year made everything brilliant, turning her favorite maples a glowing pinky-orange and reviving the excitement of going back to school each fall—new things to learn, new experiences and challenges, new people, all of life ahead. As she drove to the grocery store, she thought about her rapid swing from glum to euphoric, an instance of what she called Seattle bipolar syndrome. It was gray so much of the time that when the sun came out people acted differently—they wore shorts in December and talked about the weather to total strangers in the grocery line or at the bus stop.

At Central Co-Op, she parked her Prius among three others, confirming her opinion that Seattle was the Prius capital of the world. Inside the trendy grocery store, she worked her way through the supplements and the organic, mostly local produce, pausing before a twenty-foot-by-seven-foot display of chips. "Only in America. This is ridiculous!" she said under her breath, and, grinning to herself, she selected her favorite—non-GMO organic multigrain high-fiber baked chips with olives, on sale today.

Just ahead a tall, lean man with Teva sandals and socks, jeans, a faded blue chamois shirt, and a bad case of helmet hair was gazing at a bewildering array of chocolate bars.

Mr. Teva's cart was blocking the aisle. "Excuse me," she said.

"Oh, sorry." He moved his cart out of the way. She wheeled past and parked her cart next to his. "Do you think the world needs this many kinds of chocolate bars?" he mused.

She scanned the shelves for her favorite. "Probably no more than it needs forty-seven kinds of chips."

"There's a bar for every kind of animal—look," he said, pointing. "Turtles, cheetahs, leopards, pandas, rhinos, bears, frogs, bats—on and on."

"No baboons," she noted. "What kind of a chocolate bar would have a baboon on the wrapper?"

"Seventy-two percent cacao, with leaves and sun-dried grubs."

They both laughed.

"I think I'll stick with my cranberry-and-almond wolf," she said, putting a chocolate bar in her cart and heading around the corner and down the next aisle.

Fifteen minutes later she was unloading her full cart onto the checkout counter when Mr. Teva stopped his cart behind her. Besides his bike helmet, he had three items in it: a dark-chocolate-and-hazelnut rhino, a bottle of pinot gris, and a salmon fillet.

"Well, I see you've hit three of the major food groups," she said. "Protein, wine, and chocolate."

"Yes," he laughed, "I pay rigorous attention to my health. Look—more chocolate bars." He pointed to a nearby display.

"Have you ever been on the tour at the Theo chocolate factory? It's really interesting—and they give you samples."

"Well, I'll add that to my list of things to do. I haven't lived here very long."

She gave the cashier her co-op number. The pleasant tattooed-and-pierced young woman asked if she was Susannah, then started ringing things up.

"Got any other suggestions for things to do in Seattle?" Mr. Teva asked as he watched her finish bagging her groceries.

"If you like wine, the little neighborhood wine store a few blocks north of here has tastings every Sunday afternoon," she said. "Not to mention the usuals—Pike Place Market, the sculpture park, et cetera."

"Thanks for the ideas."

"You're welcome—have fun."

She thought about him as she loaded her groceries into the car. He was good-looking, and she liked his sense of humor.

On Sunday morning Susannah spent an hour filling the garden cart with weeds. She deadheaded the roses and dahlias, and made fresh bouquets for the living room and kitchen. Then she ate some lunch and spent a couple of hours on the sofa with the latest novel for her book club. She decided to get out and enjoy the last of the sunshine by walking up to the wine store for the tasting.

She put on her fleece and wound a scarf around her neck, then strolled past the big old houses and trees of the now-upscale neighborhood where she'd lived for more than two decades. *The neighborhood is like my house*, she thought. *It's beautiful, full of good memories, and yet so familiar—so boringly familiar. At least we paid off the mortgage, and my pension allows some travel now and then.*

The unassuming little wine store was definitely not upscale. It had a bland paint job and fluorescent lights, but the owners were friendly and knowledgeable and they had an excellent selection. She took a sample from the first bottle and joined a dozen or so people wandering around and looking at the little notes on the wine: "The best chardonnay you'll find for this price. Not too oaky." "This zin has lots of cherry overtones." "An astringent, minerally white for your raw oysters." How did they come up with these blurbs?

Discreetly disposing of the bland first sample, which she could only describe as "wimpy," she went on to a more agreeable wine that was 80 percent something and 20 percent something else, while listening to a young man talk about a wine region in Spain. Then she took a taste from a third bottle and meandered past the sparkling wines into the German whites.

"It's Susannah, isn't it?" someone said. "Are you stocking up on one of the food groups?"

She turned around to see Mr. Teva with a little paper cup of wine in his hand.

"Oh—hi! How did you know my name?"

"The cashier at the co-op mentioned it when you were checking out. I'm Peter." He stuck out his hand, she shook it, and they were formally introduced.

"So how do you like the wine?" he asked.

"I've had three of the five they're featuring. The first was rather insipid—or maybe it would be nicer to say 'subtle.' But I like the second and third. What do you think?"

"I'm only on insipid, but I'm ready to move on." She waited while he went back to the counter for a sample of the next variety. "Mmm, yes, this is better." He nodded his approval. "Wine is nice. I like it, but I *really* like beer."

"Well, here're some other items for your list of things to do in Seattle—the Belgian pub in the Fremont neighborhood, or the German pub just south of here, on Twelfth. They both have a huge selection, and the Belgian pub's right across the street from the chocolate factory."

He laughed. "Sounds irresistible—beer and chocolate!"

She bought a bottle of number two, and they went out

into the late afternoon sun. "Can I buy you a beer?" he asked. "Or have you had too much wine?"

Susannah was rather startled at this offer. "Uh, well, maybe . . . If you throw in a slice of pizza or some nachos or something, I could drink a beer without keeling over."

"It's a deal. Where shall we go?"

"The tav across the street is my favorite. They have good food and a good selection of beer."

"OK, across the street it is."

They settled into a booth with two beers and a plate of fried calamari between them. She learned that he had worked as an electrician, a financial analyst and a charter boat captain, among other things, and lived on a sailboat. She was a retired civil servant and had worked for several elected officials. While the ritual get-acquainted conversation progressed, an additional, inner conversation was occurring. She was asking herself how she came to be sitting in a tavern with a man she knew nothing about, except his name and that he liked beer. He could be an ax murderer! On the other hand, all she'd done was gather up enough courage to accept a guy's invitation for a beer—it's not like she was jumping in a car with him.

As they talked, he was fiddling with his coaster. She liked his hands, big and calloused, hands that made things and hauled sails around. He mentioned meditation as something on his bucket list. "What interests you about meditation?" she asked.

He pointed at her almost empty beer glass, and she shook her head. "Well, for one thing," he said, "I notice a lot of interest in spiritual things these days. It seems to have evolved a bit from the New Age stuff. Barnes and Noble is full of Thich Nhat Hanh and Deepak Chopra and Eckhart Tolle, et cetera. And you read about meditation being used in therapy and prisons, even training soldiers. Seems to be quite the thing. And of course it's been around for eons, so there must be something to it."

"It's interesting to see it as a cultural phenomenon," she said, "but I think most people won't really try it, or will give it up pretty quickly if they do."

"Why is that?" he asked, leaning back in the corner of the booth.

"Because of the misconceptions about what it is. That's my opinion, anyway. People think they're going to sit in lotus position and their thoughts will go away and they'll achieve bliss. It's not what happens during meditation that matters—it's how it changes your daily life."

"Has your life been changed by meditation?"

She nodded. "Mm-hmm. For example, I don't get angry as easily as I used to. I worry less. I'm less reactive. I can observe my emotions, rather than just getting caught up in them—sometimes." She laughed. "I've still got plenty of hang-ups to work on!"

"Yes, don't we all." He looked thoughtful.

"Hey, I've got to get going," she said, gathering up her purse and bottle of wine. She was amazed to find herself scribbling her phone number on a napkin and sliding it across the table. "Call me if you want some company while you're doing Seattle things. Thanks for the beer and the conversation."

He stood as she slipped out of the booth. "I've enjoyed it too." He waved his napkin. "Thanks!"

As she walked home, she wondered what she was doing giving a man in a tavern her phone number—at her age. But they had talked quite a while and he didn't say anything that set off alarms; he seemed normal. In fact, he was attractive, witty, and interesting—so why not give him her number? And if he didn't call, she'd had a nice afternoon—the most stimulating afternoon in a long time. She'd thought about the possibility of a relationship, but she didn't think the odds were very good. She wasn't unattractive, but she didn't think she could compete with the twenty-five- to forty-year-olds.

Back home again, Susannah checked her e-mail, finished writing up the minutes for her volunteer committees, and did some more weeding—a never-ending task. She wondered how long she could keep up with all the landscaping. She loved looking at it, but not so much taking care of it. It had been mostly Dave's thing.

She scrubbed the dirt from her nails, changed her clothes, and drove off for dinner at her friend Cathy's house—down from the top of Capitol Hill into Madison Valley, then up again to the Madrona ridge, where she enjoyed the view of the Cascade mountains and Lake Washington glittering to the east. Susannah and Cathy had met in their first class on their first day of college and had been friends ever since—through countless camping trips and holiday dinners, babies, teenagers, graduations, retirements, strokes, and cancer.

At dinner Susannah was telling Cathy and her husband, Max, about a book she was reading. "The author talks a lot about a 'second adulthood,' after you've had your career and raised your kids but you still have a couple of decades, if you're lucky, to do something meaningful. More and more of us are in that position, so what are we going to do with that time? You can only fix up your house and travel so much."

"You don't consider this an issue for yourself, do you?" Max said, his bald head shining in the light from the chandelier. "You certainly have meaningful things on your plate. Besides the grandkids and your meditation group, you've always got something going—lobbying for tax reform, or writing letters to the editor, or organizing seminars on the spiritual aspects of money, or whatever."

"I try to do my bit—some things I think are worthwhile. Maybe they help make the world a little better," Susannah said. "And I know how fortunate I am. I used to be so busy that I just did stuff but didn't necessarily enjoy it. It was just do this and on to the next thing. Now I'm not so busy, and

I try really hard to appreciate all the things I'm doing—rowing, dance classes, arts events, book club, and so on." She drew on the tablecloth with the end of her spoon. "I try to be more in the moment, notice more about what's happening, and not think so much about what comes next. But you know, a lifetime habit of living in the fast lane doesn't just go away. You really have to work at it, especially when everyone around you is going at warp speed."

They sat in the dining room, looking out at the garden bordered with clumps of yellow mums alternating with bronze, and the lace-leaf maple glowing scarlet in the last of the evening light. Empty plates and serving dishes cluttered the table. She covered her wineglass with her hand as Max moved to refill it. "No, thanks, Max. I'm trying to stay conscious about my eating and drinking. Last week at a dinner party, I overindulged and regretted it—awake at three a.m. feeling woozy, two extra pounds on the scale in the morning, wondering why I keep doing this. I've done it so many times, and I always chastise myself and ask why I eat too much and drink too much. But I never come up with an answer." She got up and began stacking dishes, her lips pursed.

"In all the years I've known you," Cathy said as they loaded the dishwasher, "you've been worrying about being overweight, and I've always thought you looked great. You still wear a size ten—isn't it time for you to just stop being neurotic about this?" She put on an expression of mock disapproval, swishing her fading-auburn ponytail from side to side. "I'm your oldest friend—I'm allowed to say stuff like this."

Susannah laughed. "Yes, you're allowed," she said. "And I've got the rest of my life to work on not being neurotic—isn't that what life's all about?"

When they'd finished up the dishes, Max put his arm around Susannah's shoulders. "You know, you sound a little lonely," he said. "You're busy and doing good things and all, but I think you need a man in your life. I hope I'm not overstepping the bounds of friendship . . ." He trailed off uncertainly.

"No, you're not," she said, sighing. "Having a man around would be nice, but I don't think it's likely I'll find the love of my life at my age."

"If anybody could, you could," Max replied. "You're a good-looking woman, fun, intelligent, and you're not *that* old. If I didn't have Cathy," he said, giving his wife a squeeze, "I'd be interested."

"You're such a sweetheart, Max. Thanks for the moral support." Susannah kissed them both as she left.

That night as she went through her bedtime routine—wash, brush, floss, cream—she inspected herself in the mirror. Blue-gray eyes, slightly wavy hair cut in an easy-care bob. She was glad it was a nice gray—she couldn't be bothered with coloring it, as so many women her age did. No doubt about it, more lines and age spots than a couple of years ago. Why would an attractive man like Peter want to spend time with a woman whose skin looked like hers when he could very easily be with a woman twenty years younger? He probably wouldn't. Am I old now? she wondered. *Not young anymore, certainly, but no, not old either. There's young and old and in-between, but where are the borders?* She placed herself at the upper end of in-between and turned out the light.

Susannah was rowing stroke in front of seven of the people in her midmorning rowing group. They were mostly over fifty, more than half of them women, and, with a few exceptions, had been at it long enough to row better than they were rowing today. She could hear some of the oars going into the water before hers did. "They're rushing," she told the coxswain, who should have noticed.

"Slow down, everyone," the cox said through the mike. You're rushing the stroke. Bow and three seat, you're coming in early."

Not only were they not rowing together, but the shell was continually leaning so far over to port that Susannah was having trouble getting her oar out of the water at the end of each stroke. She was annoyed but trying to be patient. There were so many things that had to be done correctly, and exactly together. It was a perfectionist's sport—some would say a control freak's sport. She asked the cox to tell the ports to pull their oars in higher and the starboards to pull in lower. When the cox did, the boat lurched to starboard and Susannah gritted her teeth. Why did she mind so much when they weren't rowing well? Why couldn't she just shrug off people's mistakes? She certainly made plenty of her own. They stopped for a break, and she was glad to be distracted from her grumpiness by the bright-yellow leaves floating on the deep-blue water.

When they were back on the dock at the end of practice, someone from another boat asked how her row had been. "Well, we had a pretty good workout," she said. And they had. She could feel the endorphins kicking in as she drove home along Lake Washington Boulevard, glancing out the window at the water ruffled by the breeze and the colorful trees glowing in the autumn sunshine. Mount Baker and Mount Rainier were both "out," as the locals liked to say when it was clear enough to see them, anchoring the Cascades to the north and south. Her pique about the bad rowing had evaporated, overcome by the beautiful setting and her love of the sport. She still got uptight when people were careless, and she was a bit strict when it was her turn to cox, but she wasn't as overbearing as she used to be. She was trying very hard to mellow. Why was that so hard?

....

He called the following day. "Hi, it's Peter. I'm ready to cross some more things off my Seattle to-do list. Are you interested?"

"Sounds like fun," she said, surprised, pleased, and

aware of a little twitch of something in her stomach. She looked at her calendar. "Thursday and Saturday are pretty clear. What would you like to do?" She tried to remember where she'd put her "Seattle for Guests" file.

"How about the sculpture park on Thursday? We're supposed to have sunshine."

"Great—shall I pick you up?" She knew he didn't drive.

"Sure, about one? I can show you the boat first." He gave her an address on the east side of Lake Union. "It's across from a little convenience store, slip twelve."

As she chopped vegetables for her stir-fry that evening, Susannah realized she had a date! She wondered what she should wear and thought that shoes comfy for a boat and walking around an art park would be good. Comfy shoes? She wasn't twentysomething anymore. And what was that twitch about? Nerves? Anxiety? She hadn't had a date in the three years since Dave died.

....

The next morning Susannah walked the ten blocks to her meditation room and sat for an hour with the other regulars. After their meditation, they talked about what was happening in their practice. Susannah noticed herself feeling mildly annoyed at the off-again, on-again presence of Sandy, who had been meditating with them for only a few months.

"I just can't sit still," Sandy said. "My back aches. I keep losing my mantra and thinking about stupid things, like what I should wear tomorrow and when I lost the spelling bee in the fourth grade—I misspelled 'separate'! Why can't my mind just be quiet?"

"A quiet mind isn't the goal of meditation," Roger, their meditation teacher, replied in his usual comforting manner. "It's nice when it happens, but most of the time it doesn't, so why get upset? Your mind is doing what minds do—it's having thoughts." As he talked, Roger was slowly running his wooden meditation beads through his fingers. "Just go back to following your breath or your mantra, and the thoughts will very likely go away."

He's only said this a thousand times, Susannah thought.

Sandy nodded and adjusted the shawl around her shoulders. "Yes, I know we've talked about this before, but it's so hard to do! I'd just like some peace and quiet, you know?" She crossed her legs, then uncrossed them and readjusted her shawl.

"Sure," he said kindly. "That's what we'd all like, but we don't get it by trying to make the thoughts go away. We watch the thoughts, don't get attached to them, and keep going back to breath or mantra when we do get attached. You have to be patient and compassionate with yourself. All of us in this room have spent a lifetime getting to be who we are now. If we want to change something about the way we are, it's going to take time, and some changes will take longer than others. As our awareness increases, we find things that we didn't even know about ourselves—and we may want to change them too."

Walking home through Volunteer Park, Susannah had mixed feelings. She was ashamed of her impatience with Sandy—after all, what was she meditating for if she couldn't be more patient? She remembered feeling the same things Sandy described, and how much her practice had evolved over the years. Roger was right about how long it takes to change. At the same time, she was aware of that familiar centeredness she usually felt after meditation, especially in a group. How could she be centered and impatient at the same time? Maybe it was a matter of levels. Perhaps you could be impatient on one level and centered underneath. She pondered this conundrum as she crunched through the dry leaves that carpeted the park's expansive emerald lawns, then finally set it aside and allowed her attention to be absorbed by the striking red and yellow of the stately hundred-year-old trees.

On Thursday afternoon Susannah stood in front of her full-length mirror, nervously inspecting her jeans and red sweater. She didn't really like the way the jeans fit. She changed to brown slacks and a brown sweater. Too boring.

She finally arrived at the marina in her favorite black cords, a lavender turtleneck, blue fleece, a scarf that tied it all together—and her comfy walking shoes. Peter had propped open the gate. He waved from the other end of the dock, where he was kneeling over a toolbox. She walked down to meet him.

"Wow, a home away from home! How big is she? Can you sail this by yourself?"

"She's forty-five feet, very cozy. And yes, I have sailed her alone for short trips when the weather wasn't too nasty."

"Permission to come aboard, Captain?"

"Permission granted," he said, standing at attention.

"Were you in the Navy?" she asked as he helped her over the gunwale and into the cockpit.

"Yup. But I doubt you were—where'd you learn the lingo?"

"My dad was in the Navy."

"Ah, that explains it. Would you like to go below?"

He showed her through the fore and aft cabins, replete with shiny brass and oiled teak. He explained the sophisticated navigational systems and showed her the solar panels and little wind turbine that generated electricity for battery storage. It was a handsome and meticulously maintained craft.

He even had a bookcase, constructed so the books would stay put when the boat was under way. She browsed, interested. Jung, Kübler-Ross, Buber, some of O'Brian's Aubrey-Maturin series, the three best of Forester's Hornblower series, the complete works of Elizabeth Bishop and Robert Frost, a slim volume of the *Rubáiyát*. "You've got quite a selection here," she remarked, pulling out Dr. Seuss's *Oh, The Places You'll Go!* "This is my favorite graduation present."

"My grandsons love it—I keep it here just for them. But I could bore you for hours with this boat," he said. "Let's go see the sculpture park before the sun goes down."

They stepped onto the dock, and Susannah walked aft. "*Este Dia*, San Francisco," she said, reading the boat's name on the transom. "Translation?"

"It means 'today.'"

"Today as in 'carpe diem,' or as in 'never put off until tomorrow what you can do today'?"

"'Carpe diem' is a little too Roman, I think. You know, conquering legions, seizing things. And the other one sounds a little too Calvinistic. My translation is more like 'You can't do anything about the past, and you can't control the future, so you'd better enjoy today.'"

"My sentiments exactly," she said as they walked to the car.

They drove down Broad Street toward the waterfront and found a spot in the sculpture park garage. The sun was glinting off the wake of a ferry in Elliott Bay, and the Olympic Mountains were visible in the distance.

"Will you look at that," Peter exclaimed as they walked down the path leading to Richard Serra's *Wake*. Five huge S-shaped curved steel forms appeared before them.

Susannah read aloud from a *Seattle Post-Intelligencer* article by Regina Hackett she'd saved: "'Five asymmetrical steel slabs advance in a staggered cluster into the valley of the Olympic Sculpture Park. . . . Moving between these sculptural slabs, each swelling as if it had an organic root, the viewer's consciousness of weight recedes, and the entire piece appears to float.' Sometimes I wonder what the art critics are talking about, but it's mind-blowing just to walk around between these huge plates of curving metal." Of all the sculptures they saw, this was their favorite.

....

As they walked back to the car, Peter invited her to dinner on the boat. "We'll have to stop at the store, though—or order a pizza."

"Have you discovered Bottleworks, at Forty-Fifth and Wallingford?" she asked as she backed her car out of the parking space and found the way to the exit.

"No, but I like the sound of it."

"Let's go check it out. There's a Belgian beer I want you to try—my favorite. On the way, you can decide if you want pizza or something else."

The parking gods were with them, and there was a space in front of the store.

"I've died and gone to heaven," Peter said in a reverent tone when they went in. "Good God, look at this selection—there must be hundreds of different brews here!"

The manager informed them that there were about a thousand different labels from all over the world. "Do you have any Rochefort 10?" Susannah asked as Peter wandered off to peruse the shelves and coolers.

"You're in luck," the manager said. "We've got some now, but we sometimes can't get it."

"Those Trappists," Susannah joked, "so undependable! I'd like two bottles, please—no, make it four, and I'll give two as gifts." At eight dollars per bottle, it made a nice gift.

Peter was filling a shopping cart, savoring all the possibilities. Thirty minutes later, the clerk rang up Peter's choices. "That's about a case," he said as he began loading the bottles into sturdy bags. "It'll be $126.73."

"I never thought I'd be so happy to spend a hundred twenty-six bucks on beer! I'll be back," Peter told the clerk.

Susannah had ordered salad and pizza while Peter was doing his beer shopping. The pizza was ready when they pulled into the Romio's parking lot, and Peter was back with it in a minute.

At the head of the dock, they unloaded everything onto a gear trolley, and Peter trundled off while Susannah found a parking spot.

Ten minutes later they faced each other over a Greek pizza, with feta, olives, and gyro meat, a green salad, two beers, and a stack of napkins.

"Oh, plates and forks." Peter sprang up to get them.

"Here's to beer and pizza," he said sitting down and clinking his bottle with hers. "Oh my God," he said after the first swallow. "What is this stuff? It's terrific!"

As they ate, she told him the story of her discovery of Rochefort 10 in a tiny restaurant in Stonehaven, Scotland. He shared a story about finding one of his all-time favorite beers in a pub in Prague—which led to talk of travel.

"I have a big trip in June," she told him. "A friend from Bainbridge Island and I are doing a French immersion class for two weeks, and then a cooking class near Avignon."

"That sounds pretty intense," he said, picking up another slice of pizza.

"Yes, it'll be challenging. I remember the very first time I traveled on my own—at age nineteen, I went to France for six months. What a mind-boggling experience! We lived with French families for the first month, and I thought if I got through that, I could get through anything life handed out! I felt so stupid, because I could hardly understand anything and I couldn't talk without a dictionary. Anyway, I'm nervous about going back, but I like all things French and I'm just going to screw up my courage and go for it!" She started her second slice of pizza. "How about you? Got any big travel plans?"

"I'll see what looks good after I work through my Seattle list," Peter replied. "Speaking of which, is Saturday still open for you? Taj Mahal is playing at Jazz Alley—there might still be a few tickets available. Or would you prefer *Madame Butterfly?*"

"My, you certainly have eclectic taste. But . . . hmm . . . Jazz Alley sounds good. There'll always be another *Madame Butterfly.*"

He beamed his approval.

"What do you do with yourself when you're not at SAM or wine tasting or sailing?" Susannah inquired.

"Sam" he questioned, eyebrows raised.

"Oh, sorry. The Seattle Art Museum."

"I'm just finishing up the wiring for a Habitat for Humanity project—that's been going on all summer. I go to the gym three times a week, stay in touch with friends and do things with them, and I've been exploring the area on my bike."

Susannah noticed the ship's clock behind him. "Oh! How'd it get so late? Much as I'm enjoying our conversation, it's time for me to go."

They walked down the dock to her car. "Thanks so much, Peter," she said. "I've really enjoyed the day."

"Me too," he said. "I'll call you tomorrow, about the time for Saturday night."

Driving home, Susannah was thinking about the amazing circumstance of having two dates in one week with a really interesting and attractive man. She'd always thought she'd be nervous if she started dating again. She *was*, but not as nervous as she thought. She wondered if she should invite Peter to the waltz ball that was coming up next week.

....

As Peter walked back to his sailboat, his cell phone rang.

"Hey!" he said. "How are you, honey?"

"We're all great, Dad. What's happening with you?"

"I went to the sculpture park this afternoon—amazing artwork!"

"Alone?"

"No, I went with this woman I met in the grocery store. You'd like her." He changed the subject, and they chatted about her sons' soccer team, their school play, and her tennis elbow. His daughter, Astri, was always after him to "find someone."

Peter went aboard, sat down with the last of a bottle of beer, and thought about Susannah. He congratulated himself on finding the right wine store, where he ran into her again; he marveled at her candor and that she didn't flirt with him. He enjoyed her wit—and liked the way her pants fit. The top of her head came about to his shoulders.

....

They arrived at Jazz Alley in plenty of time to get good seats in the balcony, just opposite the stage. Susannah watched Peter watch the arrival of a party of twenty-something women, with their long hair, low-cut tops, stiletto heels, and formfitting pants, chattering and laughing and enjoying the attention they were getting. "Pretty women, yes?" she teased.

"Pretty *young* women."

"Since when does a man have something against young women?" Susannah gibed. "It seems to me most men prefer younger women. Why is that, do you think?"

"My take on it is that a lot of older men are insecure and afraid of death, so they hook up with younger women to give themselves the illusion they aren't getting old. It's like, if they can make it with younger women, they're still young."

"You seem pretty definite about that—isn't that just a cliché?" Susannah said, surprised at his quick comeback.

"Well, clichés come from somewhere, and I have a fair number of friends and acquaintances who fit the bill."

She took a sip of her drink. "I think a certain amount of it's biological," she said. "In evolutionary terms, men needed to scatter their seed liberally for the race to continue, and young women offer the best chance of success. I know conditions are different now, but biology doesn't change as quickly as conditions. And what about the young women? Don't they marry older men because those men seem to offer more security?"

"Absolutely," he replied. "As an older guy, my experience with younger women is they want sex, or security, or both. So what I've seen many times in a couple with a big age difference is two insecure people each thinking the other is going to provide security. No wonder there're so many unhappy marriages!"

At that moment, Taj Mahal and his band made their way to the stage. Peter and Susannah sat back to enjoy the show.

"That was totally fantastic," Peter exclaimed as they moved slowly toward the exit with the crowd. "I'm really glad you wanted to come—I haven't enjoyed a show this much for years. But it gave me an appetite. Are you interested in something to eat?" he asked, slipping on his coat.

"Sure. Would you like IHOP or a burger or a chichi dessert or what? I'm up for anything."

"Lead me to the chichi dessert," he commanded, draping his arm around her shoulders.

They walked down Fifth, under the monorail and then over to Fourth to Dahlia Lounge, which was still hopping at ten thirty. As the hostess showed them to their table, Susannah noticed several women giving an appreciative glance at the striking man beside her in the turtleneck and black leather jacket.

"I have a possible addition to your Seattle to-do list," Susannah said as she took a bite of triple coconut cream pie.

"Shoot," he said, looking at her expectantly.

"I wondered if you might like to go to a ball, a waltz ball, next Saturday."

"Tell me about it. I've never been to a ball. Sounds very Jane Austen."

"Well, it's organized by the group that offers my dance lessons. They rent a big hall with a really good dance floor and hire an orchestra that specializes in playing for dancers, and everybody gets dressed up and . . . has a ball. Black tie is optional." She was pushing her glass around the table. "If it doesn't interest you, no problem. Just an idea."

He put his fork down, with one bite of chocolate stout cake left on his plate. "It sounds like it could be fun. But I have to say, it's a little intimidating going to a dance where everyone else has been taking lessons. Now if you'd offer me a brush-up course, maybe I'd be more comfortable." He leaned forward, elbows on the table.

"As a matter of fact, they offer a brush-up class every year before the ball," she replied, looking up at him. "It's this Thursday night from seven to nine at the Swedish Club. But I can't go, because I have a board meeting that night." She took a sip of water. "Maybe we should just bag this idea. It doesn't seem right to extend an invitation that requires the guest to do something besides just be the guest."

"No, the idea's growing on me. Let's do it. Give me the info on the class. I think I've got a suit down in the bilge somewhere. I accept your invitation."

He grinned at her and ate his last bite of cake.

....

Tuesday after her yoga class at the Y, Susannah went through her closet. She had a number of evening dresses, all several years old, though hardly worn. She decided to wear a black velvet gown for the ball. It was flattering and made her feel good—slinky, actually. She wondered if that word was even used anymore. The dress was formfitting and had a scoop neck, long sleeves, and a sarong-type skirt with a slit up one side.

There would be a dessert buffet at about nine thirty, but she decided she'd offer Peter a light supper, in case he was hungry after two or three hours of dancing. Something easy but filling. She made a mental menu.

As she went through the week, a busier one than usual, her thoughts kept returning to the dance. Would he have a good time? Would she have a good time? *Oh, stop it!* she told herself. *If we aren't having a good time, we'll leave and do something else.*

Then she thought, *Oh God, what if he wants to have sex?* In her mind's eye was a picture of her no-longer-flat belly and the spider veins on her legs. It was too uncomfortable to think about, so she told herself she'd cross that bridge in the unlikely event she ever got to it. Susannah had never slept with a man other than her husband. By and large, she approved of the much more open and relaxed attitude toward sex these days. But it wasn't how she'd grown up, so the prospect of fitting herself into these different mores was daunting.

They had arranged that she would pick him up at eight thirty. She figured that would get them there in time for two or three dances before the buffet. Then two or three dances after would be sufficient for appearances' sake if he'd had enough. And there was always the possibility he'd enjoy it and want to stay longer.

She had to admit it—she was getting excited. Dancing was her favorite pastime; with a good partner it could be a peak joy experience. She could also get dressed up, which she loved but rarely had the opportunity to do anymore. And, she confessed to herself, she looked forward to being physically close to Peter.

He was waiting for her under a huge golf umbrella when she arrived at his dock. "Sorry we're having such nasty weather for your first ball," Susannah said nervously.

"I don't care, as long as the ball is indoors," he said, smiling as he got into her car and fastened his seat belt. He didn't say anything about her fumbling with the controls for the rear wipers or her inattention when the red light turned green.

They found the designated parking garage on the University of Washington campus and made their way to the HUB Ballroom under Peter's big umbrella, which he checked while she sat down to put on her dancing shoes. When she had taken off her coat and checked it with her street shoes, she turned around to find him looking at her. "Very nice!" he said.

"Ta-da!" She curtsied, feeling silly. He looked very handsome in his dark suit, with his blue-and-silver tie complementing his gray eyes and hair.

Susannah took his arm and they started through the crowd toward the dance floor, where a fast waltz was in progress. "Hi, Peter," called a pretty blonde. "Remember, you promised me a dance."

"Hey, Peter, got that zigzag move down?" asked a bald guy in a powder-blue tux.

Peter gave an OK sign to both of them.

Susannah was puzzled. "How do you know all these people?" she asked as he nodded to a couple waltzing by.

"Oh, I met a lot of people at the workshop Thursday night. We bonded during cross-step waltz and pivots. We had a great time." The music stopped, and the dancers milled around, waiting to see what tempo would be played next. A slow waltz. "Shall we dance?" he asked.

Susannah thought she'd died and gone to heaven as they circled gracefully around the floor, turning right, then reversing into left-hand turns, dancing in place when people got bunched up. A little pressure on Peter's shoulder and he slowed to avoid bumping into someone.

"You told me you were a 'respectable' dancer—you're way better than respectable!" she said.

"Thanks. I'm glad you think so. I don't even feel like I'm leading, you're such a good follow," he said, smiling down at her.

The next dance was a fast waltz. She felt completely safe in his arms. They whirled around the floor, turning left and right, doing pivots and other waltz variations. He maneuvered effortlessly among the other dancers, pulling her close when a collision threatened.

While the musicians took a break, they stood catching their breath and looking at the variety of fancy dress. "Does turning make you dizzy?" he asked.

"Yes, but if you unwind me, so to speak, and turn the other way, or stop turning for a while, I'm fine. Just don't let go of me after a lot of turns!"

"I'm very dependable when it comes to unwinding women and not letting go of them," he said. She laughed but couldn't manage a comeback.

There were two more dances before the dessert buffet. They waited in the long line and then carried their cheesecake and chocolate-dipped strawberries to a table. The dessert was good, but sitting down was even better.

Peter was eyeing Susannah's feet as he ate one of the strawberries. "Those are pretty sexy shoes."

She extended her leg and said "Yes, they are, aren't they? I get lots of compliments on them, but I've never understood exactly what makes them sexy."

"Well, how about the fact that they're made mostly from see-through material," he said. "And the fact that they lace up, and can be unlaced. Pretty suggestive, I'd say."

"That's very insightful. Who knew that shoes could be so risqué? On another topic, how did you get to be such a good dancer? You're clearly a natural, but you couldn't have learned all those steps on Thursday night."

"A couple of years ago, I was seeing this woman and she talked me into going to a weekend waltz workshop with her. She met somebody else there, and that was the end of that!" He laughed. "But I had a great time and liked it so much that I kept taking classes for several months. It all came back pretty easily."

"What is it that's so special when everything clicks with a dance partner, do you think?" Susannah asked him.

"Oh, probably lots of things. One is just music. It can take you somewhere else, even when you aren't moving. And when you're moving to the music, maybe that just amps it up, so to speak."

"That makes sense. But when it really clicks with a partner, I think it's transcendence. For those few moments, you don't feel separate anymore."

"Like good sex," he teased.

She smiled but quickly bent over to retie her shoe.

The orchestra was warming up again, and people were

drifting toward the dance floor. The blonde they had seen when they first came in appeared at their side to claim her dance with Peter. Jim, a guy in many of Susannah's dance classes, happened by and, seeing her alone, asked her to dance. They chatted during a cross-step waltz, and Jim complimented her on her dress. He asked if he could keep her for a polka. "Absolutely!" she replied, and off they went.

Peter watched them from the sidelines. The couple next to him was also watching. Jim and Susannah were obviously having a great time.

As Susannah danced by, she waved. Peter nodded.

When the polka ended, Jim dropped her off at her table. She gave him a hug and her thanks, and he left as Peter arrived. "You two looked great out there," he said. "What a romp!"

"Yes, it was really fun. But I'm glistening."

"You're what?" he asked.

"Glistening. Don't you know ladies don't sweat—they glisten? Well, probably they can sweat now. I'm sure glistening went out with Title Nine. Can you imagine women's basketball teams glistening—like the Husky women, at UW, or the Seattle Storm? Anyway, I'm going to the ladies' room to dry off," she said, dabbing her face with a dainty white handkerchief. "This just isn't doing the job!"

Peter was still appreciating Susannah's sense of humor and watching the dancers when a redheaded knockout in a low-cut green sheath appeared beside him. He asked her to dance. She looked a little nervous, but she said yes, adding that she didn't know how to dance very well. "Well, we won't try anything too fancy," he said.

Back from the ladies' room, Susannah watched their progress around the room. *Poor thing,* she thought. *She hasn't got a clue.* But the next time around, Ms. Green Dress was doing much better. Peter said something to her now and then, and she would nod and look intent. By the end of the dance, she was smiling and doing a serviceable waltz.

What a gift he's given her, Susannah thought. She also felt a twinge of envy. *Oh, to be young and beautiful!*

Peter left Ms. Green Dress where he found her and located Susannah. "Just doing my Arthur Murray routine," he said, pretending it had been a difficult duty.

"It was very kind of you, Peter. She'll be telling the story for years to come about the tall, handsome guy who taught her to waltz in less than five minutes. I don't think you're all that down on young women, actually." The MC directed everyone to form a big circle. "Come on," Susannah said. "They're going to do the cross-step circle dance next—my all-time favorite. You'll really enjoy it."

He did. It was a very elegant dance, in which people changed partners through a repeated pattern, with bows to new and old partners. When they were back to their original partners, there was spontaneous cheering and applause—people loved this dance.

After a few more dances, they were ready to rest their feet and leave the overheated ballroom. "Would you like to come to my house for something to eat?" she asked. "I've got provisions for a light supper."

"I hope it's not *too* light—I'm starving!"

She laughed. "I think there's enough to keep you going."

"Hey, you know what? I got an insight into the trophy-wife syndrome. I was listening to the comments on your dress while you and Jim were dancing—they were very complimentary—and I couldn't help thinking, *She came with me.* I was kind of basking in your reflected glory. I can see how that appeals to guys."

"Hmm," Susannah said. "I'm going to have to think about that."

....

"Make yourself at home," she told Peter as they went in the back door to the kitchen. "I have to get into my slippers before I die! I'll be right back." She went upstairs, then returned wearing pink terry scuffs with her velvet gown. "I know they aren't very elegant, but they feel sooooo good!"

Peter had draped his coat over the back of a chair, taken off his tie, and loosened his collar.

"Feel free to wander around while I get out the food. Put your feet up if you like." She opened a cabinet filled with glassware. "Red wine or beer?"

"Wine and a big glass of water," he answered from the living room.

Susannah had left some cheeses and olives on the island, so that they would be room temperature. She put on her apron, got out some pâté, and cut up a baguette. She poured a glass of water for each of them and took Peter's in to him. "If you'd like music, the CD player's in the dining room. I'm fine with anything but Strauss. Oh, and just let me know when you're ready to go home, and I'll drive you back."

By the time she got the wine open, she heard the first cut of Patsy Cline's greatest hits. "You've got a good collection of golden oldies," he said, coming into the kitchen and sitting down in the breakfast nook. "I like your house."

"Thanks. People seem to enjoy being here, and that makes me feel good. And of course I enjoy having my favorite things around me—so many reminders of good times. But you know," she said, moving plates and serving dishes to the table, "I feel more and more tied down by 'stuff' and more and more bored by things I used to put so much work and money into—the curtains, the carpets, the paint colors, and so on."

"Maybe you just need a change," he suggested as she took off her apron and sat down opposite him.

"That's partly it, I'm sure. But I think it's more than that. I'm not defining who I am in the same way I used to. Susannah was the woman who lived in a house like this, in this part of town, who had a graduate degree and a career, and so on." She waved her hand dismissively. "That was important to me—that's who I thought I was—but it seems so limited now, so past tense."

Peter was listening intently as he worked his way through half a baguette and ample amounts of cheese, pâté, and olives. "So who are you in the present tense?"

Munching a piece of cheese, she considered before answering, choosing her words carefully. "I'm a person who's trying to let go of limited self-definition so I can relate to people better and be more helpful. Pretty grandiose, huh?" she said, embarrassed, playing with her napkin.

"You've thought about this a lot, obviously."

"Yes, I have. Now I have a question for you."

"No," he said emphatically, holding up his hands in the stop gesture. "You can't ask me who I am! I couldn't possibly come up with an answer comparable to yours after two glasses of wine!"

"No, no," she laughed. "Nothing so serious. I'm not going to ask you to explain Heidegger or something."

"Well, I could do that. I was a philosophy major."

"Now just listen—this isn't so hard. This question is kind of about linguistics—"

"You want to talk about linguistics when I've been dancing for hours and I'm full of cheese and bread and wine?" He burst out laughing. "You're something else!"

She persisted. "It's a very simple question. You know how the Greeks have four different words for 'love'?"

He nodded. "*Philia, caritas, eros, agape.* Except I think *caritas* is Latin."

"Right. Well, the question is, why do we only have one word? French only has one, and I'll bet the other romance languages only have one. English owes so much to Greek, so how did these important distinctions get dropped?"

"Hmm. Interesting question." He thought for a while. "English is certainly limited, having only one word. People use the same word to express how they feel about lemon meringue pie or baseball and how they feel about a spouse or God. Is it OK if I think about it and get back to you?" he said with a grin.

"Sure," she replied. "Peter, this has been a really special evening. You're a wonderful dancer, and it was such a pleasure to be your partner tonight. Thank you." His hand was lying on the table, and she touched it lightly.

"You're welcome."

She slid out of the breakfast nook and started putting things away. Every time she bent over to put dishes in the dishwasher, the slit in her skirt revealed an expanse of leg and ankle. She noticed him noticing.

"Susannah?"

She looked up, and his eyes caught hers.

"I can count on one finger the number of times I've been to a ball with a beautiful, charming, intelligent woman. Thank you."

"You're welcome," she said quietly, with a little smile.

By this time, Patsy Cline was over and they were halfway through Elvis's greatest hits. They went into the living room just as "It's Now or Never" came on.

"One more dance," he said, holding out his arms. She put down her wine, and he pulled her to him, putting his arms around her waist.

She hummed along, her cheek against his chest. It was one of her favorite songs, though a little suggestive, given the situation. *But so romantic,* she thought dreamily.

"Susannah?"

"Mmm," she replied.

"When do I get to sleep with you?"

She started to pull away, but he held her close. Suddenly, there they were—all her inhibitions and fears. She tried to stall. "You want to sleep with me?"

He laughed. "Of course I do! Why wouldn't I? I've been thinking about it since I met you in the grocery store."

His hands moved slowly up and down her back, from her hair to her hips. Her body hadn't felt these feelings for a long, long time.

He kissed her neck below the ear, then her shoulder. She

was completely melting. "Susannah, do you want to make love with me?"

After a pause, she said, "Yes, I do, but . . ." She wouldn't look at him.

"Let me guess," he said gently. "It's been awhile, right?"

"Yes, it's been awhile . . . and I feel awkward . . . and a little scared."

"But willing?" he asked, kissing her hair, her eyes.

"Yes," she said softly after a moment, and kissed him.

They went up to her bedroom. "How shall we do this to make you comfortable?" he asked, unbuttoning his shirt and pulling off his watch.

"Um . . . I'll get undressed . . . and brush my teeth . . . and meet you in bed," she suggested shyly. She went into her walk-in closet, pulled her dress over her head and hung it up, took off her panty hose, bra, and jewelry, and put on her robe. She couldn't believe this was happening!

He was already in bed as she went to the bathroom. She turned out the bedside light on her way.

She brushed her teeth, looked at herself in the mirror, and took a deep breath. Then she turned out the bathroom light and walked into the dark bedroom, illuminated only by the dim glow from the streetlights. She dropped her robe on the floor and slipped between the sheets, into his arms.

The hidden sun was making the gray sky slightly less gray when Susannah awoke Sunday morning. She propped her head on her hand and looked at Peter, sleeping on his belly with one arm under his pillow. She liked the muscles in his back and smiled at his feet extending beyond the end of the bed—he was so tall. A list of adjectives went through her mind—was she content, euphoric, happy, surprised, changed, desirable? *All of the above,* she thought.

When he opened his eyes sleepily, Susannah was gazing at him. "Good morning," she said. She ran her hand through his longish gray hair. "Sleep well?"

He rolled over to face her. "Very well, thank you. And how are you this morning?" He picked up her hand and kissed her fingertips.

"Hmm. I feel like a woman again. Or a new woman," she answered, quietly happy.

He stretched luxuriously and said, "I feel like a satisfied man. Well, almost satisfied. Come here, Woman Again, or New Woman, or whoever you are now. Kiss me."

She did.

After a leisurely breakfast, Susannah offered to drive Peter back to the boat. "No, I think I'll walk, thanks. An hour's walk will feel good—and it's downhill all the way." She gave him a long, lingering kiss at the door.

Throughout the day she was distracted by thoughts of him: his expressions, his laugh, his lovemaking. She tried to do some desk work and read the new *Atlantic*, but her mind kept wandering. He was so stereotypically male—tall, strong, in charge—and he made her feel very feminine. *We're down to evolutionary basics here,* she thought. She assumed he must have had lots of practice in bed. He was an ardent and considerate lover.

At about four in the afternoon, the phone rang. Time for her son's weekly call. "Hey, Mom, how was the big date?"

She told Alex about the incredible dancing, Ms. Green Dress, the good conversations, the post-dance meal, and that she couldn't remember the last time she'd had so much fun.

"Well, Mom, I'm not going to ask any, um, impertinent questions, but you sound really happy—happier than you've been in a long time. Whatever happened, I hope it keeps happening!"

"Me too!" she said, laughing. They caught up on work and the kids and plans for Thanksgiving, and ended their call.

Susannah went through her usual routine on Monday: rowing in the morning, groceries and errands in the afternoon. She was still on a lover's high. She kept checking her voice mail, but there was nothing from Peter. Nothing again on Tuesday. She imagined all sorts of possibilities but didn't want to call him. She didn't want him to think she was chasing him.

By Thursday, she was in a state. *Why hasn't he called?* she kept thinking.

That afternoon he finally did. "Susannah, are you busy? Could I come over? I need to talk to you."

"Of course. Come any time."

He arrived at about seven thirty, giving her a quick hug. He looked distracted and unhappy.

"Peter, what's happened?" she said. "Is your family all right? Are you all right?"

"My family's fine, but I'm not. There're some things I need to explain, Susannah. Sit down. This will take a while."

She sat down on the sofa, mystified.

"I'm leaving tomorrow, flying back to San Francisco."

Her heart lurched.

"Some friends of mine are going to sail the boat back in a few weeks." He started pacing up and down. "I can't stay, Susannah."

She was trying very hard not to let her feelings get in the way of hearing him. If ever she needed to listen well, it was now. "Peter," she said as calmly as she could, "tell me why."

He sat down across the coffee table from her. "Five years ago, I lost, I think you'd call her my soul mate, Andrea. We'd been together ten years, and a drunk driver crashed into her one night when she was coming home from dinner with friends. Killed her instantly. We were best friends as well as lovers. We had lots in common, had such fun together. It was so easy with her, in comparison to my marriage—which was clearly a mistake." He picked up a coaster and put it back down, then looked over at her.

"I went off the deep end. I'd work fifteen-hour days and then I'd sit in a stupor for days. I couldn't concentrate. I'd get angry for no reason. Finally, my daughter dragged me to a grief counselor. He helped me understand what was going on and told me my anger and my inability to concentrate were common symptoms of grief. That helped. He said I should face the grief and allow myself to feel all the feelings—time doesn't just take care of things. I'm finally at the place where I'm only sad every once in a while. I try not to think about it, because I get so angry that she left me, even though I know it wasn't her fault. There were so many things I wish I'd said, or said more often—how much I loved her and all the little quirks that made her so special." He paused.

"And then about six months after the accident, I had a pretty severe heart attack. I was told I had some kind of cardiac condition—sudden cardiac death syndrome is what it's called. They can't do anything about it. I could drop dead tomorrow, or I could live another twenty years."

It was all Susannah could do to keep the tears from falling—her crying wouldn't make this any easier for him. He got up and started pacing again, and when his back was turned, she quickly wiped her eyes on her shirtsleeve.

His voice was strained. "I'm not the type to sit around waiting to die, afraid to do anything. I might as well be doing something I enjoy when I kick the bucket. So I decided to travel and enjoy my friends, do some helpful things where I could—you know, with Habitat for Humanity, tutoring kids, some other organizations I've been working with. But no entangling alliances, Susannah. I can't face the possibility of another loss like Andrea's. And I don't want to be the cause of someone else's grief. Up until now, there was no danger. But there's a real possibility I could fall in love with you, and if you were to fall in love with me, it would be too risky for both of us."

Too late, dear one, she thought. *I've already fallen.* She said nothing, but her eyes followed him as he paced.

"So, that's why I have to leave."

In as steady a voice as she could manage, she said, "I think your decision to do the things you care about is the right one. It's what we should all be doing, even if we aren't facing a life-threatening situation. But even if you didn't have a heart condition, you could still drown in a storm or be electrocuted in some freak accident. Should you deprive yourself of love because of all the bad things that might happen? Isn't that the question, Peter? Would you rather not have had your ten years with Andrea? Would you rather not have had your daughter and grandsons?"

He looked stunned by the question.

"I wish you didn't have to go." Her voice was a little unsteady. "But I can see that you need some time and space to work on all this some more. I hope you'll consider what I've said. And I encourage you to find someone to talk to—it seems to me you still have a lot more grief than you think you do."

She went to him and put her arms around him. "I'm here if you decide you want to take the risk," she said, and kissed him.

He kissed her forehead and left without another word.

Then she cried—for herself and for him.

It was a week before she could trust herself not to break down in public. As more weeks passed, her hope dwindled. She kept positive thoughts for him in her consciousness. But there was a sad place in her heart. She missed him.

....

About six months later the mailman brought a big package to the porch. It was from San Francisco. *What on earth?* she wondered.

Inside she found an elegant box from Saks Fifth Avenue. And within that box, wrapped in silver tissue paper, was a beautiful full-length black evening coat, with a hood and black satin lining. There were also two envelopes. She opened the larger envelope and read:

Dear Susannah,

   Dad told me all about you when he came back to San Francisco last fall. I think being with you helped him get over the loss of Andrea. He seemed to be doing a lot of 'processing' about all that in the two or three months after his return. Then he told me he was planning to go back to Seattle. I think he was ready to give love another try.
But we lost him three months ago—the heart condition I'm sure he told you about. It happened aboard Este Dia, and he was gone immediately, no suffering.

   I'm sorry it's taken so long to get this in the mail to you. From the receipt, I can tell that he bought it just before he died. But there were all the things to do, decisions to make, and tears to shed. So I'm only now getting this gorgeous coat off to you. I know you'll wear it with pleasure, and I hope it brings you happy memories.

   Sincerely,
   Astri Weston

She could barely see for all the tears. She opened the small card.

It read *Love, Peter.*

CHAPTER TWO

Some Enchanted Evening

Friday evening Susannah sent out an e-mail to her rowing friends. "Car trouble—can anyone pick me up for Otter Island tomorrow morning?"

She got a reply right back from Marty. He must have been sitting in front of his computer. *I'll pick you up at 8:00.* He cc'd everyone, so no one else needed to reply.

Marty McAlistair was a quiet but well-liked fellow among the midmorning masters rowing group. Of average height, stocky but fit, his once-copper hair was still thick but now a burnished auburn-white. His friendly smile, ready wit, and caring manner made everyone like him. He was always supportive of his crewmates, never one to carp about so-and-so's timing being off, or people's other rowing foibles.

Susannah's duffel bag was loaded by seven thirty the next morning. She liked to find that sweet spot where she was prepared for almost everything but still didn't have too much. She considered herself a consummate packer, but that was due to her lists: a camping list, a Costco list, a retreat list, a rowing list.

From the items on her standard-rowing-gear list, she'd chosen what she'd need for a fall outing: waterproof gloves, hat, sunglasses, water bottle, rain pants and parka, and vest. To avoid taking a handbag, she settled for some cash and a credit card, hankies, and a comb.

When Marty arrived punctually and rang the doorbell, she was ready.

"Good morning. Thanks so much for picking me up on short notice."

"My pleasure," he said. "I'm glad for the company. I was so busy last week I didn't get into the carpool arrangements."

"Well, you're a carpool now, at least as far as the freeway is concerned."

They walked out to his car, a shiny black BMW Z4. "Oh, wow! One of the three classiest sports cars in the world. I've never ridden in one—what a trip!"

"What are the other two?" he asked, opening the door for her, taking her bag, and tucking it behind the seat.

"A Porsche Carrera and a Corvette," she answered

They got in, and he started the engine. "You like Corvettes?" He sounded a little incredulous.

"Oh, yes, that rumble the engine makes is really neat. It's probably a holdover from my high school days. My first boyfriend was a greaser—he drove hot rods."

Marty laughed. "I never would have guessed!" He put the car in gear, and it purred sedately down the street.

"How did you happen to choose this car? I would have pegged you as a Camry or Saab kind of guy."

"Oh, I did all the research on engineering, performance, safety, and so on. And I decided I should be bold and different. This is what I came up with. I really am a Camry or Saab kind of guy deep inside," he said. "This is fine. It handles well and has plenty of power. But it's a car, you know?"

Susannah laughed. "Well, I'm sure going to enjoy this ride," she said. "A BMW and good company! Have you been to the Otter Island Regatta before?"

"No. This is my first time. Have you been?"

"Yes, I went once and swore I'd never go again, but the coach talked me into trying it one more time."

"Why? What happened?" he asked, sounding a little alarmed.

"One of the juniors was coxing our eight. She could steer OK, but she couldn't, or wouldn't, tell people what to do to fix the balance. I was rowing port, and we were down on the port side for two hours—we could hardly get our oars out of the water. It was awful!"

"It *sounds* awful" he said.

"Well, we've put together an eight from Mount Baker that we know won't have that problem, even if the cox can't cox. So I'm sure we'll be fine."

They had a two-hour row around Otter Island, along with about a hundred other rowers from clubs in the area. The Everett Rowing Club provided a delicious salmon barbecue after all the boats were in. It was fun to get together without having to compete.

On the way home they talked about how they got into rowing, what Susannah did with herself now that she was retired, why Marty had chosen cardiology, and other topics. As they turned onto her street, he said, "Would you like to have soup and a sandwich at my house this evening? I doubt either of us will be hungry for a regular dinner after that huge salmon feed."

She was a little surprised at the invitation but had no plans, so she accepted. He dropped her off at home, arranging to pick her up again at about six.

He lived on the east side of Mount Baker ridge, with a view of the lake and Mount Rainier. It was a small house that had been remodeled to give a more spacious feeling and to accommodate his art collection and his grand piano.

"You're welcome to look around while I put the soup on," he said, going off to the kitchen. She walked around the living room/dining room area and down the hall, and peeked into a bedroom. Art everywhere, and by some noted Northwest artists.

"Marty, you have an amazing collection!" she said, going into the kitchen, where he was pouring a can of Campbell's tomato soup into a pan and adding milk.

"Thanks," he said. "I really enjoy it. I bought most of the paintings when the artists were just getting established. I could never afford to buy them now."

"Can I help with anything?" Susannah asked.

"Sure, you could make grilled cheese sandwiches, if you don't mind. I'll set the table."

"Cheddar or Swiss?" she asked, finding the cheese in the fridge. "And how do you do them—broiler, grill, skillet?"

"Cheddar, please. There's a grill down there." He pointed to a lower cupboard. In it she found every conceivable appliance: a food processor, a regular blender, an immersion blender, an ice crusher, a rice cooker, a juicer, a Crock-Pot, an electric grill, and even an electric crepe maker.

"Goodness! You're quite the cook, Marty."

"Oh, I never use any of it. I get a new toy and play with it a little and then put it away. But I'm really accomplished with a can opener and a microwave."

"OK, the grill is hot. I'll put the sandwiches in. Oh, Marty, stir the soup or it'll boil over!" He quickly pulled it off the burner and gave it a stir.

After they had eaten, he offered to make her a latte. "I'd love one—if it can be decaf."

"Oh, darn, I only have regular coffee." He frowned, looking worried.

"Well, how about a steamed milk, then," she suggested. "That will set me up for a good sleep."

He busied himself at an espresso maker that looked like it must have cost a zillion dollars and soon had a latte for himself and a steamed milk for her. They took their cups into the living room. "Tell me about the piano," she said. "I assume you play?"

"Yes, I do, as much as I can. I took piano lessons as a child—all through school, even some during college. Of course I don't have much time to practice now. I'm lucky if I get in thirty minutes a day. But I do keep trying. It's very relaxing—gets me unwound."

"What are you unwinding from?" she asked, sipping her milk.

"Well, I have a busy practice. I see patients from eight

thirty to six four days a week. The fifth day—which often stretches into the weekend—is for desk work, professional reading, meetings, and so on. I do take Friday mornings off for rowing, and I try to work out in my basement gym. Oh, and I'm on the board of Seattle Opera, so that has some duties. Mostly pleasant, but it still takes time."

"What do you do for fun besides playing the piano and rowing?"

"If I can squeeze it in, I go to a concert or a gallery opening," he said. "But I don't get to go as often as I'd like."

"Are you happy?" she asked. "Oh, sorry. That just popped out! That's way too personal a question for me to ask. Sorry, Marty."

"No, it's OK. It's something I should be asking myself anyway. I do, about every ten years, then I forget about the answer and just keep doing what I always do."

She thought she should change the subject. "Would you play for me?"

"Sure," he said. They moved to the piano bench, and she sat down beside him. "What would you like to hear?"

"What do you usually play?"

"Mostly classical and Broadway musicals."

"How about the theme from *Elvira Madigan*—Mozart, isn't it?" He nodded and began the haunting melody. She was almost in tears when he finished.

"It's so sad—probably because of the story."

"Music can be sad even when there's no story associated with it. I've never heard a scientific explanation, but it seems to be a universal experience."

She asked him to play "Some Enchanted Evening," and he launched right into it. They both knew the words, so they sang it all the way through together.

Susannah clapped her hands in delight. "We sound pretty good together, don't we?"

"Yes. That was amazing," he said quietly.

"Thanks for playing for me, and for the dinner, Marty. I

think I should go now—we've both had a strenuous day." It was a quiet but companionable ride back to her house.

Susannah thought Marty seemed rather shy and a little ill at ease that evening, though he never seemed that way at rowing. She wondered why some woman hadn't snapped him up—a nice, cultured, well-off man like that. Perhaps he preferred men. In any case, he seemed lonely or sad.

....

The following Friday they were all coming out of the boathouse after putting the last boat away. Jane's grandson, about five, was riding his bike on the tarmac in front of the boathouse. He and his grandfather Sam were there to pick Jane up after practice.

Suddenly the boy hit a bump and went flying over the handlebars, hitting his head on the pavement, his loosely fastened helmet askew. Everyone came running, and Marty was the first one there. He ordered everyone to stand back so he could see. The child wasn't moving, and his head was bleeding. "Who's got a cell phone?" Marty said.

Two people held theirs up.

"Both of you call 911 and tell them to send an aid car." He pointed at two other people. "Go in the office and get the first-aid kit and some blankets. Tell Joyce I need something clean to stanch the blood—towels, whatever, as long as it's clean." They ran off to get the items he requested. Meanwhile, someone had laid a fleece jacket over the boy.

Marty asked Jane, who was very pale, kneeling beside her grandson, what insurance the family had.

"Group Health," she answered.

"OK, they'll take him to the Swedish ER. One of you should go in the aid car with him, and the other should call his parents and arrange to have one of them meet you there. Tell them to remember his medical card."

Someone came running back with blankets and towels and a first-aid kit. They could now hear a siren in the distance. The little boy's eyes opened, but he didn't speak. Marty said in a calm, friendly voice, "Hi there. You had a fall and bumped your head. It's going to be OK, though. You get to do something most little boys never get to do. *You* get to ride in an ambulance with some firemen!"

"Are you going with him, Jane?" he said.

"Yes, I'll go. Sam can drive to the ER."

"Will someone volunteer to go with Sam?" Marty said.

"I'll be fine, Doc."

They heard the big engine of the aid car. Several people had stationed themselves in the parking lot to direct the firemen quickly. The medics arrived, strapped the boy to the stretcher, and disappeared into the back of the aid car, which drove off, lights flashing.

It was over very fast. Everyone was jittery but Marty. "How do you stay so calm?" someone asked him. "Years of practice," he said, with a self-deprecating smile.

....

Sunday evening Marty called Susannah and asked her to attend the opera with him the following Saturday night. "They're having a reception for board members afterward, and I thought you might like to go. I've been to dozens of these affairs, and it would be nice to have someone else to talk to—not that I don't like the opera staff and the other board members—they're really great people. Anyway, would you like to go?"

He'd made something of a hash of the invitation, but she didn't know him well enough to tease him. She accepted. "I assume this is dress-up?"

"Yes, it's black tie," he replied. "I'll pick you up at six thirty, because the traffic will be terrible."

"Thank you for the invitation, Marty. Will I see you at rowing on Friday?"

"Yes, I plan to be there. I'm glad you want to go with me—to the opera, I mean. See you Friday."

Susannah found Marty a study in contrasts. Awkward, competent, shy, supportive, friendly. She wondered about his background, his family, how he saw himself.

Susannah was looking forward to the event. She hadn't been to the opera for several years, and they were doing *Rigoletto*. Marty appeared on her doorstep right on time and escorted her to the car, opening the door for her. She felt pampered.

"You're looking very debonair, this evening, Dr. McAlistair," she told him. "The tux is quite a change from the way I usually see you—in sweatpants, a rain parka, and an old baseball cap."

"Yes, my ex-wife used to tell me I 'cleaned up pretty good.'" He laughed.

"Tell me about the reception for board members," she said.

"Oh, it's the perk for helping the opera raise money. That's what board members do, you know."

The traffic *was* terrible, but they got into the parking garage by 7:10. He had a reserved space on the same level as the skybridge. "Good evening, Dr. McAlistair," said the usher, handing them programs. As they went to their seats, Susannah noticed heads turning. Several people waved to Marty or spoke as they settled into their box, front row center.

"This is certainly the high-rent district," she whispered to him.

"Yes." He smiled. "I like to have good seats."

The conductor entered, the music began, and the audience settled into the performance. Out of the corner of her eye, Susannah could see how engrossed Marty was. She was enjoying the performance, but he seemed totally immersed.

At the first intermission he asked if she liked the performance so far.

"Yes, I do!" she said. "It's particularly special because this is the very first opera I ever saw—in Paris when I was nineteen. It was a huge thrill. I hadn't thought I would like opera, but I really did—the music was very moving."

They stood up to stretch their legs. She was warm enough now, and he helped her off with her evening coat and draped it around her shoulders. "That's a beautiful coat," he said. "Looks like it was made for the opera house, or a ball or something."

"Yes, it is a beautiful coat, isn't it?" she replied.

Just then someone came up to greet Marty, and she was introduced to the chairman of the board. "I look forward to chatting with you at the reception, Susannah," he said genially. She noticed that they were still getting lots of appraising glances and couldn't figure out exactly why.

At the second intermission, they went out to the lobby, where Marty introduced her to more board members and some of the opera staff. One hearty fellow slapped Marty on the back and said, "Nice to see you here with someone for a change, Doc!" Marty blushed.

After the last strains of the music died out, then the applause, it was time for the reception. "That was a wonderful performance," she told Marty. "I really enjoyed it."

His face lit up for a moment, and then the slightly anxious look he'd had all evening reappeared.

They moved into the Allen Room, where waiters were circling with trays of champagne glasses and platters of canapés. Across the room Susannah saw one of her meditation friends and her husband. Alice waved and moved through the expensively dressed crowd to greet them. "Well, hello! I didn't know you and Marty knew each other."

"We row together," Susannah explained.

"For heaven's sake," Alice said. "What a coincidence! Marty, Susannah and I meditate together—when I get there, that is."

Just then the chairman of the board called for their attention. "I'd like to introduce our general director, who will say a few words." The general director then commended the board for all they did for the opera and expressed how much they were appreciated. Then the chairman announced that they were presenting a special award tonight. He said the board had never done this before, but they were all agreed that special recognition was due to one board member who had gone above and beyond the call of duty. "Dr. Martin McAlistair, would you please come to the podium." Enthusiastic applause followed.

Marty crossed his arms, then put his hands in his pockets, then took them out and clasped them behind his back as he stood beside Mr. Chairman, who delivered a handsomely worded tribute in recognition of Marty's work. He was presented with a hand-blown art glass bowl by a well-known local artist. Marty said his quiet thanks, and there was more applause. Many people came up to congratulate him. As Susannah watched and sipped her champagne, Alice appeared beside her again. "Not only did Marty get the recognition he so richly deserves tonight, but there's another reason this is an occasion."

"Why is that, Alice?" Susannah asked.

"Because he's never brought anyone with him to a performance or a board event in the ten years he's been a board member."

"Oh, that's what all the stares were about! So what's the gossip, Alice? Have they married us off yet, or am I his sister or cousin or what?" She and Alice laughed.

"Well, there's certainly a buzz," Alice said. "Women have been chasing him for years, but he seems oblivious."

"He's an awfully nice guy. I hope he'll find someone" Susannah said.

"You're not the one, then?" Alice asked, smiling.

"No, no, we're just friends," Susannah replied.

The party was breaking up, and Marty helped Susannah on with her coat. It was cold as they walked over the skybridge, and she was happy to pull the hood up. Marty let her in the car, put his carefully wrapped glass bowl behind the seat, and got in. "Thank God that's over!" he said. "Where can we eat at this hour? How about the Burgermaster on Forty-Fifth? It's too late for someplace nice."

"Dick's, on Broadway, is closer," she said.

"Good idea—let's go there!" he replied.

They arrived in fifteen minutes. "What would you like?" he asked, getting out of the car.

"A cheeseburger and a diet something to drink, please," she said, and he left to order, looking a little out of place in his tux among the hipsters and goths. Soon he was back with several bags of food. "When was the last time you ate?" she asked.

"Let's see, last night, I think. I get nervous, and then I can't eat. But now I can relax. I'm beginning to feel like a human again. By the way, you look really nice tonight. I noticed—I was just too distracted to say anything. Red's a good color on you."

She gave him an awkward smile of thanks, pointing to her mouth full of cheeseburger, and they both laughed.

After they had finished their burgers, Susannah said, "Can I make you a cup of coffee, Marty, or is it too late?"

"It's never too late for me. Caffeine doesn't keep me awake. Yes, I'd love a cup of coffee."

When they arrived at her place, she motioned him to a stool on one side of the counter that separated the kitchen from the living room, and draped her coat over a chair.

She set out a mug and turned on the electric kettle. "Marty, I never had a chance to tell you how impressive you were, handling that accident with the little boy." Getting out her French press, she went on. "You were so calm and competent, and you kept him from getting too scared. It *was* scary, but at the same time, I felt everything was under control."

"Well, thanks for the compliment. But it's just what I do."

"Another thing that was really impressive was the respect your fellow opera board members have for you, and the work you've done to earn it. Why did you have so much angst about this very nice affair?"

"Being in front of people makes me nervous. I'm fine with two or three people, or in a meeting, but I'm just not comfortable being 'on.'"

"Cream or sugar?"

"Black is fine." He took a sip. "Hot and strong—perfect. Thanks."

"Alice said something interesting to me. She said that in the ten years you've been on the opera board you've never brought anyone with you to any of the events or performances. Why is that?"

"There's never been anyone I wanted to take—I mean, I didn't know anyone to ask. After my wife and I split up, I didn't have any interest in another relationship for a long time. And by the time I was ready to consider it again, I was too busy. And shy."

"That's just another way of saying relationships aren't important," Susannah said. "If you want one, you have to make time." She bit her lip—she was out of line again. "I can't believe I just said that! I'm sorry, Marty. That was really inappropriate. I sound like a therapist or something."

"I'm not taking offense," he said. "I know you're right. It's just years of inertia to overcome. It's a daunting prospect."

"Is it more daunting than saving people's lives or raising millions for the opera?"

"Yes, it really is." He drained his coffee cup. "I'd better go and let you get to bed. Thanks for going with me and being my moral support."

"It was a lovely evening," she replied. "I enjoyed it very much."

As she got ready for bed, Susannah wondered how she could have been so inappropriate, with personal questions and comments on his private life. She resolved to be more careful—if he ever wanted to talk to her again.

Marty drove home full of thoughts and emotions. He'd had his first date in years! He was probably more nervous about the award ceremony than about having a date, so that made it easier in a way. Susannah was fascinating. He was a little surprised at some of the things she'd said, but not annoyed. While it wasn't intentional, she was making him think about things he'd been avoiding for too long. He liked her perfume, and being close enough to her to notice it.

....

At rowing the following Friday he was chatting and laughing with Brenda, a lovely thirtyish woman with a great figure and beautiful thick blonde hair. She was a good rower and a fun person to row with. "See you next week, Brenda," he said, heading toward the parking lot, where he invited Susannah to coffee, not Brenda.

"Sorry, Marty. I wouldn't be caught dead looking like this anywhere but the boathouse! But I have a counterproposal—how about my fixing dinner for you? Are you free tonight?"

"Yes, I am—that would be great, thanks!"

The details were arranged: he'd come to her place at seven; he ate anything and would bring wine.

When he arrived at her condo, he had a red wine, a white wine, and a bunch of daffodils. "How thoughtful, Marty—thanks! If the way to a man's heart is through his stomach, the way to a woman's is through flowers," she said over her shoulder as she went into the kitchen to find a vase.

"Sure smells good—what are you cooking?"

"Coq au vin, a green salad with walnuts and raspberries, and crème brûlée."

His approval of the menu showed in his face as he followed her to the kitchen.

"Did you buy this unit, or are you renting it?" he asked.

"Actually, I'm house-sitting for a few months, to see if I like living in a smaller place. I'm talking with my son and his wife about their moving into the family home, and buying a condo for me. With two children, they need a house. And I'm tired of maintaining one. But before we do anything irrevocable, I decided to try condo living."

"How do you like it?" he asked.

"Well, it's hard to get used to the limited space, but I'm getting tired of having lots of stuff, and moving to a smaller space would force me to get rid of some of it. Another plus is the change—after thirty years in one place, change looks pretty good, even if you have to leave behind a place of good memories. So, it's a mixed bag, but I'm pretty sure I'm going to do it, especially for my son and his family."

They drank nearly the whole bottle of red wine during dinner and conversation over the next two hours. Talk ranged from health-care reform to charter schools to the latest exhibit at SAM. Susannah mentioned that she was going on one of her semiannual silent retreats the following week.

"Why do you go on retreats?" Marty said. "What do you get out of them?"

"I wrote a little newsletter article about retreats that might explain it—I'll get it for you. You can read it while I make the coffee." She went to her computer and printed off a copy of the article.

What Happens in Silence

You might wonder why people would go away together for a week and not talk to each other.

Well, there are lots of reasons. One person said, "I've never been silent in seventy-six years, and I want to see if I can do it." Another person said, "I want to know people in a different way, without the conscious and unconscious social conventions that go with conversation."

I've been on many silent retreats and enjoyed them all. Silence removes a huge amount of distraction. And what do you find? Heightened awareness of many things—colors, smells, feelings you didn't know you had. Take carrot soup, for instance. It's amazing how *orange* carrot soup is, how pleasing it is to see those chopped green onions sprinkled over the top of the potage next to the intense green of the romaine on my sandwich.

One year there were scores of college students present for a cross-country race. They hopped and flapped and pushed up and sprinted and stretched in the alternating sun and rain as I watched them from the porch of our retreat house. Stripping off their brightly hued warm-up suits, they dropped them helter-skelter and took off in a horde at the sound of the gun. The runners first circled the parade ground, a luminous, brilliant grass-green that fairly glowed in the fall sunshine, before they raced off up the road and into the woods. Later I walked through those pine-smelling woods, and when a small group of runners jogged by, I caught a whiff of fresh laundry, as if their shirts had been just washed in Tide and brought in from the clothesline. If I'd been talking with someone, I'd have missed these colors and smells, or they would have been far less vivid.

There are also the long walks on the beach at Fort Casey, overlooking Puget Sound. Once, as the clouds came and went, I noticed how the color of the water changed from blue to gray and back again. I sat for a long time and watched the gulls, especially how they come in for a landing, stall, and drop right down in the midst of a tightly packed flock without touching each other. Amazing—how can they do that? All those feathers and ligaments working just so! I continued my walk downwind as a young couple came to the beach from the cliffs, and the smell of her perfume puffed by in the breeze and was gone in a second. Then there was just the clean, cold saltwater air to breathe.

I would have liked to ask how my fellow retreatants were. Instead, I watched the expressions, the body language. You know that lots is happening in an inner way, but you must bide your time until the end, when we have time to share our experiences. Meanwhile, there are smiles and hugs and other gestures of support and companionship.

I think we all noticed the intensification of what came to us through our senses when we weren't distracted by talking. But we also noticed a lot going on internally. On a silent retreat, you have time to *really notice* your emotions, to be with them, to see how your behavior is affected by them, to see how they come and go, to examine and reflect.

Silent retreats are wonderful experiences. Silence is truly golden.

Walking between Meditations at Fort Casey

Wind whips up waves
Polishes my face
As water polishes rocks
Only faster

In the lee of the hill
Peace and quiet
At the crest turbulence
Wind noise and wave noise

Walking into the sun
Only white, blue,
Glistening Irish green
And black

Sun strikes a shaft of trunk
A patch of grass
A lighthouse roof

Black letters on a white board
On a gray bunker
Who was the Reuben Turman I've
Honored summer and winter
Going on two decades

With my back to the sun
Burgundy window trim
Faded yellow office
Gray green barracks

Seaweed green river green
Olive green, salmon pink, coral
Cordovan and a hundred hues of brown

Rocks of white, gray with stripe
Mauve, dun, mottled
Green blue, gray blue, no true blue
Wet and lustrous, dry and ordinary

Tufts of fallen pine needles
Clean salt water air
Flapping flag
Bird song

  She made coffee while he was reading, and then they adjourned to the sofa.
  "This is really interesting, Susannah. I've never been in a group that was trying not to talk. I can see what you could get out of it, but I can't imagine doing it myself. I'd probably go crazy!" he said, taking a sip of coffee. "Your poem is

lovely—I can almost smell the saltwater."

"Thanks. It was fun writing it." She sensed that this wasn't a topic that he'd enjoy pursuing, so she changed the subject.

"Now I have a question for you, Marty. I'm doing a survey. Why do you think men are attracted to younger women?" She looked at him over the top of her coffee cup.

"Are they? It seems to me they'd prefer someone from their own generation."

"Come on, Marty! Haven't you ever heard of a trophy wife?"

"Well, sure, I have. I can think of a couple of men I know professionally who've married women much younger than they are. I don't know what their reasons were, but I'm not attracted to young women. They're nice to look at, of course, but what would I talk to them about? I don't know what Twittering is, and I wouldn't know the music they would know. It just seems like the age gap would make relating difficult."

"Thanks for the input—I'll add it to my research data." She put her feet up on the coffee table. "On another topic, something just occurred to me. You asked me to go out for coffee after rowing—what about work?"

"I'm cutting back my schedule. You were right—I can't have relationships if I don't give them more priority." Then he said, "That's partly what happened to my marriage. We met during our residencies and seemed compatible, and it was time to take the next step in life. So we got married. Two careers, professional obligations. Busy, busy. We just kind of drifted apart. But in retrospect, I don't think we were ever really close."

Susannah didn't know what to say. She wanted to commend him on cutting back his work schedule, to be encouraging, but she couldn't think of the right words. She just said, "Good for you," and kissed him on the cheek.

"Is there a man in your life right now, Susannah?" he asked, carefully studying his coffee cup.

"No, not now. There was, about a year ago. We were only together for four weeks, then he had to go back to San Francisco. He had a heart condition, and he died suddenly, before he could come back. I didn't realize how in love with him I was until he left."

"I'm sorry, Susannah."

She smiled a sad smile. "More coffee? Crème brûlée?" she asked.

"No, I couldn't possibly," he said with a groan.

"I'm sending you home with a care package." She bustled around in the kitchen and came back with plastic containers filled with noodles and coq au vin, and a box with four ramekins of crème brûlée. "They're five hundred calories apiece," she said. "No way am I going to leave them in my fridge to tempt me."

"Great—this will keep me going for a couple of days. It's been a wonderful evening. Thanks for the dinner and conversation. I really enjoyed myself. I hope your retreat goes well."

....

Meditation accoutrements littered the front room of the big old house in which they held their six-day retreats: blankets, shawls, woolen socks, slippers, pillows (foam, feathers, or buckwheat hulls), water bottles, mugs of tea, Tiger Balm, books, journals. Definitely not a Zen dojo. But it worked.

Susannah's meditation group had been coming here for years and had it down to a science. It was a silent retreat, except from about six to nine on the five nights when they talked at dinner and in the following "process" meeting. Wednesday night they didn't talk. Over the years they'd figured out that by Wednesday, after three days of concentrated meditation, people's stuff was "hitting the fan," and it would come out in what they jokingly called "nonproductive interpersonal interactions" if they were talking. So they just remained silent.

Susannah reflected on how reactive she had been years

ago, when she started going to meditation retreats. It was almost painful to remember the judgments she made about people, how irritated she'd get at people's little foibles or how they set the table, the compulsive cleaning up she did to establish the order she needed to feel comfortable. She was relieved that she'd been able to leave a lot—if not all—of that baggage behind.

Thursday evening Susannah got the chance to watch her level of reactivity and compassion—or her lack of it—when they broke their two-day silence. Roger asked his standard question for starting the discussion, "So, what's up in your meditation?"

It was customary to let those go first who seemed to have a need to talk, and not to monopolize the conversation. Sandy started right off describing her difficulty maintaining her mantra, and the tangents on which her thoughts sped off. She also described in some detail the dreams she'd had the past two nights.

After about five minutes, Roger interjected. "Sandy, remember on Tuesday night, we talked about how to handle thoughts, and that the goal wasn't 'no thoughts'? Did that guidance come to you during these last two days?"

Sandy said nothing for a moment and then answered. "Yeah, a couple of times I remembered, but mostly I just got absorbed in the thoughts and then got very frustrated because I was absorbed." She squirmed a bit in her chair.

"Meditation is called a 'practice' for a reason," Roger replied. "We just keep practicing. It doesn't matter what happens during the meditation—it's just as worthwhile an experience if there are lots of thoughts as when there are few or none. If you keep practicing, you'll notice there are changes in your life, whether or not there are changes in your practice." He looked around the room at the rest of the group. "Are there other experiences to report?"

Someone asked a question, and before Roger could reply, Sandy launched into her answer to the question—which she had completely misunderstood. By this time, people were fidgeting and no longer looking at her when she spoke; they were just waiting for her to stop talking. She didn't get the cues.

Susannah noticed herself getting annoyed. An inner conversation was going on:

Poor thing, she's so insecure and self-absorbed she doesn't even see how she's affecting others.

Well, yes, but she's also being rude. I wish she'd just shut up!

Where is all this coming from, this anger I have?

They say people who "push your buttons" are a mirror— they reflect back something in yourself that you don't like, that maybe you don't want to be reminded of.

Maybe she's reminding me of my own insecurities and that's why I dislike her.

Finally, Roger was tactfully able to wrest the conversational space away from Sandy so that others could participate.

The next day Susannah walked along the beach between breakfast and their coming meditation session. She was thinking about the daily interactions that were occasions to practice a healthier attitude to life. Was it useful to get angry about people who cut in front of her on the freeway, or who took up two spaces in a crowded parking lot, or yelled at their children on the bus, or tagged the new restrooms in the park? She didn't excuse bad behavior, but was it worth getting angry about?

Could she look a panhandler in the eye and smile at the person within, instead of feeling guilty about her good fortune compared to his? Could she feel compassion for people who believed lies and spouted nonsense because of their fears? Could she ignore the cultural emphasis on youth, and feel good about her health and what looks she had? Could she get past her dislike of Sandy to hear what Sandy had to teach her?

Susannah continued down the beach, watching the eagles

and the waves, and the ferry chugging to Port Townsend.

As she walked, her thoughts turned to her marriage. There had been many good times, but in retrospect it wasn't what she wished it had been. What had she wanted and expected when she married right out of grad school? Someone to make her feel secure. And she thought Dave would do that. Of course, this was unconscious—it took years for her to figure it out. And she still didn't know what he wanted and thought he was getting when he married her.

She still surprised herself with the amount of anger about her marriage that occasionally welled up. They were who they were, products of their upbringing and their times, and they did the best they could. She grieved, looking back at what they might have done differently, had they been able.

Their unhappiness came, she thought, from their separate insecurities, each wanting the other to change so they could be comfortable together. The older she got and the more she could see how she was limited by her upbringing and experience, the more she realized she needed to change. And she could only change herself—difficult though that was. If Dave hadn't been willing to change, then she would have had to decide if she needed to leave, or if she could find a way to stay with him that was workable. She was in the latter mode when they discovered the tumor, and he was gone in three months.

Her grief included both regret and relief. The years of accumulated unresolved issues and feelings hadn't just dropped away, and now there was no way to resolve them with him. She would never know if they could have grown enough to work through their problems. At the same time, a source of tension and worry was gone.

Susannah wondered how long it takes to really know another person. She thought probably a lifetime. If we didn't have to commit for a lifetime, would we give it the same amount of effort? There were certainly good reasons to end some marriages, but she guessed that many people gave up too soon, not willing to do the inner work required to grow personally and develop deep relationships. And even if people are willing to do the work, a happily-ever-after outcome is never guaranteed.

She also grieved for Peter and the clichéd "what might have been."

So now what? At her age, the odds that she'd find another partner were pretty slim, although being completely honest with herself, she admitted that's what she'd like—another chance. She didn't want to expect anything, but she did want to stay open to possibilities. She wanted to love and be loved.

....

Susannah and Marty saw each other every week or two for the next few months: dinners in and out, concerts, walks, a couple of day-trip picnics.

What was this relationship about? Was he wooing her? He never said anything suggestive, even in a humorous way; he never made a pass at her. And yet she didn't think his interest was entirely platonic. And what was her interest? She certainly liked him, respected him, enjoyed being with him. At her age, how could she expect more? To have even this much was pretty rare. But something was missing. She thought of Peter. Was that what was missing—a romantic experience like that? *Well, forget it, honey,* she told herself. *You were incredibly blessed to have had that, and lightning isn't going to strike twice!*

"What attracts people to each other, do you think?" Susannah asked Marty as they were having dinner one night in his favorite neighborhood Thai restaurant.

"There's lots of research," he said. "For example, various personality typologies, or the pheromone thing. Then there's the conventional wisdom—men choose women who remind them of their mothers, karma, and so on."

"You think karma is conventional wisdom?" she asked.

"Sure," he replied. "Kind of like the concepts of heaven

and hell, something to make people feel better, or scare them into good behavior."

She reflected on what he said and then replied. "But back to the main topic, don't you think it's a mystery why some people 'click' and others don't? Two people could have lots in common—family background, likes and dislikes, values, assumptions about life, and so on, and they just don't click. And people who have very little in common may click."

"Yes, I know what you mean. It's like the line in 'Some Enchanted Evening' about why people fall in love. Fools will give you reasons but wise men don't bother.

....

In June, Susannah went to France for three weeks for a French language immersion class and a cooking class, a trip she'd planned for a year earlier and postponed. Given the intensity of the experience, she was surprised how often Marty came into her thoughts: how much he'd like this particular dish, how interested he'd be in a certain French expression that would convey in two or three words what needed a sentence in English, how he would have enjoyed the concert in the square of the little town where they stayed. She and her friend Patrice had a wonderful time, but she was exhausted by the time she got back to Seattle.

Marty had insisted on picking her up, even though it was late and he had to work the next day. She met him at baggage claim. *"Bonsoir, mon cher,"* she said. *"Je suis très heureuse de te voir!"* She greeted him in the French manner—kissing one cheek, then the other—and gave him a big hug. "You're a sweetheart to pick me up. Let's go right now so you won't have to stay up any later than necessary."

"We have to get your luggage, remember?"

"Oh, yes—I guess I'm pretty rummy!"

"I'll pick it up," he said. "You go walk around or get a drink or something. Come back in fifteen minutes—that will be eleven thirty."

"It's sort of a purply-blue bag with a yellow ID tag on the

top handle," she said, handing him the baggage claim stubs and wandering off. When she came back, Marty had her luggage. He took her arm and steered her toward the escalators to the parking garage.

He paid for the parking at the machine and pointed toward the car, just three spaces in from where they stood. "You have good parking karma," she told him.

"Just luck." he said, contemplating her massive bag. She collapsed into the passenger seat, and he managed to wedge her suitcase behind the front seats.

"What have you got in here?" he said. "Bricks?"

"I just couldn't pass up these oils—one was from the olives of the farm where we stayed, and the other is from a nut mill we visited."

"You can't get olive and nut oil here?" he teased.

"Oh, Marty, you know it's not the same. I couldn't get *these* particular oils here. Anyway, you don't have to carry my suitcase—I managed it all the way to France and back." She yawned and was asleep before they got out of the parking garage.

Next thing she knew he was shaking her shoulder. "Susannah, you're home. Wake up." Her mind was blank for a moment, and then awareness seeped in.

"Marty, I'm so sorry. I couldn't even keep you company for thirty minutes—after all the trouble you went to."

"No problem—I know what jet lag feels like. And I'm glad to see you home safely. I'll help you in with your bag," he said, which he did, promising to call in a few days to see how her reentry was progressing.

When he called, she was still having trouble sleeping and was very tired. "But why don't you come over for a glass of wine tonight," she told Marty. "I have a little *cadeau* for you."

"OK, I'll be over around eight, but I won't stay long."

When she opened the door that evening, he said, *"Bonsoir, madame,"* and kissed her in the French manner.

"You sure picked that up fast!" she said, laughing.

After pouring them each a glass of chilled rosé, she disappeared into the bedroom, returning with her hands behind her back. "Hold out your hands and close your eyes, and I'll give you something to make you wise." He closed his eyes, and she put a package into his hands.

He opened his eyes and then the box. It was a coaster for a wine bottle, and a cork topped with a clump of grapes as a handle.

"Actually made in France! What a perfect gift—you know I need a wine coaster. Thank you!"

They drank their wine, and she told him a little more about the trip. When she stifled a yawn, he said, "I can see you're fading fast, so why don't you go to bed and I'll let myself out."

It sure is nice to have someone to come home to, she thought as she dropped off to sleep. *Maybe we'll click after all.*

....

One evening they were parked in the ferry line, waiting to return to Seattle from Bainbridge Island. Susannah said, "Marty, what do you think about death?"

"In general, or mine in particular?"

"Both," she said.

He thought for a moment. "In general, it's sad. Especially a child's death—that's such a wrenching thing. All that possibility just disappears, all that potential for enjoyment of life. With an adult, it can be different. In some cases, death is a relief, for the dying and the survivors. But usually it's not. Pain, regret, anger, sadness—not a pretty picture. As for myself, I haven't thought about it much. It's a natural process. We all have to die. I hope there isn't too much pain, but that's about it."

"Has someone close to you died?" she asked.

"My parents died when I was in med school. My mom died of cancer, and then a year later my dad died of a heart attack. Not the best couple of years of my life. Now that I think about it, maybe that's why I got married—to help deal with the grief."

"One time you said that you thought karma was conventional wisdom, a platitude," she said. "What do you think comes after death?"

"Nothing," he said. "Why? Do you believe in karma?"

"It makes more sense to me than the idea that we only get one chance. The conventional understanding of heaven and hell doesn't make much sense to me, but the idea of karma seems just. You get more than one chance, and the next time around you have to deal with the consequences of what you did the last time around."

"Well, I've never thought about it that way, but I still feel that all these ideas about the afterlife are motivated mostly by grief, or people's fear of death," Marty said. "This is a gloomy topic! Can we listen to some arias?" He rummaged through the console for a CD.

....

As the music filled the car, Marty thought about Susannah. In some ways she was downright kooky—Corvettes and karma! He was very conventional in his own habits and thinking, and she challenged that conventionality—that's one of the things that attracted him to her. But really, karma? That was a bit much.

....

A couple of weeks later, Seattle was in the midst of a heat wave—in the nineties for several days running. Marty called Susannah on a Friday evening to see how she was doing in the heat. "I'm dying," she complained. "It's still ninety degrees in the condo, and I barely slept last night."

"My place is fine," Marty said. "The air-conditioning really works, but I can't imagine what my electricity bill is going to be."

"Air-conditioning! I didn't know you had air-conditioning. Could I sleep on your couch or use the guest room tonight?

It's supposed to cool off tomorrow."

"Sure," he said. "I'll come pick you up, and we can go wade in the lake."

"I can drive down," she said. "You don't have to pick me up."

"No, I don't have much opportunity to drive with the top down, and the breeze will feel great. I'll be there in thirty minutes."

Susannah had just taken a shower in an effort to cool off. She put on her coolest dress—white linen with a gathered scoop neck, short puffy sleeves, and knee-high slits up the side seams to let the air in. She sorted through her collection of designer shopping bags and found one from Parfumerie Raingeard—a small bag made of heavy black paper with a fancy logo and dainty gold rope handles. She put in a few cosmetics—she didn't wear much makeup anyway—and her toothbrush and her nightgown.

Marty knocked, and she let him in. He was wearing swimming trunks and a faded tank top. "I'm ready," she said, grabbing her handbag and the little shopping bag.

"Isn't that a little dressy for *wading?*" he asked. "We aren't wading at Versailles, you know."

"I know, but it's the most comfortable thing I have and I don't care if it gets a little wet or wrinkled. You can't care about wrinkles if you're wearing linen. I'll just hike up the skirt," she said as she pulled the front door closed.

It was wonderful to feel the breeze as they drove down Madison and along Lake Washington Boulevard. The beaches at Denny Blaine, Madrona, and Mount Baker were overflowing, with people of all ages enjoying the cool lake water.

They found a place to park at the northern end of Mount Baker beach, where it was a little less crowded. As soon as they got to the water, Susannah kicked off her sandals, hiked up her skirt, and waded right in up to her knees. "Oh, this is heaven—it's so cool!"

Marty pulled off his shirt and ran into the water, splashing her as he dove under.

"Hey," she yelled as he surfaced. "I said I didn't mind getting a *little* wet, not *drenched*!" He just laughed and swam back and forth for five minutes.

"That's enough. I'm cool now," he announced, wading out. They sat on the steps and dripped dry, watching the water-skiers and the sailboats. "Ready to go?"

"You're going to get your leather car seat all wet," she said.

"No, I've got a towel in the car," he replied.

"You're always so prepared, Marty! Do you ever forget anything?"

"Never," he joked. They got in the car and drove up the hill.

"Gin and tonic?" he asked as they got out of the car and went into his pleasantly cool house.

"Lovely!" she replied. "Heavy on the tonic and lime, please. It feels just right in here—air-conditioning is a godsend, even in Seattle." She set down her sandals, handbag, and shopping bag by the sofa. "Thanks for saving me from my sweltering apartment."

"Wish I'd thought of it sooner. I'll get your drink and then change." He disappeared into the kitchen, returning shortly with her G&T.

"Oh dear," Susannah said a few minutes later, when Marty came back from exchanging a wet swimsuit for dry cotton gym shorts. "I didn't drink enough water today." She was looking with chagrin at her almost-empty glass. "I'd better slow down or I'll be swacked!"

"I'll get you some water," he said, laughing.

Coming back, Marty paused in the kitchen doorway and watched her. She had set aside her glass and stood looking out at the thinning crowd on the lakefront and the twilight sky turning pink. The top of her dress reminded him of those blouses the waitresses wear in some Mexican restaurants. He imagined sliding it off her shoulders. It had buttons all the way down the front. And he could see through it as she stood in front of the window.

He came up behind her and put his arms around her waist. "Susannah, that damned dress!"

"What's wrong?" She turned around, startled.

"It's so provocative!" He kissed her, and kept kissing her.

....

Susannah was surprised. *Should I be doing this?* flitted through her mind. But it felt so good: His skin was cool from the lake. His shirt smelled like fresh laundry. He tasted like lime.

She noticed her hands slipping up around his neck and into his thick damp hair. *Oh, why not?* she thought as she kissed him back.

When they stopped kissing, Marty pulled Susannah closer and said, "I've been wanting to do this for months!"

"Sometime," she said, "you can tell me what took you so long."

He didn't need any more permission than that. Several kisses later, he started unbuttoning all those buttons.

....

When Susannah woke up Saturday morning, she could smell coffee. She wasn't on the couch; she was in Marty's bed. And she felt delicious. Marty came into the bedroom, wearing a terry robe and carrying two lattes. She was trying to prop up pillows, sit up, and keep the sheet over her front, all at once. He laughed at her and set the lattes on the nightstand. He sat down facing her on the bed and reached around to arrange the pillows behind her. Then he kissed her gently. "Does *madame* require anything else?"

"Marty, what happened?" she burst out.

"Lots of things happened," he said with a look of contentment. "Don't you remember?"

"Yes, I remember very well," she said as he gave her the latte and picked up his own. "You know that's not what I mean. Why did the whole thing happen last night? We've been spending time together for months, and I thought we were just friends."

"I was attracted to you the first time I saw you, years ago. But I was shy and in a rut, so I didn't do anything about it. Then when you sent out that e-mail asking for a ride to Otter Island, I saw my chance. And that night when you came over for soup and we sang "Some Enchanted Evening" together, it was all over—I was head over heels."

"Well, you sure fooled me!"

"I was being very careful. I didn't want to make a wrong move, so I just went very slowly. But it was getting harder and harder as I fell more in love with you. And then last night, that dress was just the last straw! Susannah, come live with me. You can have your own room, and rearrange the furniture or redecorate, or we'll buy a new house. We can make love as often, or as seldom, as you want—"

"Marty, wait, wait, wait!" she said. "This is going way too fast!"

His hopeful look disappeared, and Susannah was afraid she'd hurt his feelings. He had obviously been giving this considerable thought. In an effort to lighten things up a bit, she said with a smile, "Dr. McAlistair, are you asking me to be your *mistress*?"

"I would have asked you to marry me, but I thought you'd say no, at least right now, and that if we could live together for a while, it might be more likely that you'd eventually say yes."

"Marty, this is completely overwhelming! You're moving from friends to lovers to marriage, and I'm still halfway between friends and lovers. I need time to think and try to sort this out. Does that sound reasonable?"

"Of course, of course. Just don't say no right away. Then I can hope."

She smiled and kissed him. "I won't say no right away. Now, how about some breakfast, and then you can take me home."

....

She blew him a kiss as he dropped her off in front of her building. He drove home, thinking about the past twenty-four hours. She was so uninhibited—at least compared to him. Wading in a linen dress. Using a shopping bag for a suitcase! She was intelligent, fun, and interested in art and music; she made him think about things he didn't usually think about. His life was so much more interesting and lively since she'd come into it. And, God, it was good to have a woman in his bed again! He was pretty sure she'd enjoyed their lovemaking, and he was impatient for more.

....

Susannah was rattled. She had enjoyed making love with Marty, but was bowled over to learn how strongly he felt about her. Everything seemed different now. After meditating for an hour, she felt more centered. She checked her e-mail, worked on a fund-raising letter for a nonprofit, and put in some laundry. She made herself a chef salad for dinner and tried to think methodically through her feelings about Marty and his offer.

He's responsible, competent, considerate, friendly in a quiet way, good with kids, generous, cultured, financially well off—and he's in love with me. We seem to be sexually compatible. And I really do care for him. She was sure that some women wouldn't have any scruples about going after Marty, even if they didn't truly love him. He was quite a catch.

So why didn't I just say yes immediately? She thought about that for a while. *I think I need more assurance that it will last. He'd be devastated if I found out later I'd made a mistake. But how do we know? There's no way you can know everything about a person before you commit to a relationship.*

The next morning in the middle of her meditation another thought occurred: *It's not about needing more assurance that it will last.* She returned to her mantra until she had finished her hour. Then she began to mull over the new thought. If she didn't need assurance that the relationship would last, what was it about, her hesitation? It slowly dawned on her: it was too easy, too comfortable. At her age, it was very compelling to have the prospect of a comfortable—beyond comfortable—life with a man who loved her and desired her. There were so many intelligent, attractive women out there, and it seemed as though there were so few eligible men. She was fortunate to have this opportunity. But she wanted more than a comfortable life.

Maybe she could make Marty happy, but would he challenge her? Would she grow as the result of the relationship? She thought back over many of their conversations about life, about death and the afterlife, about karma. On these big issues, they had very little in common.

She wanted a partner who cared about his spiritual life and spiritual questions. Someone who was coming from the same philosophical perspective as she was, or at least understood the concepts she was talking about. That wasn't the case with Marty. She could be with Marty while she was on her own spiritual path—she had been—but spirituality wasn't something they had in common, and it was something of primary importance in her life.

Over the next few days she thought continually about whether they could be happy together. She weighed pros and cons. But increasingly, she was of the opinion that something was missing. On her part, there was no passion, no longing, no sense that she could hardly wait to see him again. She was well aware that passion and longing alone weren't enough for a long-term liaison, but somehow, as much as they enjoyed each other's company, something was lacking for her. Maybe she should be practical and take a good deal when it appeared, but she just couldn't look at it that way.

As it became clearer to her that this was not going to be a long-term relationship, her thoughts turned in another direction. Had she been leading him on? Not intentionally. But he was so easy to be with, and since it took so long for him to declare himself, she was caught unaware. Not totally unaware, she admitted, but she had allowed herself not to think about where their friendship might be leading. He could have misinterpreted some things she'd said and done. *Damn! I should have been more careful, and I shouldn't have slept with him!*

On the other hand, she reflected, maybe she'd broken the ice for him. Maybe he wouldn't be so shy now. He knows how to date; he knows he can do it, that it's worth the effort. And he knows he can satisfy a woman in bed.

Susannah invited Marty over for dessert on Friday night. She made his favorite—crème brûlée. They sat at the table and chatted about this and that, both a little tense.

"Marty, this is very difficult for me to say, because I know you're not going to want to hear it. I can't live with you or be your wife, though I'm deeply honored that you've asked me."

He appeared to be examining his coffee cup with great concentration. She put her hand over his and went on.

"You're a wonderful man, Marty—considerate, gentle, competent, intelligent, witty, a very satisfying lover. I *do* love you. It's just not in the way you want me to."

He wouldn't look at her, but she continued, more and more upset as she realized this was much harder for him than she had hoped it would be. "There's something missing, that spark we talked about. It's nothing that's wrong with you, that you could change or become. That 'click' just isn't there between us. You can't have a one-sided click. Do you know what I mean, Marty?" She made a silent plea that he would understand.

He glanced at her briefly and then back at his coffee cup. "I can't really take in all you're saying. All I'm hearing is 'no.'"

"I'm so sorry, Marty," she said with tears in her eyes as he withdrew his hand from hers. "I'm very fond of you. I would never have intentionally led you on. I would do almost anything to avoid hurting you, but I don't feel what you want me to feel."

There was a moment of silence, and then he said, "Well, I guess that's that, then. I don't know what to say, except I'm sorry too, Susannah. I think I'd better go now."

After he left, she went to bed, tossing and turning for hours, wondering if there was anything she could have said differently to make things easier for him.

For two days she labored over a letter, hoping he would read it and reflect on it and that in time he would be able to appreciate the good things that came out of their relationship. Finally, she put it in the mailbox. Then she called Alice, their mutual friend.

"Alice, I have a request to make. But first, I have to ask for your discretion. Will you keep this between us?"

"Of course I will, Susannah. It will be just between us."

"Marty and I won't be seeing each other anymore. He wanted something I couldn't give him, I'm truly sad to say. My request is that you'll be on the lookout for a nice woman for him. I know people have tried to fix him up before, but he wasn't interested then. I think he will be now—he's more self-confident and clearer with himself that he does want a relationship. He'll get over me, and he'll get over me faster if there's someone else in the picture. So be on the lookout for him. I'd really like him to find someone perfect for him."

"I'll be discreet in every way, Susannah. I'll do my very best—he's such a dear," Alice said. "And you'll be happy to know I can think of a couple of prospects right now."

Marty didn't come to rowing for several weeks, and then he was back again. He seemed to be his old self, but he and Susannah didn't talk much.

About three months after their "breakup," he walked

with her to the parking lot after rowing. "Susannah, I want to thank you for your letter. It was very wise, and honest. I didn't want to hear those things at first, but I know you were right. And I thought you'd be pleased to know that I'm dating a woman I like very much."

"I'm so glad to hear that, Marty!" She gave him a hug, and they went their separate ways. She hoped he'd found his true love. But she also hoped she wouldn't spend the rest of her life dreaming all alone.

CHAPTER THREE

Only Connect

They noticed each other at Gate 12 as they were waiting for their row numbers to be called for the flight to Seattle from Boston.

He had the easy stride of a natural athlete. Stopping by an empty seat, he struggled out of his small backpack. It looked heavy. He was wearing chinos and a blue dress shirt, open at the collar with rolled-up sleeves, and he carried a brown corduroy sport coat with elbow patches that made it look like it had seen better days. He was about six feet tall and had a good physique. His graying dark hair needed a trim.

She had only a handbag and a book for carry-on luggage and was wearing a black pantsuit that looked comfortable but was a cut above what's commonly seen on planes these days—classy in a quiet way. She was about average height, attractive, not too heavy, not too thin.

As their paths converged at the ramp, they smiled slightly and he motioned her to go ahead, catching a faint whiff of her perfume. It happened that they were sitting next to each other, he in the middle, she in the aisle seat. "Looks like we're together for the duration," he said, pushing his backpack under the seat and maneuvering into his place.

"Yes, it looks like it," she replied, smiling.

Neither of them buckled their seat belts, since Window Seat hadn't arrived yet. The flight attendants were shutting the overhead compartments when a breathless young woman hurried down the aisle toward them. She was wearing a zip-up sweatshirt proclaiming "Harvard" across the front, a skimpy tank top, and the ubiquitous low-slung jeans that exposed a narrow swath of belly. Tossing her long blonde hair over her shoulder, she tried to shove one of her bags into the already-crowded overhead bin. A flight attendant came to help her, and Susannah and Middle Seat got out, letting her in. Within fifteen minutes they were in the air.

Susannah began reading a new novel by John Irving that she'd picked up in the airport bookstore. She liked his quirky writing. Middle Seat was reading *The Quiet American* by Graham Greene. Window Seat appeared to be asleep, wearing her headphones. After a while, Middle Seat asked Susannah if she had read much John Irving. "Pretty much everything he's written, I think. I like *Cider House Rules* the best."

"Yes, I like that too, and they did a good job adapting it for the movie."

"Do you read much Graham Greene?" she asked.

"No, this is my first since *The Power and the Glory*, and that was ages ago."

"*The Quiet American*'s pretty dark, as I remember. I read it for my book club."

"What else have you read in your book club?"

"We've been together for years now, so it's hard to remember all the books we've read. Let's see: *The Amazing Adventures of Kavalier and Clay*, *The Kite Runner*, *The Sparrow*, *The Poisonwood Bible*, *Reading Lolita in Tehran*, *Team of Rivals*. I can't remember more."

"That's quite a selection!"

"It's a very well-educated group of women with very eclectic taste—which is great, because on my own I'd never pick out a lot of those books," she said. "Do you read a lot?"

"Yeah," he said. "I've always got my nose in a book. I've read many of the ones you mentioned. I also read mysteries, crime thrillers, and so on."

"Who are your favorite mystery writers?"

"P. D. James, Elizabeth George, and Tony Hillerman come to mind first."

"I've noticed that a lot of mystery writers have a formula," she said, "and after you read three or four of their books, you can predict the ending pretty quickly. Have you noticed that?"

"Yes, I have—except I can rarely predict Tony Hillerman. In a way, I think a formula would be understandable. Imagine trying to think up all those plots. It must be easier to write a novel if you have some organizing principle and then fill in the blanks."

"Well, maybe it works that way for some writers," Susannah said, "but I think the creative process is generally not very formulaic. When you hear writers describe how they work, they're all over the map. I write stories for my own amusement, and it's fascinating how they come out. Maybe I start with just a sentence or just a vague idea of a plot, and then stuff just comes. Sometimes I'll write several paragraphs and not change a word. Other times I edit like crazy. It's really quite amazing how it happens. And I've learned never to think I know what the ending will be. I may have a general inkling or feeling, but I try to leave it wide open."

He looked at her intently. He had very blue eyes. "But it's your story—you can do what you want."

"No, it's only partly my story. The details, the description maybe, some things would be called 'mine,' but basically it comes from the 'field' and I'm just trying to give it birth, so to speak."

"What do you mean by the 'field'? By the way, my name is Will Ryan."

"I'm Susannah Emory," she replied. "Hmm, we're getting into metaphysics or philosophy or something. Does this *really* interest you?"

"Sure it does. I teach comparative religion and philosophy at the University of Washington, so this is definitely up my alley."

"Well, that's rather intimidating! If you told me you taught math or biology or something, I'd be more comfortable talking about this stuff."

"I teach math at the U," he said, and they both laughed.

"OK. I'll do my best," Susannah said. "Consciousness manifests in an infinite number of ways and with an infinite number of possibilities. That's the 'field,' and that's where stories come from—and all art."

Just then the flight attendants arrived with snacks and drinks. Susannah pulled a turkey sandwich out of her purse, and Will pulled a foot-long sub out of his backpack. Window Seat took a package of sushi and two energy bars out of her duffel. He politely conversed with both of them. Susannah could see that the young woman was actually flirting with him—he was old enough to be her father! But, he *was* good-looking.

After they'd finished eating (he put half of his sub back in his pack), Susannah got up so Will could get out. When he was gone, Window Seat leaned across his seat and said, "Hi, I'm Pam. You know who he is?" Susannah shook her head, mystified at this conversational gambit. Pam went on. "He's one of the most popular profs on campus. Half the girls in his classes are in love with him, because he's so handsome and, like, intelligent and funny—and he doesn't sleep with any of his students. My sorority sisters are going to be so jealous when they hear I sat next to him for five hours, like, thigh to thigh!"

Susannah was taken aback—amazing what you could hear on an airplane!

Will came back, and Susannah stood up to let him in. She didn't want to initiate conversation that he might not welcome; they'd already talked for two hours or more. So she closed her eyes and thought about what Pam had said. *Isn't it interesting how you learn things about people? And isn't it nice to know that girls still fall in love with men who are intelligent and witty and ethical? It's probably easier if they're handsome too.* Mulling all this over, Susannah fell asleep, something she never did on airplanes. When she woke up nearly an hour later, her head was inappropriately close to Will's shoulder. She sat up and apologized for impinging on his space and inconveniencing him.

"No problem," he said. "I'm happy to be a pillow for a well-read woman. He grinned at her, and she smiled back.

"But if I read *People* magazine and bodice rippers, would you still be happy to be my pillow?" She realized immediately what a snobby remark she'd made. "Sorry, that was really inappropriate."

She was glad he was correcting papers and she could hide behind her book. *Where did that come from?* she wondered. *I've probably ruined whatever positive opinion he might have had of me. Thoughtless, conceited woman!*

As they started the descent into Seattle, he stuffed all the papers back in his pack and got out a big box of Junior Mints. He offered some to Susannah and Pam, both of whom accepted. The three of them sat there enjoying their mints in companionable silence. Susannah thought it would make a delightful vignette for a story.

They all three walked together to baggage claim, chatting about travel, lost luggage, et cetera. One of Pam's sorority sisters picked her up. Pam gave Susannah a conspiratorial look and went off with her friend. Will and Susannah collected their luggage, walked to the light rail link, and took the train into Seattle, talking the whole time.

Susannah stood up as they approached her stop. "It's been really nice talking with you. It made the trip go faster."

"Do you have time for coffee?" he asked.

"Not right now, but could I take a rain check? Let me give you my phone number." She rummaged around in her bag and found a card for him just as the train doors were opening.

"I'll call you," he said as she left the train and waved.

Susannah waited outside the station for her bus, and then

walked the few blocks to her condo, all the while pondering her faux pas. It was kind of him to pretend to forget about it. He probably wouldn't call. She sighed.

As she unlocked the front door, she again experienced how odd it felt to call this new condo home. She and Alex and her daughter-in-law had worked out a novel arrangement. They paid for her condo, and she gave them her house—it would be theirs one day anyway. She was putting the finishing touches on her unit; there wasn't a lot to do, but she was enjoying making it her own.

································

Will thought about Susannah as he walked to his house in Montlake. It had been a long time since he'd enjoyed a conversation with a woman so much. And what color were her eyes anyway? Were they blue or blue green, or blue gray, or what? Her quip about bodice rippers was revealing—she was quick and funny, but she recognized a bit of snobbishness in herself and was embarrassed. He was sorry she didn't have time for coffee but glad to have her phone number.

································

Will called her about a week later. "Remember when we were talking about non-dualism, unicity, and all that, on the plane? Eckhart Tolle is going to be on campus Thursday night, and I wondered if you'd like to go hear him. I don't expect to learn anything new from what he says, but I'm interested in how he comes across and who comes to hear him."

Susannah smiled at that little bit of academic arrogance. "That sounds interesting—yes, I'd like to go. Shall I meet you there or pick you up or what?" She knew he didn't have a car.

"I'll meet you at Kane Hall at seven fifteen," he said. "Let me give you my phone number, in case you need to reach me."

Thursday afternoon she got an urgent call from her daughter-in-law, Sylvianne, asking if Susannah could babysit one of the boys. Sylvianne needed to take the other one to see his doctor about an earache, and Alex was out of town.

"Of course," Susannah said. "I'll be right over." She immediately called Will and left a message. "Sorry for the last minute change of plans, Will. I can't come tonight—family emergency—non-life-threatening. I'll call you tomorrow."

When she called him the next day, she caught him during his office hours. "I'm really sorry I had to cancel at the last minute. How was the lecture?"

"Oh, I decided to bag it after I got your call. Is your family OK?"

She explained the situation and then said, "I was wondering if you've ever seen *V for Vendetta*? If not, would you like to come over and watch it with me? It's got some interesting ideas in it."

"Sure, that sounds like fun. When?"

"How about Wednesday night? Come about seven thirty."

"Wednesday's soccer night. I've been playing with a bunch of guys for several years, all about my age. We have a good time, huffing and puffing up and down the field. But it keeps us in pretty good shape. How about Thursday night?"

Movie night arrived, and after they'd finished watching the DVD they sat munching popcorn on the sofa and talking about the film. "I loved the acting and the political commentary, but I think the violence was gratuitous," Susannah said. "I think all the violence in movies is gratuitous. It's just there to titillate, and make money. Violence is never right—they know from all kinds of studies that torture doesn't work, that spanking doesn't work, and so on."

"Well," said Will, "you may be right, but it's also true that violence is real, it's happening, it has some meaning. So what's the meaning? Isn't it just evidence that people are screwed-up, that whole cultures are screwed-up? It's how some dysfunctionality in the person or culture gets expressed, like a lack of love, or fear, or excessive emphasis on authority or honor."

"Yes, I agree with you, but that point isn't made in the movies—violence is just spewed out like . . . like . . . I don't know what," she spluttered. "As though it's just something fun to watch, like sports or the cooking channel!"

Before he left that evening, Will invited Susannah to go with him the following week to one of his periodic get-togethers in a tavern with any students who wanted to come. She was game to go, but she wondered what she could talk about with his students and how to dress.

....

She didn't want to look like a grandmother, but she wasn't going to dress like a college student either. She decided on jeans, boots, a turtleneck, clunky earrings, and her old leather coat. Will was waiting on the sidewalk in front of his little Montlake house when she drove up. They went over the Montlake Bridge and down Pacific to the Speakeasy. *It hasn't changed in thirty years,* she thought as they went into the noisy dark tavern. She liked the feel of Will's arm around her shoulder, guiding her to the table in back where his students were waving at him. They scooted over to make room.

"Susannah, this is Ashley, Jason, Brittany, and Samuel—everyone, this is Susannah."

They were all chatting when the waiter arrived to take their orders.

"Do you have Moose Drool?" Susannah asked.

Conversation at the table stopped.

"No," said the waiter, "sorry."

"Black Butte Porter?" she asked.

"No, sorry," he said again.

"Mac and Jack's?" she asked hopefully.

"No, we only have Bud, Coors, Corona, PBR, and Boundary Bay."

"OK. Boundary Bay, please. Thanks!"

Will ordered the same thing, and conversation resumed.

Susannah noticed the easy relationship Will had with his students. They joked a lot and moved back and forth from serious to light topics. She threw in a quip once that drew laughter, but she mostly listened and watched.

They were having an intense discussion of Aristotelian logic versus paradoxical logic, which wandered into the similarities in Taoism and dialectical materialism. She had to concentrate very hard to follow the conversation. Then Brittany surprised her by asking, "What's your philosophy of life, Susannah?"

Susannah blanked for a moment, then she said slowly, "Hmm. Well, I guess I'm with Socrates and Jesus: 'The unexamined life is not worth living,' and 'Love your neighbor as yourself.' I take that directive in a non-dualistic way, like we *are* our neighbor. I guess that pretty well sums it up."

They nodded thoughtfully and the conversation wandered on to other topics.

As they were walking back to the car Susannah asked, "Will, why did you invite me to come along?"

"I enjoy your company," he said easily, "and I wanted them to see I have a social life."

"Well, did I pass inspection?"

"Oh, yes, I could see the wheels going around in their heads." In a professorial manner, he reeled off his idea of what his students thought of her. "One, you drank beer. Two, you knew at least four different kinds. Three, the tavern didn't have three of them. When you asked for Moose Drool, you got extra points! Four, you're quick and have a sense of humor. Socrates and Jesus and non-dualism—that knocked their socks off!"

"Whew, what a relief to know I made the grade, so to speak. I was interested to see your relationship with them. It's sort of 'parental lite.' You care about them, and they'll listen to advice from you, because it's not coming along with all the emotional baggage there is between parents and kids."

"Yeah, it's one of the biggest rewards of teaching," he

said. "When I came to the U, I published just enough articles and went to just enough conferences to get tenure. I do enough of that now to keep from becoming stale to my students and myself, and of course there're always tons of interesting things to learn. But I'm not heavy on the research and publication. I'm not one of those faculty members who don't want anything to do with students."

Susannah dropped him off and continued home. *What was all that about,* she wondered? *He wanted them to know he had a social life? Is that code for something else? That he's gay? That he likes women his own age?* Or was she being used as a prop somehow? It was puzzling.

....

Two weeks later, Will asked her to come over for dinner. "It'll have to be pizza or Thai takeout or something—I'm no cook," he laughed.

"I'll bring soup, salad, and bread," she said, "if you'll do wine and dessert."

"I think I can manage that. What kind of wine?"

She thought a moment. "Do you like curry?"

"Sure."

"In that case, get a dry Riesling. I don't have any dessert preference"

Monday, Susannah went through her daily routine of meditation, rowing, and a couple of hours at the computer working on her stories. In the afternoon she made a mulligatawny soup and a green salad. She put a loaf of French bread in a shopping bag, along with a few last-minute ingredients, fastened the lid onto her stockpot with a small bungee, so it wouldn't spill in transit, and arrived on Will's doorstep holding the hot soup, with her handbag over one shoulder and a shopping bag on the opposite wrist.

"Hi," he said, opening the door before she could figure out how to knock. He took the soup from her and carried it to the tiny kitchen. She put the rest of her dinner supplies on the counter next to a dripping bottle of the wine she'd suggested, opened but untouched, and two plastic cups.

"Welcome! I didn't try to fancy up the house," he said proudly. "This is how it looks pretty much all the time. Shall I pour us some wine?"

"Yes, please," she said, "and I'll finish up the dinner."

"I've cleared off one end of the dining room table." One end was covered with books and papers, and he had set the other end with mismatched flatware and paper towels for napkins. She put the soup on the stove to reheat and gave him the bread.

"Here, cut this up for me, will you? Half a loaf is fine. And I need a small knife, please."

He rummaged around in a drawer and came up with a small dull knife for her and a large dull knife to cut bread. She couldn't help grinning.

Susannah cut up an apple, dumped it into the soup, and poured in some half-and-half. "OK, ready in two minutes." Opening various cupboard doors, she found two plates, two bowls, and a saucer for the butter. She ladled the soup into bowls using a coffee cup, and they carried their food and wine to the table.

"This smells terrific—what is it?"

"Mulligatawny—chicken and rice with curry, basically."

"It's delicious!" he said after a few spoonfuls. "And it's nice with this wine."

As they ate and talked, she took note of her surroundings. Fairly fresh paint, all beige. Absolutely nothing else on the walls. For furniture: a lumpy couch, a battered coffee table, a torchiere, and a TV with DVD player. There was also one enormous bookcase—full. Later when she went to use the bathroom—which was pretty clean for a bachelor pad—she peeked in his bedroom. Mattress on the floor, but sort of tidy, a reading lamp, and one frame on the wall. It was his BA diploma from Notre Dame, summa cum laude in philosophy.

He was putting the dishes in the sink when she returned. "I was looking at all those fancy desserts in the QFC bakery," he said, "but I couldn't figure out how to get home with them on my bike without squishing them. Then I found the perfect solution. My old favorite—maple bars!"

"Oh, good. I haven't had one of those for ages," she said, smiling to herself. He was so cute—off-the-charts intelligent, but so unsophisticated.

He nodded when she asked if he'd like tea.

"Do you have a teakettle?"

"I just use a pan," he said. She got out two mugs, and they sat down again to tea and maple bars.

"How long have you been here?" she asked. "It's certainly convenient for your work."

"My folks left this place to my sister and me. She and her family live in West Seattle—on Alki Point. We rented this place out for years, but then I did the math and realized it was cheaper and bigger than where I had been paying rent, so I moved in here. Sis is a lawyer and married to a lawyer and she doesn't need the rental income. So it's a good deal."

"Will, the other night when we went to your favorite Italian restaurant, you were speaking what sounded like fluent Italian and you said you'd lived in Italy. How long were you there, and what were you doing?"

He looked like he was trying to decide what to say, so she quickly interjected, "I don't want to pry—don't feel you have to answer. I'm sorry I asked."

"No, it's OK. I've been thinking about telling you this. I just wasn't sure where to start. I was a Roman Catholic priest for about twenty years, including seminary and my PhD. I was working my way up the ecclesiastical ladder. I was going to reform the church from within, et cetera, et cetera. I was in Rome for several years." He paused and fiddled with a spoon lying on the table. "I won't go into all the reasons that led to my decision, but I couldn't stay in the church. I'm glad my parents were gone when I left. They would have been so disappointed, and it would have been impossible to explain everything to them. The Notre Dame diploma on the wall in my bedroom is kind of a memorial to them—they didn't go to college and they were proud of me. Want another maple bar?" She shook her head as he reached for another.

"So maybe the best thing I got out of all that was fluent Italian! And now you'll understand when you see some of my eccentric behavior," he said, laughing.

She sat with her elbows on the table, fingers laced beneath her chin, and listened intently. Between bites, glancing at her now and then, he continued. "When I left the church, I was kind of unstable for a while. I was so angry and disappointed that what I'd idealized, what I'd sacrificed so much for, didn't live up to my expectations." He got up to pour more hot water into their mugs. "There are some good things about organized religion, but there's a dark side too. It just wasn't the place for me. Shall we adjourn to the couch?"

They brought their tea and settled on the couch. She kicked off her shoes and curled up with her legs under her as he went on.

"Anyway, I guess I thought I needed to make up for lost time, so I was sleeping around. I had a few flings that might loosely be called 'relationships,' but not really. I'd been seeing this one woman for about a month, Betsy, and it was pretty hot and heavy. We always used protection, but one night we'd had a lot to drink and we were careless and she got pregnant. She wanted me to marry her, and I wouldn't do it. She wanted to have the child, so I agreed to pay child support. I've never missed a payment—and I'm paying for half of his college expenses. His name is Derek Bailey, and he's twenty-one. He's a junior at Reed, majoring in English." He took a sip of tea.

"Did she ever marry?"

"Yes, she married a guy named Steve Bailey when Derek was about three, and he legally adopted Derek. She says her husband has been a real father to him, but Derek knows I'm his biological father. She says he has no interest in me, which doesn't surprise me. I haven't pushed it. But I've been feeling more and more over the last year or so that I should try to establish a relationship with him. It's easy to let it slide—I have a fair amount of guilt about the whole situation."

"Yes," Susannah said, "but you should certainly try. If you regret now that you haven't done it, you'll regret it even more later."

"When I'm honest with myself, I admit I'm procrastinating because I'm afraid he won't want to have anything to do with me. He must feel I've rejected him, which is certainly understandable." Will shifted his position and put his feet up on the coffee table. "So now you've heard the whole sorry story. I've dated a few women over the past few years, but nothing ever came of it."

"You live a rather Spartan life. No women, minimalist living conditions—just reading, soccer, and your students. Is that intentional, or did you just kind of fall into it?"

"I guess I just fell into it. I've never really cared about things, about stuff. I enjoy being in places that are beautiful, or tasteful, like your home, but I have no interest in doing anything to this place—I don't notice it very much. I do recognize that other people would find it rather austere, though," he said with a grin, looking around at the bare walls and floors. "I spend time with my sister and her family. I have dinner with them about once a month, and we go skiing, take bike trips with the kids, and so on. She has two girls, and when they were little I used to take care of them every so often, so Allie and Greg could have a getaway, or go to a function or something."

They sat without talking for a while. Then she said, changing the subject a bit, "I noticed a rosary hanging on the lampshade in your bedroom. Have you rejected everything about the church, or just some things?"

"I guess I'd say I've rejected the institution but not all of the spiritual practices. You probably know about prayer beads, how they're common in lots of religious traditions because they're calming and they help you get into a meditative state. You don't have to attach any theological story for them to work—kind of like a mantra. I meditate every day. We have that in common," he said, smiling.

"That's a lot to take in!" Susannah didn't know what else to say. "And I think it's time for me to go home." She slipped into her shoes and went to the kitchen to put her pot and plastic boxes in her shopping bag. Will walked out to the car with her.

"Thanks for cooking," he said, touching her arm lightly.

"Thanks for the wine and maple bars," she replied, and kissed his cheek.

Susannah was thinking about Will's situation as she got ready for bed. He was a tenured professor with medical insurance and no mortgage or rent payment. Paying for half of tuition at Reed was probably cutting into his income considerably. Money or lack of it, however, didn't account for the way he lived. She could understand having little interest in material things, but she still wondered if his lifestyle was the residue of a priestly life.

And she wondered what it meant that he had been so candid with her about his personal background.

....

They settled into a comfortable routine. They'd go out for dinner, or she'd cook dinner at her place—his kitchen was impossible—and then they'd watch a DVD. Tonight he'd invited her to his soccer game before dinner and movie. She enjoyed meeting his teammates and getting acquainted with the girlfriends and wives who were sitting with her on the bleachers of the Montlake Playfield. It was a good game, the score was close, and Susannah was interested in Will's role on the team. He seemed to be the unofficial coach, encouraging the others and suggesting strategy now and then.

After the game ended, the guys were joking, rehashing their plays and gathering up their gear. Laughing at something a friend had said, Will pulled off his sweaty jersey, stuffed it into his duffel bag, and put on a dry sweatshirt. The woman sitting beside Susannah said, "God, I wish Joe looked like that—and he's ten years younger than Will!" Susannah had definitely noticed Will's flat belly and the muscle definition in his arms and back. *Nice,* she thought. *Maybe I should come to more soccer games.*

Tonight's movie selection was *Notting Hill*, which Susannah found romantic and poignant.

"Pretty lightweight," Will sniffed.

"Yes, it was lightweight, but it was about love, which is about as basic as you can get. And that scene where the Julia Roberts character says she's always hungry because her career, her image, depends on her being slim—that bit was very moving. But if you're inclined to a weighty topic, Professor, what do you think about death?"

"Are you serious?" He looked at her quizzically.

"Yes, of course I'm serious."

He settled further down into the sofa and clasped his hands behind his head. After a moment he said, "Death is a rearrangement of the borders of reality."

"Well, is that all? Aren't you going to say more?"

"Of course I am. I'm a professor—I couldn't possibly stop with one sentence, even if it is brilliantly succinct."

"You're so humble!"

"Remember on the airplane you said something like, 'Consciousness manifests'?"

"I'm amazed you remember that," Susannah said.

"Well, I was amazed you said it. What're the odds that I'll sit next to an attractive woman on an airplane who says something even remotely close to that? I was just blown away. Anyway, I digress. We talked before about different kinds of consciousness. The thing I call 'I' can be conscious in various ways—waking, sleeping, dreaming, and so on. But the 'I' is still consciousness. And when the body dies, the consciousness is still there. So death is just a transition to another form of reality or consciousness. In a nutshell."

"I'd say that was a pretty big nutshell."

"Of course, this is just my view," Will said, "but it's backed up by a great deal of philosophical, spiritual, theological, and religious thought. As are other points of view, I hasten to add." He looked at her with brows raised. "Did I pass the test?"

Susannah pretended to think about her answer. "Even with all your caveats, you passed. I'll even give you an A for your answer—probably because I agree with you." Refilling his popcorn bowl, she said, "Now I have a different topic for you. I've been conducting a survey. Why is it that middle-aged and older men seem to prefer younger women?"

Will laughed and said, "You're asking the wrong guy. I avoid younger women like the plague!"

"Well, I understand your specific situation," she said, grinning at him. "But you must have some thoughts about the phenomenon in general."

He considered her question and then said, "I'm remembering a conversation in the tav after soccer one night. Mostly guys were just BS'ing, but one guy was pretty candid. He said that when he was young and just getting interested in girls, he was too shy to ask a girl for a date. All those women, but he never got one. He finally did get married, and he loves his wife, but he said he's still kind of stuck in adolescence, noticing the pretty girls and wishing for them, thinking about what he missed out on in his youth. I thought that took a lot of guts to admit."

Susannah went out to the kitchen to get more sparkling water. When she came back, she said, "Will, remember when we were leaving the Speakeasy after that evening with your students?"

He nodded.

"I asked you why you asked me to come, and you said something about wanting your students to know you had a social life. What did you mean by that?"

"This is kind of embarrassing. For several reasons," he said, examining his fingernails. "Sometimes my students—both male and female—make, um, inappropriate advances. I've developed my standard 'thanks, but no, thanks' response, and that usually works pretty well. But I thought maybe I could head some of this off at the pass if everyone knew that . . . that there was a woman in my life. I hope you don't mind. I was kind of taking advantage of our friendship." He looked at her to assess her reaction.

"Would you like me to call you 'honey bun' and pat you on the butt the next time we're around your students?"

He looked startled and then laughed. "I wouldn't mind that at all, but I don't think it's necessary. I think the word is out. You're funny," he added.

Susannah told him about Pam's revelations on the airplane. "So I already knew you had temptations. And I was impressed to hear that you didn't sleep with your students."

"Well, it's a no-brainer, isn't it? But you'd be amazed at how often teachers succumb," he commented ruefully. Will slipped on his shoes and stood up. "Time for me to go." He put on his coat and got his bike helmet. "I enjoy movie nights with you," he said at the door.

And then he kissed her, a long slow kiss, and she kissed him back.

"That was just like I thought it would be. Thanks, Susannah. Sleep well."

Well, he's been thinking about kissing me, and he finally did, she thought. *That's progress—I guess. Be patient.* An image of his naked torso as he changed into his sweatshirt zipped through her mind. She didn't feel very patient.

The first week in December, Susannah planned a housewarming. There would be only about ten people—she didn't have room for more. Her friends enjoyed seeing her new home; many of them were also contemplating a move to a smaller place, so they wanted to know how she liked it. And there was the usual conversation about local politics, house prices, terrorism, and the latest books read. She was pleased that Will seemed to be enjoying himself. There was lots of talk and laughter and consuming of wine.

  He stayed after the others left to help her clean up and put things away. Then they sat on the sofa and put their feet up. As he was telling her anecdotes of the evening—witty things people had said, arguments over what to do about the latest financial crisis, and so on—he was absent-mindedly running his hand up and down the inside of her arm. She teased him about how much wine he'd drunk. He sat up suddenly. "Am I drunk, Susannah?" he said. "I'm really sorry."

  "No, no, you're not drunk," she said, laughing. "You're fine!"

  "No, I think I'd better go home." He went to the closet, got his coat and helmet, and said, "Thanks so much! It was a great party—you have nice friends. I'll call you soon." And off he went before she knew what was happening.

  Susannah thought this relationship was like chaos theory. When was a pattern going to emerge, when was it going to make some sense? One minute he was a suave professor; the next minute he was almost like a teenager. Then she remembered his story about how he came to have a son, and it made a little more sense.

....

Will was twenty minutes into his two o'clock class on Lao-tzu when the classroom door flew open and Fred, one of his students, stepped into the room. His hair was dripping, and his clothes were soaking wet. There was a strong smell of gasoline. He had a matchbox in one hand and a wooden match in the other.

"OK, Professor Ryan, you're always talking about the importance of deeds of conscience, and right action, so you're going to see one right here and now!"

"God, help us," Will prayed instinctively.

Fred waved the matchbox at the class. "Get out your fucking cell phones, you bimbos and dickheads," he yelled, "and get ready to take some action shots. You can sell them to the TV stations for beer money!"

"Hey, let's talk about this, Fred," Will said as he started moving toward the young man. "Give me the matches."

"No! You're not going to talk me out of this. Someone has to protest this fucking war!"

"Fred, what you're proposing is a courageous act. It's coming out of a concern for the world, for the innocent. I know how you feel—we've talked about this a lot." Will kept moving slowly toward Fred. "But there're lots of ways to deal with violence and oppression. Give me the matches, Fred." Will could see Fred's hands shaking. "Look at Gandhi or Martin Luther King."

"They died for what they believed in," Fred shouted.

"Yes, but somebody else committed the violence. Not them. What you're proposing is violence, Fred, against yourself." By now Will was very close to Fred, who was trying to hold his ground. "You don't have to do this," Will said quietly. "We can find better ways to protest the fucking war."

There was a commotion in the hall, and behind Fred, Will could see a dozen UW police officers in riot gear come charging up the stairs and down the hall. Someone must have texted 911. When Fred turned and saw the cops, he began backing away from Will, tears running down his face.

Will knew he had to get his attention back. "Come on, Fred, let's go someplace quiet and talk." In two steps he was close enough to gather him into a bear hug. Fred began sobbing. Will released him, took the match and the box, and put his arm around Fred's shoulders, gently moving him out of the room and down the hall.

The cops had stopped abruptly as Will motioned for them to back off. "It's OK, folks," he said calmly. "Just a little misunderstanding. Everything is fine." They watched warily, surrounded by the strong smell of gasoline.

"Jake, could you join us?" Will had recognized one of the police officers.

Jake came immediately, and there was a five-minute conversation in the hall. Then Jake's arm replaced Will's around Fred's shoulders. "Come on, son," Jake said. "Let's get you some clean clothes." Followed by at least two police officers, he and Fred disappeared down the stairs.

Will went back into his buzzing classroom. The students, on an adrenaline high, cheered and clapped. "Way to go, Professor Ryan!" "Fantastic, dude!" "Thank you so much, Dr. Ryan!" Some of them were crying. Will leaned against the blackboard and motioned for everyone to sit down and be quiet.

"Ladies and gentlemen," he said after a minute, "what you've just seen is what's called in textbooks 'alienation.' But it was nothing like a dry textbook, was it?"

The room was very quiet.

"This is what happens when people feel alone, separate, disconnected, unloved. This is where terrorism and all kinds of violence come from. What Fred did was wrong, but can you imagine how unhappy he must be to try something like this? You're going to have some exciting stories to tell your friends and family. You'll be the center of attention for the next few days. But what about Fred? He'll be locked up in a cell or a psych ward."

Will was silent for a while, staring at the floor. Then he said, "I have a question for you—you don't need to raise your hands or answer out loud. Just think back to what was going on inside you ten minutes ago. Were you praying? If so, who were you praying to? If you don't usually pray, why do you think you did just now—if you did?" He looked down again and then, after a moment, back at the class.

"Whether you prayed or not, I'll bet everyone was afraid for a few minutes—I certainly was! What were you afraid of? That you were going to die . . . that you might get burned and be in pain . . . that you were going to witness a suicide? Did you wonder if you had the courage to try to jump Fred before it was too late? Did you realize that you didn't have that courage?"

Now he was looking over their heads, out the mullioned windows at the adjacent old brick building and a century-old fir tree. "These are the kinds of situations and questions that religions were invented to address," he said. "And that philosophers think and talk about. At its most fundamental level, this stuff isn't dry and empty—it's relevant! Why were you in this class today, instead of some other class? Why are you having this experience? What are you going to get out of it? Do you have the self-awareness to recognize that there's something to get out of all experiences, not just the in-your-face ones?

"I'll find out where Fred is, and if he can have visitors, and I'll let you know. I hope some of you will at least write to him. Who knows, a gesture on your part might turn things around for him, start him in a healthier direction. OK, that's it for today." The students filed out quietly.

Will took off his gasoline-soaked jacket, rummaged around in his pack until he found a plastic bag, and stuffed the coat into it. The chief of the UWPD appeared to tell him that crisis counselors would be available for him and his students, and they talked for a while about how those services could be accessed. Then Will gathered up his notes and put them in another compartment of his pack, went outside, and got on his bike. The whole thing was over in thirty minutes.

Back at his house, he threw the jacket in the outdoor garbage can and jumped in the shower, trying to decompress. Then he dressed, put the rest of his smelly clothes in the washing machine, and stood dumbly in the laundry room. He decided he'd ride up to Susannah's; even if she wasn't there, the ride would do him good.

....

Susannah was surprised to see Will standing at her door, ashen and exhausted. "Will! Come in—what's wrong?"

"I'm glad you're here—you're not busy, are you?"

"Just doing laundry," she replied. "Can I get you something—tea, coffee?"

"I could use a glass of scotch," he said wearily, sinking into the couch.

"OK, coming up. Ice?"

"No, thanks."

She was really surprised now—other than wine with dinner, Will rarely drank. She poured a glass of Chivas and a glass of water, and set them on the coffee table. He sat up, took a big sip of scotch, grimaced, and sank back against the cushions.

She curled up in the corner of the sofa and waited expectantly.

"I'm glad you're here," he repeated, "because I wanted to tell you this myself, before you heard it on the news or saw it in the paper." He told her the whole story.

She listened very intently; it was so much to grasp: that poor kid who was going to set himself on fire, the students' reaction, Will saving the day, the media frenzy that would go on for a few days.

"What do you feel?" she asked.

"Drained . . . sad for Fred . . . glad to be alive . . . mad at Fred . . . thankful for angels or whatever helped us get through that . . . angry at all the things in the world that lead to this kind of situation."

She moved behind the sofa and rubbed his neck and shoulders, which were very tight. "Why don't you stay for dinner?"

"I'd like that," he said. "I can't face a restaurant, and I don't want to fix anything myself."

He sat on the couch, staring into space, his feelings and thoughts bouncing all over. Meanwhile, she broiled some sausages and steamed some potatoes and broccoli, and poured them each a glass of red wine. He ate and drank absentmindedly; she didn't try to engage him in conversation, but he did seem to be relaxing a bit.

"Will, you know what's going to happen next, don't you?"

He looked at her questioningly.

"You're going to be a hero, and the press is going to be after you like crazy."

"Porca miseria!" he said with disgust, shaking his head.

"I don't think I want to know what that means in English," Susannah said, eyebrows raised. "Anyway, they're probably already at your house, waiting for you to come home. They'll certainly be waiting for you on campus before your first class tomorrow. I have a suggestion for you to think about. Why don't you make a statement? You can read it on camera, or just release it to the media. And then you can say you have no further comment. After a few days, it will quiet down."

As he pondered, his expression changed from disgusted to hopeful. "That's a really good idea. May I use your computer?"

"Sure," she said. "You can sleep in the guest room tonight if you don't want to go home to hordes of TV cameras."

"Thanks. I really appreciate the offer—and the scotch and the dinner."

Susannah cleared away the dishes, and Will sat down at the computer. He looked more his usual self. She brought him some tea and went back to her novel. About an hour later he came out and read her the statement. "What do you think?"

"Never one to miss a teaching moment, are you, Professor Ryan?" she teased. "I think it's inspired! I especially like the part about 'the fucking war.' Fred will be glad to read that."

"I put it in just for him, even though I know it'll get deleted."

"How are you going to do this? Just e-mail it to the media or have a press conference or what?"

"I hadn't thought about that." He looked perplexed.

"Why not wring everything out of it you can?" she said. "Call the university PR people right now and ask them to arrange a press conference tomorrow. They can take care of getting your statement out. They have all the contacts and so on. You can e-mail your statement to them right now. They'll probably be thrilled—it's a PR bonanza. No one got hurt, one of their professors is a hero, and the university gets worldwide press. There will be all kinds of crazy, unexpected questions at the press conference—if you do it. But you're used to that. You deal with questions every day."

Looking energized, he went off to get in touch with the university and put the wheels in motion. By nine o'clock he looked totally tapped out.

"You'd better go to bed here," she said. "You look like death warmed over."

"Susannah, I should go home, even if there are reporters there. I'll need to wear something decent tomorrow, and I just threw away my only sport coat. I guess I could wear a suit, but my students wouldn't recognize me."

"How about a dress shirt, with or without tie, and a sweater?"

"I can manage that."

"Just arrange things so you arrive looking like you want to look. Are you going to ride your bike to the press conference? The PR people will pick you up, if you want them to, I'm sure. What time is the press conference anyway, and where is it?"

"It's at ten a.m. on the steps of Suzzallo Library. In the president's conference room if it's raining."

"Good luck, Professor Ryan. I'm sure you'll knock 'em dead!"

"Thanks for everything. I never would have thought about any of this."

"You can thank me by letting me take you shopping for a new sport coat!"

He hugged her and went out the door.

As she had anticipated, the next day was a media circus. The front page of the *Seattle Times* had a very poignant photo, taken on a student's cell phone, of Will and Fred walking down the hall, with Will's arm around Fred. Many of the students who were there were interviewed, and one of them had an audio recording of the whole exchange between Will and Fred, and Will's comments to the class. It was quoted verbatim. The students were raving about Will's composure and his handling of the situation.

Susannah watched the press conference on TV and thought it went off beautifully; Will had just the right amount of nervousness and articulateness.

At three o'clock he called her. "Would you rescue me again? Can you pick me up at the Fortieth Street entrance to the campus? Then let's go to a movie—people won't know me in the dark."

She arranged to pick him up at four. They drove up to Sundance Cinema, sure they could find something worth seeing with ten films to choose from. At the box office they were greeted with, "Hey, you're Professor Ryan, aren't you? I saw you on TV. Tickets on the house—nice job saving that guy!"

Will thanked him, and they went into the darkened theater. "What are we seeing anyway?" he asked.

"A romantic comedy—I didn't think a thriller was quite what you needed."

After the movie, she asked, "Now what?"

"Let's go out to dinner," he said.

"Are you sure?" Susannah asked. "You'll probably be recognized again."

"It's OK. I can deal with it."

She chose a creperie on Capitol Hill, because it was very small, and they didn't have to wait long for a table. It was clear within five minutes that everyone in the restaurant knew who he was, but no one was intrusive.

He had two glasses of cider, everything was delicious, and they splurged on dessert crepes. When he asked for the check, the proprietor beamed at him and told him there would be no charge. He tried to insist on paying, but she was firm.

"I'll bet you're ready to go home," she said.

"Yeah, I'm bushed!"

"It's not over yet, you know. It'll probably be a few more days till it dies down. You may even get a call from Oprah," Susannah said, laughing.

The next day he phoned to tell her that he had talked to Fred. It looked as though no criminal charges would be filed, and his parents had come from Eastern Washington to be with him while he was undergoing psychiatric evaluation. Fred was surprised and quite moved that several of Will's students had been in touch with him.

....

The week after the Fred incident, Susannah spent a lot of time thinking about her feelings for Will. *Do I want to have a long-term relationship with him? Yes. Why? Because he's a nice guy, intelligent, witty, ethical, fun to be with, interesting to talk to.* And she was physically attracted to him. She wanted the relationship to be more than it was. *If I tell him that, and he's not interested, would the relationship end? Or could we go on as friends? Do I want to take a chance on losing the relationship altogether?* She decided on an in-between approach. She'd push it a bit and see what happened.

Susannah took the bus downtown to Nordstrom. A helpful salesgirl found just what she wanted. It was a light-blue knit top with three-quarter sleeves and a low neckline. But Susannah wasn't used to the décolletage, and when the clerk came to the dressing room to see how she was doing, Susannah said, "Are you sure this is the right size? It looks awfully low-cut."

She was assured that the neckline was very fashionable and not excessively low. So she bought it.

Will wanted to take her out to dinner someplace really nice in appreciation for the support she provided him during the Fred event. They decided on Il Terrazzo Carmine, in Pioneer Square. As she gave her coat to the maître d', she noticed him and Will appreciating her new purchase. With the blue top, she was wearing a long black skirt, and silver earrings with blue crystals.

"You look terrific," Will said after they'd been shown to their table.

"Thank you. You look very handsome in your new Harris Tweed. A new tie too?"

"Yes, I go shopping every ten years for shirts, ties, and underwear—whether I need them or not!"

They had a delicious dinner and an Italian waiter. Will was delighted to speak Italian again.

"Would you like coffee or tea at my place?" Susannah asked as they walked back to the car.

....

On the way home there was a debate going on in Will's head. He'd never felt this way about a woman before—he thought about Susannah all the time; he could hardly wait to see her when he was away from her; it was all he could do to keep his hands off her! *But,* he thought, *what if she doesn't feel the same way? Well, she always sits close to me on the couch, and she kissed me back when I kissed her the other night. And she must have known what effect that blue top would have on me. It sure seemed like a signal.*

....

They went into Susannah's condo arguing about whether the panna cotta had been better than the zabaglione. She went to start tea. He hung his coat on a doorknob, pulled off his tie, unbuttoned his collar, and followed her into the kitchen. Resting his hands on the sink on either side of her as she was filling the electric kettle, he began kissing her neck and shoulders. She mentally cheered Nordstrom, then closed her eyes and leaned back against his chest, reveling in the sensations that were flowing through her body. The erotic wiring was still in very good condition. She'd been longing for this to happen!

He said between kisses, "I thought I'd be a little rusty at this. I'm kind of out of practice, but it all comes back pretty quickly. Um . . . your teakettle is overflowing."

"This is extremely distracting behavior, Professor Ryan. I'm never going to get the tea made if you keep this up."

"OK, OK," he laughed. "I'll give you a break." He went into the living room and stretched out on the sofa with an audible sigh. Susannah came in a few minutes later and set two cups of tea on the coffee table.

He pulled her down beside him on the sofa. "You know, I really don't want any tea." He slowly traced his finger around the neckline of her low-cut top. "I have a new appreciation for the term 'plunging neckline.' It makes a guy just want to plunge right in." He kissed her hair, her collarbone, the inside of her wrist. "I want you Susannah, and I've wanted you for quite some time now."

"I'm so glad to hear that," she said softly. She gave him a radiant smile, slid her arms around his neck, and kissed him.

Time passed, there on the sofa, and as it passed, their kisses gathered intensity; then her shoes were off, her shoulder bare, his shirt untucked, their hair mussed. "God, I'm drunk with you," he said, his voice husky. "I could do this forever!"

OK, she said to herself. *I can do this.* She untangled herself, stood up, and took his hand. She tugged him in the direction of the bedroom.

He stopped in the doorway. "Are you sure, Susannah? You aren't doing this just because you think I want it, or it's the modern thing or something. . . ?"

She stopped, amazed—had she totally misread him? After she'd screwed up her courage to be a modern woman who could ask for what she wanted, did he not want her? She was totally embarrassed. "I . . . I . . .You don't have to if you don't want to. I'm sorry. I guess I thought—"

"No, no, no! Don't misunderstand—this is what I've been waiting for! I want to make love with you more than anything. I just need to make sure it's what you want, I don't want to make a mistake." There was an almost desperate tone in his voice.

Oh, the relief! "It's what I want too, Will," she said slowly, her gaze holding his. "There's no mistake to be made." She still held his hand, which she kissed, then he enveloped her in his arms.

....

Jane's words to Lizzy after Bingley proposed in *Pride and Prejudice* (which Susannah had read six times) came to her when she awoke the next morning: *"'Tis too much . . . I do not deserve it. Oh! why is not everybody as happy!"*

She lay very still, not wanting this moment to end. They were lying spoon-fashion, with his hand on her hip, and she felt totally content. When he woke up, they lay together without talking, until he said, "It was the Fred thing that finally did it. I realized there was this amazing woman in my life, and what was I waiting for? I don't want to live like I have been anymore. It's kind of like I've been living on the surface, and never going deep. My students keep me going, trying to relate to them, give them knowledge in a way that's useful to them, help them sort out the world. That's rewarding, but it only goes so far. With you I can go deep. Can we be together, more together than we have been?"

She turned over to face him. "Do you remember the first words you said to me, on the airplane?"

"Haven't got a clue."

"We were getting into our seats and you said, 'Looks like we're together for the duration.'" She kissed him and said, "I'd be really happy to be together with you for the duration, Will."

He put his arms around her and kissed her tenderly. Then he leaned back on the pillow and sighed. "I feel like a parched garden that's finally getting watered . . . or a drowning man who's finally made it to the surface." He was quiet, thinking and running his fingers through her hair. "I feel like I've just discovered this big empty place. But at the same time, I'm so content. And euphoric. Is it possible to be content and euphoric at the same time? It must be—that's how I feel."

Tears came to her eyes. "I love you, Will. I love the way you care for your students, and your introspection, and your willingness to talk about your feelings, and your blue eyes, and how you help me untangle things, and how I feel when you touch me. You've been so long without love, Will, It makes me sad. But that can all be over, if you want." She looked into his eyes as she spoke, but her hands were twisting the sheet.

"If I want? Yes, I want!" He pulled her closer. "I've never been in love before, but this must be what it is. You're always in my thoughts, my stomach lurches when I see you again after we've been apart, I want to make mad passionate love to you. You are so lovely in every way, Susannah—your smile, your eyes, your body, your manner. Yes, this is what I want."

"Now *I'm* euphoric!" She snuggled closer to him, and they lay quietly together for some time. Then she ran her hand back and forth slowly across his belly. "Could we go back to the part about your being mad and passionate about my lovely body?"

CHAPTER FOUR

A Better Version

Will Ryan wanted to be a father to his son of twenty-one years whom he had never met. He didn't regret not having married the boy's mother—that would have been a mistake. He didn't regret paying child support and his share of his son's college expenses. But he did regret what he considered his emotional and physical abandonment of the boy. Now he was trying to figure out how to make contact, to see if Derek would be willing to have some kind of relationship with him. Will had spent many hours on a letter, attempting to get just the right tone.

Dear Derek,

Through your mother, I have kept up with some aspects of your life—class photos, graduations, soccer awards, and so on. But I have increasingly felt that I would like to know you in person and be in your life in a way that works for you. From what your mother has told me, your stepfather has been a real father to you, and I would never expect or want to affect that relationship in any way. However, I would like for us at least to be acquainted, and, hopefully, over time be more than acquaintances.

I'd be happy to come to Portland for a visit. We could go out for lunch, or dinner, or just meet for coffee, if that's what you prefer. If you're willing to meet, please write, call, or e-mail me and suggest a time. I look forward to hearing from you and seeing you.

Sincerely,
Will Ryan

Susannah had come into the office they had made for him in the guest room and was looking over his shoulder at the laptop screen. "What do you think of the latest version?" Will said.

"I think it's fine. And your last three versions were also fine. It's understandable that you're uptight about this, but you've done your best, and a word change here or there isn't going to make the difference in his response. Why don't you just put it in the mail?"

So he did.

After dinner they were sitting together on the sofa. Will was perusing an essay written by Susannah's meditation teacher, Roger Marklun. "What does he mean by 'self-imagination'?"

Susannah put her book down and her feet in his lap. "Self-imagination is how you define yourself—who you think you are, based on your life experience. Most people aren't aware of it, but that definition changes all the time, depending on who you're with—parent, lover, child, sibling, colleague, boss, or whoever. It also changes according to your life circumstances, particular events, and so on. And how you see yourself isn't necessarily at all how other people see you. So who are you, really?"

"So," he said, rubbing her feet, "the point of being aware of your own self-imagination, and how it changes, is what?"

"If you're aware of what's going on, you can see where you're limiting yourself, or giving yourself grief. For example, if you see yourself as homely, because your mother said you were, you're more likely to present yourself to others that way, to act like others couldn't find you attractive. And that could become a self-fulfilling prophecy. That's a gross simplification, but I think it illustrates the point.

"Take me, for example," she said. "For most of my career, I needed to be seen as competent, the successful career woman. I had a very high anxiety level. To a certain extent I sacrificed my family to my work, and I wasn't really happy. I was just burning myself out. So I was making myself and my family unhappy because I had some idea of myself that I thought required me to act in a certain way."

Will said, "In Buddhist terminology, you were attached to desires."

"Right, and the point is to get unattached, and I can't do that until I'm as conscious as possible of what's going on in myself, and in others. That's why I meditate: the awareness increases, and my reactivity decreases."

"It all boils down to love, though, doesn't it?" he mused. "We do everything for love, or because we don't have love. I became a priest to make my parents happy. Fred was going to incinerate himself because he felt no one loved him."

"Mmm, I guess I'd put it differently," Susannah said. "I think loving and being loved and feeling connected is our natural state. But it gets obscured by our life experience. We get these quirky ideas about who we are and what life requires. They're very constricting—and they lead to all the bad stuff in the world. How's that for a philosophy?"

"We've gone from self-identification to evil. That's quite a jump! I think I need some ice cream to help me process all this."

The following week, Will waited anxiously to hear from Derek. Finally, two weeks later an e-mail came.

Hey, Will.
Sure, why don't you come down for a visit. I'm always looking for a free meal. If you're not busy on the 17th, I'll meet you in front of the Gray Campus Center at noon. I'll be wearing a blue parka.

See ya,
Derek

"OK, he's going to take the 'I don't really care about this' approach, with a little jab thrown in for good measure," said Susannah. "It could be that he doesn't care, but I doubt it. I'd interpret this as meaning that he doesn't want to *appear* to care but really does want to meet you."

"God, there are so many possibilities! I don't know what his mother's told him about me, about why we didn't get married. He may want to know me if I'm someone he can admire, but not if I'm someone he doesn't admire. Who wants a jerk for a father? So for him there are all these unknowns." Will paced around the living room.

"But there are all sorts of unknowns for you, too, Will. Maybe he's an immature, self-centered kid. Maybe you won't really like him as a person. That's very possible."

"I know it's possible. But that doesn't change the fact that I should try to be a father to him, however I can."

"Yes, I agree—you have to try. Why don't we go to Portland for the weekend? I'll make a hotel reservation, and you can drop me off downtown and go out to Reed to meet Derek. I'll go shopping or something. If you two want to spend the rest of the day together, and even have dinner, just the two of you, that's fine with me. Or I can stay here. Whatever you prefer." She watched him pace back and forth.

"I'd like you to come," he said. "I know I'll want to talk with you about how it went, while it's fresh in my mind. And it would be fun to see Portland—I haven't been there for years."

They left about seven thirty on the morning of the seventeenth. While it was only a three-hour trip, Will wanted to allow for traffic jams, road construction, getting lost, and so on. He had a good map, and he and Derek had exchanged cell phone numbers, in case there was a problem.

He dropped Susannah off at the Benson Hotel at eleven, promising to call her between two and three with an update. He was nervous.

"Will," she said, "he's going to find out that you're a good man who's trying to do the right thing. But it might take a while for that to come through to him, so you may need to be patient."

He kissed her and drove away.

It wasn't difficult to find the college; his map and the directions were easy to follow, so he got there thirty minutes early. He sat in the car in a parking lot near the campus center, thinking about his motivation to meet his son after all these years. There was clearly a lot of guilt involved, but where did that come from? Underneath the guilt was a belief that all children should know they're cared for, and he hadn't provided that knowledge to Derek.

He was standing in the appointed place exactly at noon. About ten minutes later a young man in a blue parka came sauntering up the sidewalk with a pretty coed. She waved good-bye, and he came up to Will. "Hi, I'm Derek. You must be Will."

Will extended his hand, and Derek shook it. "I'm glad we can do this, Derek," Will said. "Where would you like to go for lunch? I've got a car, so we can go anywhere."

"Why don't we just eat in the cafeteria," Derek replied. "The food's OK, and we don't have to drive anywhere." Will got the sense that Derek wanted to be able to leave quickly, in case the visit turned into a debacle.

"Sounds good," said Will, smiling. "Lead on." As they walked, Will commented that Reed had a beautiful campus, and asked Derek why he had chosen this college.

"Well, it's got a good reputation," Derek said.

An understatement, Will thought.

The conversation paused as they picked out their food and sat down at a table near the windows.

"Anyway, I wanted to go to a small liberal arts college, I wanted to be in a city, and it's just far enough from home—did you know I grew up in Ashland?"

"Yes," Will replied. "I knew that."

"Just exactly what do you know about me?" Derek asked, with a trace of defiance or hostility in his voice, or something else that Will couldn't quite name.

Will put his napkin in his lap and picked up his fork. "I

know what your mother's told me. She's sent a few photos of you over the years: your graduation photo, a clipping when you won your soccer team's most valuable player award. She told me that she'd married when you were about three and that your stepfather has been a great parent to you. She also said, some years ago, that you had no interest in knowing me. On top of that, I deduced that you had to be a good student and bright, or you never would have gotten into this college. And that's it," he said. "What do you know about me?" He began eating his salad.

Derek put down his hamburger. "Mom said that she was in love with you, but you wouldn't marry her, that you live in Seattle and are a teacher or something, and, let's see, that you're helping with my college expenses. That's pretty much it."

There was a long silence while Will studied his plate and chose his words carefully. "Well, I guess we've both got a lot to learn about each other. Shall I start?"

Derek nodded.

"I grew up in Boston and Seattle in a very Roman Catholic family, got my BA from Notre Dame, became a priest, got my PhD, lived in Rome for several years, and left the church about twenty some years ago." Will could see the surprise on Derek's face.

"I was pretty wild and irresponsible after I left the church, making up for lost time or something. Your mother and I had known each other for about a month when you were conceived. It's true she was in love with me, or thought she was, and it's true I wouldn't marry her. I didn't love her, Derek, and I didn't think that we suited each other, aside from the physical attraction. I agreed to pay child support, which I have done without fail, and I'm paying for half of your college expenses."

Derek looked quite taken aback, and it was no wonder. This was a lot of information to digest. Nothing contradicted what his mother had said, but he was probably beginning to see that he hadn't heard the whole story.

While they were talking, students were coming and going, many waving or nodding to Derek. A pretty dark-haired girl came up to the table and said, "Hi, Derek, are you going to introduce me to your father?"

Derek blurted out, "How'd you know he was my father?"

She laughed. "Well, it's pretty obvious—you look just like him. Hasn't anyone ever told you that?"

Will held out his hand, which she took. "Hi, I'm Will Ryan. Do I detect an Italian accent?"

"Yes, she said. "My dad's the Italian consul in Portland."

He asked her, in Italian, if she liked Reed, and they carried on for a few minutes, until she said good-bye and left to join friends. Derek looked like he was still trying to take it all in.

"So, what do you do in Seattle?" Derek asked.

"I'm a professor at the University of Washington. I've been there for going on twenty years. I teach quite a few classes on comparative religion and philosophy. I'm not into the research stuff that much. I like being with the students." Will looked around the bright, noisy room. "This is a really pleasant building. I was hoping when we're done, maybe you'd take me for a tour. I'd like to see your dorm, a classroom, whatever you especially like about the campus."

They walked out into the cold, sunny January day, and Derek showed Will around. In one of the classroom buildings, they passed a woman carrying a big stack of books, which she looked like she was about to drop. "Can I help you, Professor Lundberg?" Derek said, hurrying to take the books.

"Thanks so much, Derek! I was trying to make as few trips as possible, and I took too many. I'm moving into a new office."

They followed her to her new office, where she indicated a spot for Derek to put the books. She looked at Will and waited for Derek to introduce him.

"Oh, uh, Professor Lundberg, this is Will Ryan. He's a professor at the University of Washington."

"I'm pleased to meet you, Dr. Lundberg. I take it Derek is one of your students."

"Yes, he's in my physics class. We have lots of interesting discussions about quantum mechanics and string theory."

"Well, they're pretty elementary conversations," Derek put in. "I hardly know anything about physics."

"You know enough to ask good questions, and that's what a teacher always likes to see. Thanks for the help with the books."

Derek and Will went on to see his dorm room, and then to the athletic fields. "Do you still play soccer?" Will asked.

"Yeah, I do. It's a good antidote to the books."

"I agree," said Will. "I play with a group of guys every Wednesday night."

As they were walking back toward Will's car, Derek asked him if he was married.

"No, I'm not. Never have been. But there is a woman in my life. We've been seeing each other for about four months, and it looks like it's going to be a long-term thing. I'm nuts about her!" He laughed.

Derek laughed too. "Yeah, I know how that is. I've been with my girlfriend, Trisha, for about a year, and I still can hardly wait to see her every day. And I hate it when she goes away to a regatta or something."

They stopped at the car and shook hands. "Thanks for meeting me, Derek. It means a lot to me," Will said. "And I hope we can get together more often. If you and Trisha would like to come to Seattle, we've got a guest room. You're welcome any time."

"Thanks, Will. I'll be in touch."

It was two thirty, so Will called Susannah. "I think it went pretty well. I'll tell you all about it at dinner. I'm coming back to the hotel for a nap. I'm wiped out!"

Derek walked to Trisha's dorm, where they'd agreed she'd hang out until after the Big Lunch. "Well," she said, "How was it?"

He plopped down on her bed. "It was OK. Better than I thought it would be. I guess I was afraid I wouldn't like him, or he'd be a nerd or something. But he's not. He's a professor at UW, and he plays soccer. And he told me some stuff about his life that fills in some of the blanks. There's more I'd like to know, but it was plenty for a first meeting."

"Like what?" she said. "I'm dying to hear everything!"

"Well, the most embarrassing thing was when we were having lunch, Tomasia Lombardi came up and asked me to introduce her to my father. I was floored. She said I looked just like him!"

"You do," Trisha said. "I snuck a peek through a window where you couldn't see me. He's handsome, just like you." She left her desk and came to sit on his lap. "But you can't get conceited—I'll make sure to keep you in your place."

"He was a priest for about twenty years, I guess."

"No kidding!"

"Yeah, then he left the church about twenty years ago. Never married, but he says there's a woman in his life now that he's nuts about. And, we've got an invitation to stay in their guest room if we want to come to Seattle."

"Fantastic! Maybe we could drive back with him, or them, tonight!" They both laughed.

"I've got a lot to think about before I see him again," Derek said. "This is pretty weird, having an extra father show up in your life. I didn't tell Mom about this meeting, so I have to sort that out too. Hey, you know I could Google him—that never occurred to me."

When Derek Googled "Will Ryan, University of Washington professor," he was shocked at all the hits, most related to the near self-immolation of one of Will's students, and Will's defusing of the situation. "God, my father's a freakin' hero!" he said in wonder. "How did I miss this? Oh, I know why. It happened when I was on my semester abroad."

Derek read other articles: about Will's popularity as a teacher, his publications, and campus involvement. "Hmm, this is interesting," said Derek.

Trisha went back to her desk, and Derek lay on her bed, thinking about his meeting with his biological father. He seemed sincere, seemed like a nice guy. But where was he for the past twenty-one years? He obviously had resources. Lots of divorced dads still managed to see their kids, even if they weren't a big presence in their lives. So what's the difference between an absent divorced dad and an absent biological dad—if any? He remembered a close call with a high school girl he'd been dating—she missed her period, and he was terrified that he'd gotten her pregnant. It turned out to be a false alarm, but he remembered how appalled he was at the idea that he might have to marry her. Could he blame his father for not doing something Derek wouldn't have wanted to do either?

Marrying was one thing, though, and being a dad outside of marriage was another, and Will hadn't done that, other than financially. He wasn't sure how he felt about Will's absence from his life for all these years. He hadn't thought about it much, but that didn't mean he didn't care.

....

Will was sound asleep when Susannah came back to their hotel room with a stack of used books she'd bought at Powell's, and shopping bags from Whole Foods and an Asian department store. She got a book and sat down in a comfortable chair to read until he woke up. Then she climbed on the bed and snuggled in beside him. "Tell me all—I'm dying to hear everything!"

"I'll have to think about it first. Wouldn't want to get things out of order or anything. So while I'm thinking, I'll just put my arms around you, and . . . cogitate."

"This doesn't fit the definition of cogitating—but that's OK with me," she said, moving closer.

Later, as they were looking at the dinner menu in a trendy restaurant she wanted to try, he said, "You know, the most amazing thing—it was just stupefying—was to see myself sitting across the table! You have a son, and you've had his lifetime to get used to the ways he resembles you. But for me, I was blown away. I never saw the resemblance in his grade school pictures, but now that he's a young man, it's very strong. It had a physical effect on me—for a moment I thought I might not be able to speak. One of his friends stopped and asked him to introduce her to his father—she saw the resemblance. Then it was his turn to be blown away!" He paused as their salads arrived.

"He told me what his mother had told him about me, which was very little and left a lot of room for him to read in both good and bad. So I filled him in, and I could tell that it was a lot for him to deal with. I think maybe it was dawning on him that things could look very different than what he might have imagined. But we didn't actually talk about why I had never tried to get in touch with him. Well, not exactly—I did say that his mother had told me that he had no interest in knowing me."

"I gather you didn't learn as much about him as he may have learned about you?" she said, breaking off a piece of bread.

"Yes, that's true. He still plays soccer, he has a girlfriend named Trisha—he's been going out with her for about a year—and he seems to have an inquiring mind." He told her about the encounter with Derek's physics professor. "By the way, I've invited Derek and Trisha to use the guest room if they want to come to Seattle. I hope that's OK with you."

"Of course it is," Susannah said. "It would be a really good way for you to get better acquainted—for him to see you on your own turf, so to speak. And there are tons of things to do to avoid awkward times."

They enjoyed walking around downtown Portland after dinner, bundled up against the cold. After a leisurely breakfast the next morning, they drove home.

....

One day a couple of weeks later, Susannah asked Will, "Do you think I should try to have my stories published?" He was working at the computer they had set up for him in the guest room.

"Why're you asking me—it's your decision?"

"I just need to talk to someone about it."

"Well, what are the pros and cons? I'm sure you've thought about it." He turned around to face her as she leaned against the doorframe.

"People keep telling me—a few people anyway, not very many have read them—that they're good enough to be published. That's a nice compliment, and maybe it's true, but I'm not writing them to try to make money or become famous."

"Why *are* you writing them?"

"Because it's fun," she said. "And because it's fascinating to see how the process works—how ideas just come. Also, I'm told that doing some kind of creative work helps the spiritual process."

"Well, writers apparently write for a variety of reasons, but if they were never published, we wouldn't have anything to read! So why not go ahead and see if a publisher is interested?"

"Probably because I'm afraid of rejection."

"Susannah, you know that self-imagination stuff you've talked about? You're wallowing around in it. How are you defining yourself that makes publishing your stories an issue?"

She considered what he said. "You're right. I am wallowing around in it. I guess I need to imagine myself as competent, and having the stories published would demonstrate that to be true and then I'd feel good about myself.

"But it really doesn't matter whether other people actually *like* the stories or not," Susannah said, sitting down on the chair beside the desk. "Of course, if they don't like them because they're badly written, then I should just write for myself or give it up. But if they're written well enough, then some people will like them and some not. And that's fine. I don't like everything I read. So why not submit them for publication? I still don't know whether I will or not, but you've helped me sort it out a bit."

"Happy to oblige, any time,' he said, turning back to the keyboard.

She kissed him on the back of the neck and left for the grocery store.

....

Friday night one of Will's colleagues and his wife came over for dinner. Sam taught sociology at the U, and Julia taught history in a public high school. Dinner conversation ranged from state funding for higher education, to the relevance of education in a democracy, to the difference between students now and a couple of decades ago.

Susannah asked if any of them had read the review of a book about marriage some time ago in the *Atlantic*. The book was by an academic couple who taught at the University of Chicago. They argued that Americans are both romantics and anti-romantics at the same time, and that the high value placed on individualism doesn't really mesh with the idea of a committed relationship, in which people sacrifice for the good of the relationship. "What do you think about that idea?" she said.

Julia was the assistant coach for the girls' soccer team at her high school; she had spent many hours on buses going to games and listening to conversations about all kinds of things. "Well, many young women are very sophisticated in some ways. They say things like 'Why get married when half of marriages end in divorce? You don't have to be married to have a child—there are lots of single parents. Why not just have sex and enjoy it when you have contraceptives and abortion—why the big deal about tying sex to a long term relationship? If I get married, my husband might pressure me to give up my career in favor of his.' Yet, they want to be in love, they want the white dress and the honeymoon and the soul mate. It's really schizophrenic!"

"That's the point this article was making," said Susannah. "People think of themselves as independent, and they place a high value on independence, but at the same time they long for union with another, and that requires thinking of the other person instead of yourself, and some compromise—both people's desires can't always be met."

Will was thinking about this conversation during his office hours the next Monday, when he should have been correcting tests. It seemed so clear to him, perhaps because he'd already lived two-thirds of his life—relationships were always the most important thing. For younger people, who had career possibilities and potential child-rearing ahead of them, it was perhaps more complicated.

Will asked himself why, if he knew relationships were so important, he had spent so many years alone, except for his sister's family and his students and soccer friends. There were plenty of women around—several had made their interest known—but with few exceptions, he hadn't followed through. Even when he had dated someone, it never went anywhere. Why? And now what had changed?

It was partly the Fred incident, he knew; a brush with death usually occasioned a reassessment of what really matters in life. Meeting Susannah had changed things big-time. But he suspected there was more to it. Over the past year he had been thinking more and more about his desire to know his son and, if possible, to make up for his absence in his son's life. Perhaps his increasing determination to deal with this issue was dissolving a sense of guilt that had kept him from finding a partner. Maybe his celibacy after leaving the priesthood had been an unconscious penance. There must be some psychological reason. Why else would a perfectly healthy, decent, well-educated straight guy go on year after year with no women in his life?

He remembered with chagrin his promiscuous behavior after leaving the priesthood. Rejecting the church as an institution didn't mean rejecting all his values, but he'd conveniently forgotten some of them for a while. Fathering a child woke him up. He'd used sex as rebellion and recreation—no matter that his partners were willing—but he didn't believe that was what sex was about. It might be old-fashioned, but for him, sex needed to be with someone he cared about, someone he could consider a relationship with. Very few of those possibilities had arisen in the years since Derek had been conceived—for whatever reason.

....

"Will, don't forget the carpenter is coming tomorrow morning to talk with us about your bookcases," Susannah said that evening after dinner. "Have you got some idea how much your books weigh, or how many there are? Maybe you should just take him over to your house and let him see them, so he'll know what he's dealing with."

Will hadn't totally moved in with Susannah, but over the past few months he spent less and less time in his "hermitage," as she called it, and more time at her place. He needed to refer to his books a lot, though, and it was inconvenient to be running back and forth between his house and hers, so she'd suggested they put some bookcases in the guest bedroom they'd made into an office for him. He expressed his doubts.

"Good grief! Moving all those books over here is a really big deal. You'd never get rid of me if I had to move those books again!"

"On the other hand, you could never leave," she joked, "because I'd have your books!"

"Susannah, should we get married?" he said suddenly. "What do you think?"

She stood there for a moment with her mouth open, and then she said lightly, "I'm taking that as a question, not as a proposal. But since you ask what I think . . . I don't think there are any relevant 'shoulds' anymore. At least for us. What would be the pros and cons? Or maybe the question really is, what do each of us think marriage is about?"

"Well, this is certainly a very modern discussion," Will said. "But as long as we're having it—marriage for us wouldn't be about children, or what our families want, or making an honest woman of you, or either of our financial futures, or every successful man needing a woman behind him, and so on. It's not about those things, so what is it about?"

"I think it's about bookcases!" she said. She poked him in the ribs and went into her office to attend to her e-mail. She sat there at her desk, thinking about the exchange that had just happened. She was in love with him and sure he loved her, but she wondered if it was too soon to be thinking about marriage. They hadn't known each other for six months yet, and had never even argued about something. Why had he brought this up in the way he did?

....

Will was asking himself the same question. It wasn't just about bookcases! But they did raise the prospect of the future. He loved Susannah—and she was intelligent, insightful, fun, sexy. She helped him think things through. She was a good partner. He could imagine growing old with her. He knew she loved him, but it seemed to him she didn't care about marriage all that much, judging from the discussion that had just occurred.

....

Will got an e-mail from his son at the beginning of February; Derek wondered if he could bring his girlfriend and come for a weekend. After checking dates with Susannah, Will wrote back suggesting that Derek and Trisha come Valentine's Day weekend. Will proposed that they arrive in time for dinner Friday, and that they should feel free to go out by themselves for a romantic evening on Saturday night, if they wanted to. He also asked if there was anything in particular that they would like to do and anything they didn't eat.

Derek replied that they liked Will's suggestion. Trisha was from San Diego and had never been to Seattle, so they were up for anything. They planned to arrive by six that Friday evening—and they ate anything.

Will and Susannah discussed the possibilities. Friday night they could walk down to Broadway for an informal dinner. There was every kind of food, and interesting little shops to poke around in. That might be easier than making conversation at home, at least to start out. Saturday they could do Pike Place Market, the art museum, the university, or a walk around the Arboretum or Green Lake. If the weather was horrible, they could always go to a movie. Susannah would be prepared to cook dinner for everyone Saturday evening, but she thought they would be ready for a break from each other by then. They'd probably only have half a day on Sunday, because of the drive back to Portland in the end-of-weekend traffic.

The appointed day arrived about two weeks later. D&T, as Susannah referred to them, called around five thirty, saying they were stuck in traffic in Tacoma, and expected to be in Seattle around six thirty. Will told them not to worry about being late, and that a beer or glass of wine was waiting to take the edge off the traffic experience. Will was absent-mindedly wandering around the house, straightening things, sitting down to read, then jumping up. "You're the one who needs a beer," Susannah told him.

They arrived around seven. The bags were deposited in the guest room, the bathrooms pointed out, and D&T were invited to have something to eat and drink. Susannah listed the beverage choices; Derek asked for IPA and Trisha for white wine.

"Tell us about your trip," Susannah said, as she gave everyone napkins and little plates for the hors d'oeuvres she'd prepared.

"It was fine until we got to Tacoma," Trisha said. "Getting out of Portland was no trouble, and it's a pretty scenic drive most of the way." They were both munching away like there was no tomorrow, Susannah noticed with an inward smile. *Wish I could still eat like that!*

Derek added that he'd had a paper due today, and he had been so focused on getting it done that he forgot to get gas, which slowed them down a little.

Susannah asked him what the paper was about.

"Believe it or not, I'm taking a class in gender studies," he said, a little sheepishly. "I'm an English major, and the paper was about how women writers were treated in the eighteen hundreds."

"That sounds fascinating," Susannah said. "I want to hear all about it, but first we need to decide what to do about dinner. We were thinking of walking down to Broadway, about fifteen minutes from here. You probably feel like a good leg-stretch after all that time in the car. How would it be if we eat and drink a little more here and then go?"

When they went out for dinner, Susannah managed to walk with Derek, who seemed a little uptight. Trisha was talking with Will about the Fred incident and seemed quite at ease. "Do very many guys take gender studies classes, Derek?" Susannah asked.

"Actually, it's a popular class," he replied. "We have this really great teacher, Professor Tunbridge, and she made the case that since fifty percent of the population is female, and most guys have or will have moms, sisters, girlfriends, wives, and daughters, it's a topic guys should know about. Seems reasonable to me."

Susannah nodded. "What's surprised you or impressed you the most about what you've learned?" she asked.

"It's only a one-semester class, so I haven't learned much yet, but I guess what I've thought about a lot is what it must feel like to be discriminated against. Since I'm a white male from a middle-class home, going to a very selective college, I don't have any experience of discrimination. It's hard for me to imagine what it must feel like to know that you can't do something—like get a certain kind of job, or even walk in a certain part of town—because you're a woman, or because of your skin color or religion or something. I mean, it's bad enough in this country, but I just can imagine what it's like in Afghanistan, or Somalia, or places where women are considered just chattel. I'd be so pissed off! I guess that's what they're used to, but I'll bet it still makes them angry, at least some of them." They stopped and waited for a traffic light to change.

"I read somewhere that the suicide rate for women in Afghanistan under the Taliban was much higher than it was in other Muslim countries," Susannah said. "I don't know how they get these statistics, and how believable they are, but it's pretty sobering if it's anywhere near accurate. Have you read *Reading Lolita in Tehran*?"

Derek said he hadn't.

"It's about a group of college age-women, students of literature, who meet at the home of their female professor, and they read things that can't be read on campus because of censorship. They had a joke about the first line of *Pride and Prejudice*, which you may know." She quoted from memory. "'It is a truth universally acknowledged, that a single man in possession of a good fortune must be in want of a wife.' Their variation of the first line of this classic was something to the effect that it's known everywhere that a Muslim man, no matter his fortune, must be in need of a nine-year-old virgin wife. A macabre kind of humor. Sort of makes you sick to your stomach, doesn't it?"

They moved on to other topics, and soon arrived at Broadway, where they were lucky to get into a popular Mexican restaurant when no one was waiting, and just as a table was being cleared. After they had ordered, Will asked D&T what they did for a break from their studies.

Trisha said that her big thing was exercise. If she didn't get a good workout regularly she didn't sleep well and was cranky.

"You can say that again," Derek commented, and they all laughed.

"So how do you like to work out?" Will asked her.

"I row," Trisha said. Will glanced at Susannah, who looked like she'd just won the lottery, and said, "I think we're in for it, Derek—we've got two rowers here."

"Oh no," Derek groaned. "I suppose we'll have to hear about being down to starboard, and all that nautical talk!"

"OK, everyone," Susannah said. "I think I know where we should go for a walk tomorrow. We can either go to my boathouse and walk along Lake Washington, or we can go to the Green Lake boathouse and walk around Green Lake. Maybe Green Lake, then you guys can go across the street and inspect the soccer fields. Either way, I can show Trisha a boathouse."

....

On the way home after dinner, the women walked together, trading rowing stories, and it was Derek's turn to ask Will about the Fred incident. He'd read all the articles in the papers, but it was different to hear from Will how he felt as it was happening and after it was over. He also wanted to know what happened to Fred.

"He was released after a few days of psychiatric evaluation, and no charges were brought," Will said. "Several people from my class contacted him, and he's even dating one of the girls—a very unlikely pair. But I'm really happy for him. He seems to have turned a corner—which is a huge relief!"

When they got home, Susannah informed Will and Derek that she and Trisha were going to walk at about nine, because Susannah knew that rowers would be out at both boathouses. If the men wanted to come, breakfast was at eight, and if they didn't, they could get their own breakfast.

"Can I decide in the morning?" asked Derek.

"Sure," said Susannah. "Now I'm going to bed—I rowed this morning! Sleep well, you two."

D&T closed their door and got ready for bed. "I like them," Trisha said, after she'd snuggled under the covers. "They're comfortable to be around. They're not parental, even though they're parental age."

"Yeah, they don't seem to need to impress or anything. And they talk about interesting stuff." Derek yawned. "I'm really tired. OK with you if I decide to sleep in tomorrow?"

"Absolutely," she said. "Susannah and I will get our exercise, and talk rowing and girl talk, and you guys can do what you want. I would like to be just with you in the evening, though. It is Valentine's Day, after all."

"Mmm," he replied, already half-asleep.

....

"How are you feeling so far?" Susannah asked Will sleepily the next morning.

"So far, so good," he replied, pulling her close. "It really helps that you're here. This would be a lot harder without you. I think they like you."

"Are you going to be OK this morning if it's just the two of you guys?"

"We did OK the last time, and I can't always have someone running interference for me. We'll just have to see what happens. For now, I think I'll snooze some more."

....

Susannah and Trisha had a quiet breakfast, so that the men could sleep, and left about nine. They were lucky to have a sunny day, so they drove down to Lake Washington to the

Mount Baker boathouse. As they arrived, the weekend masters class was just putting its boats in the water. Susannah showed Trisha through the sailing facility and around the shell house. They got on the ergometers and had a short workout, and then walked down the lakeside path toward Seward Park.

"It's quite a place," Trisha said.

"Yes," Susannah replied. "It really is nice now that they've finished it all up. They have a huge juniors program here. It's such a trip in the summer when there're about a hundred teenagers here, with all their hormones and airheadedness. You wonder how they can even get a boat in the water sometimes!"

Trisha laughed. "It wasn't very long ago that I was one of those airheads. It was so good for us—to work really hard physically, and to be on a team and learn what that's about. I think kids who row, or do any sport, have an advantage over those who don't."

"Do you compete, Trisha?"

"I do. I went to the Head of the Charles last year. We didn't place, but it was a huge thrill just to be able to row in that race. It'll always be a high point in my life, I'm sure."

"Congratulations—that's really impressive! I could never do something like that. Competing just ruins the fun for me. You and Will have the competition thing in common."

"You're retired, I gather?" Trisha asked. "What do you do with your time?"

Susannah gave her an overview and then added, "I can hardly believe what a lucky person I am, to be doing what I want to be doing. And now that Will's come into my life, things are just about perfect. What are your plans after Reed, Trisha? Or are you still sorting that out?"

"No, I'm planning to go to med school. I've wanted to be a doctor since I was in grade school. I loved my pediatrician when I was little, and admired her when I was older, and I've always been interested in the biological sciences.

So that's what I've got my heart set on. I've done all my 'due diligence' to be as sure as I can that's what I want to do. I've volunteered in hospitals and clinics, and taken EMT courses, and been on a search-and-rescue team, and talked with practicing physicians. So I think I know what I'm getting into."

"You're very thorough! But with this kind of decision, I can see why you'd want to be. It's a long row to hoe, and so expensive—you need to be sure."

The two of them walked and talked for about two hours, then stopped at a coffeehouse on the way home.

....

Will got up shortly after the women left and put the coffee on. Susannah had left juice, muffins, and orange slices, and Will could manage the rest. He was reading the paper and drinking coffee when Derek came into the kitchen.

"I hope you slept well," said Will. "How about scrambled eggs and bacon for breakfast?" Derek said that sounded good, and helped himself to coffee.

"What's on the agenda for today?" he asked.

"Lots of possibilities," Will replied, and ran through a list. "I don't know how much walking Susannah and Trisha will want to do after their morning jaunt. We could go to a movie, or we could go to Alki and walk along the beach—lots of places to eat and drink coffee there."

"I'm pretty open," said Derek, watching Will beat the eggs and add seasonings. As Derek was setting the table, he asked, "So what made you decide to be a priest, and then . . . not be a priest?"

"I think I mentioned to you in Portland that I come from a very Catholic family. My folks were really devout, and in their families, having someone join the priesthood was really important. I have lots of cousins in the East, and several of them became priests. Anyway, my folks didn't insist or lay a trip on me, but I wanted to please them. Besides, I was very devout myself, and drawn to the idea of serving God and my fellow man. Very idealistic and all that." He stirred the eggs.

"But the reality was very different from the ideal," Will said. "Priests are people just like everyone else—same problems, issues, faults, gifts. And the institution as a whole just can't cope with the difficulties and realities of human nature. I couldn't do much about a lot of the things I saw that shouldn't have been happening. So I left." He put the scrambled eggs on the plates along with the muffins, and they sat down to breakfast.

"What was it like, after you . . . uh, became a civilian?"

"It was a pretty confusing time for a while," Will said. "I was angry that the church hadn't lived up to my ideals, and felt that I'd wasted a lot of my life, so I was acting out, you could say. I slept around—I guess these days they call it 'hooking up'."

"And that's how I got here," said Derek, with a touch of hostility in his voice.

Will didn't try to avoid the implications of Derek's tone. "Yes, that's how you got here, ashamed as I am to admit it."

"Well, it's nice you're ashamed," Derek said sarcastically. "Is that why you never showed up when I was a kid?"

"Yes," Will replied. His face was tense, but he looked Derek in the eye. "I was ashamed and guilty." He paused and then went on. "What was your understanding, as a child, about me and your stepdad? Do you mind my asking?"

"No, it's OK. I've been thinking about that too, trying to remember. I can't remember when Dad wasn't my dad, so I don't have any conscious memory of not having a father, or losing a father. I think it was probably in grade school that Mom told me about you. And it was very low-key—she didn't make a big deal out of it. She just said that you lived far away and couldn't take care of me, and Dad could, and that was that." He studied his plate, and Will fiddled with his spoon.

"I didn't think about it much until I hit my teens," Derek said. "And then, I guess I imagined the worst—that my biological father was someone who got my mom pregnant and left her, and didn't care about being in my life. I did tell Mom that I wasn't interested in knowing you. I figured I didn't want to know a guy who didn't care to be in my life and would treat my mom that way. And it feels good to say so!"

Will grimaced. "Well, it's natural for you to feel that way," he admitted. "But, unfortunately, it gave me an out, a reason not to make the attempt I should have made sooner. I felt very guilty—that's why I procrastinated. And I told myself that I didn't want to get in the way of your relationship with your stepdad. All excuses, I know, but that's how I let myself off the hook. And the more time passed, the more difficult it was to act." He looked directly at his son.

"But one thing is really clear to me, Derek. I needed to meet you, to try to establish a relationship with you and try to make up for the time that I wasn't a father to you. If you don't want that, it's your choice. But it's the responsible thing for me to do, and besides, I want to do it. I like you, and that makes it easier, but I would have tried anyway, even if it seemed we didn't have much in common or didn't like each other."

"Well, I'm glad you don't seem to be a jerk," Derek said. "But I'm still pissed off, and it's going to take me a while to sort all this out. I was telling Trisha that it's weird to suddenly have an extra father show up in your life, especially when he's not like what you thought."

Just then Trisha and Susannah arrived, bringing in with them a blast of cold air from the winter day. They had rosy cheeks and were very animated, telling Will and Derek about the eagles they had seen hunting ducks on Lake Washington, and the golden lab jumping off the end of the fishing pier to retrieve a stick.

"We've had lattes and other goodies, so we're ready to

go exploring," Susannah announced. "Have you guys made any decisions?"

"Nope," Will said. We were waiting for you two, so Trisha can decide. Derek says he doesn't have any preferences."

"Oh, so you're going to put it all on *me*," Trisha said. "Well, I can take the pressure. I want to go to the Pike Place Market and have lunch downtown. After that, Derek has to decide. And I want to have a romantic dinner with my sweetie this evening."

....

They enjoyed looking at the colorful and artfully arranged fruits and vegetables in the stalls and listening to the palaver of the fishmongers as they encouraged buyers. Trisha got a photo of a fish being thrown to the cashier for wrapping. They meandered through all the little shops in the market, and Susannah bought halibut and brussels sprouts. Then they had lunch at the brewpub.

By this time it was after three, and they all decided that a nap or reading a book and sipping tea sounded pretty good, so they got back on the bus and went home. Susannah curled up with her book club selection, and everyone else took a nap. She thought the group seemed fairly relaxed, and she was grateful. She liked D&T and hoped that things had gone well between Will and Derek that morning. She looked forward to a report at dinner.

Susannah was getting a foot rub from Will on the sofa when D&T emerged from their room, yawning and looking rested. "It's so relaxing being here," Trisha said. You'd better be careful, or we'll be up here all the time!"

"We're glad you're enjoying yourselves," Susannah said. "I'm sure your classes are stressful, so it's good you can have a break. Have you decided where you're going to go tonight?"

"We'll probably just wander around Broadway until we get hungry, and then see if we can get into a restaurant,"

Trisha said. They left at about seven with Will's key.

....

D&T walked down the misty streets hand in hand, exchanging impressions of the day. "I told Will how pissed I was about his not being in my life for so long," Derek said. "He handled it pretty well. Said he'd felt guilty for years, but that he'd finally gotten his shit together and decided to try to be a father, on whatever terms I'd accept. I still have mixed feelings. I like him, but I'm still mad that he wasn't around when he should've been." They waited for the traffic at a crosswalk. "How was your morning with Susannah?"

"She's really neat. It's kind of like having a much-older sister, or an aunt or something. She treats me like an adult, and listens to my opinions, and is just fun to talk to. And I love to see her and Will together. Just watching that foot rub turned me on! They have quite the thing going. Nice to know that can still happen when people get older."

....

Will set the table and poured two glasses of wine while Susannah cooked the fish and followed an elaborate recipe for roasted brussels sprouts. "Every time I make this recipe, I swear I won't do it again," she grumbled. "But they taste so good, I just keep doing it. Tell me about your morning with Derek."

"It sounds like he didn't really know about me until he was in grade school," Will said, "and didn't really understand the implications until he was older. Then in high school, he kind of assumed the worst—that I'd deserted him and his mom—and so he didn't want to know me. But he still resents the fact that I didn't even try to be in his life. And I don't blame him. It never fails to amaze me how people can rationalize their sins—more specifically, how I've rationalized mine. I'll just have to see how we can go on from here, and if he can work through his resentments and disappointments."

The next morning they walked around the UW campus. Susannah packed a lunch for D&T, and they left around noon, wanting to get back to Portland before the traffic got bad. Hugs and promises for another get together were exchanged, and they were off.

"I'm going to meditate," Susannah announced. "I think this visit has gone pretty well, but it's taken a lot of energy and I need to get back into my routine. She disappeared into the bedroom. Will got himself a beer and sat down on the sofa to reflect on the visit with his son. He, too, thought it had gone fairly well. He was cautiously relieved that Derek didn't seem to be screwed-up by not having had him around, though he knew that emotional wounds could show up later in life. He pondered what he should do next. Maybe he'd wait to hear something from Derek, and if he didn't hear anything within a few weeks, he'd make contact again.

Susannah had a morning ritual: shower, cream, hair drying, clothes, makeup, perfume. One morning as she was at the cream stage, dressed only in the towel on her head, she looked up to see Will leaning against the bathroom doorframe. "I like your headdress," he said with a grin. "Mind if I watch?"

"I like it that you like to watch," she said with a brave smile, "but I have to say it makes me a little uncomfortable. I've spent my whole life wishing my body were different, and even though I know our culture is sick when it comes to women's body image, I can't totally escape it. But I'm trying."

"Let's talk about this some more when I don't have to go to class and you're wearing more than a towel," he said. He gave her a little farewell salute and left to catch the bus to campus.

That evening after dinner they were sitting on the sofa

reading. Will put his arm around Susannah, kissed the top of her head, and said, "Now, tell me about this body-image thing."

Susannah sighed. "I know you like to make love to me, I know you enjoy my body, and that makes me very happy." She paused in her explanation to kiss him. "But there's this voice in my head reminding me that I have fat on my belly and thighs that I shouldn't have, that there are age spots and broken veins, and wrinkles. There are ads everywhere about all these things, and the not-so-subtle message is that the natural effects of getting older are not OK. I know it's ridiculous, but I'm influenced by all the hype. Most women are. And it doesn't help that a lot of men marry significantly younger women. So there's another message—you'd better look good or you won't have a man in your life."

"Ah, I see," he said, and was quiet for several minutes.

"You know that last message isn't true, Susannah. There're lots of women who don't fit the ideal image who have men in their lives. So the advertising industry and the film industry, and whoever else stands to gain financially, are perpetrating a lie and a lot of fear. Right? So it seems to me you're succumbing to the fear. Is that true?"

"Now that you say it, it's obvious it's fear, and yet I never thought about it that way."

"So how do you deal with fear?"

"A lot differently than I used to," she said. "It's been such a big thing in my life, something I've been working on very hard. It sounds a little silly and hokey, but when I feel fearful, I try to consciously welcome it by saying to myself, 'OK, little fear, I'll be your friend. You don't have to worry. We'll get through this together.' So if I'm uptight about some deadline, or some event that I'm involved in, and I realize I'm fearful, that's what I try to do. And I try to figure out where the fear is coming from. Am I afraid I'll look incompetent, or stupid, or what? Sometimes I can tell what the fear relates to, but a lot of times I can't. And the strange thing is that this approach often works—it sort of defuses the fear. It wouldn't work if a bear were charging at me or if a loved one were in danger, but it works for psychological fears, at least for me."

"I guess you have to keep working on the fear thing. I can't do much about that," Will said. "It's irrational, and you know that, and you've developed some ways to defuse it or transform it, or whatever happens to it. So you have to work on that consciously. But I think I can help too. I'm the man in your life, aren't I?"

She nodded.

"I have no intention of going away," he said. "I love you, and I love your body. You might be surprised how often I think about making love with you, how I like to watch you get dressed—and undressed! Men just like to look at women, and I like to look at you. Think about that the next time you're feeling self-conscious. OK? I would really like you to stop worrying or being afraid, or whatever it is."

"OK, I'll try," she said, giving him a hug and an appreciative smile.

She lay awake that night, after Will had gone to sleep, thinking about the past few years and the men in her life. Dave, Peter, Marty, Will—all four of them were so different, and yet all four of them helped her see herself in a new way, become a better version of herself, more capable of enjoying life. She was wondering, as she dropped off to sleep, if her attempts to examine her life, to face her fears and faults—to be open to life—had brought more life to her.

....

Early April was the traditional time for Will's departmental office party, Susannah was looking forward to meeting more of Will's colleagues. She expected there would be good conversation with so many intelligent, well-educated professors and their spouses. Will's eyebrows went up when she expressed this expectation. "I guess I've been to too many of these parties," he said. "They may be smart and well educated, but they play the same games as everyone else. I'll be interested in your observations afterward."

She decided to wear her blue knit top (Will's favorite), a knee-length floral print skirt, and sandals. The outfit would be springy, but warm enough for the April chill.

This year the party was at the home of Tom Bagshot, the department chair. Everyone brought a bottle of wine and an appetizer, and the host and hostess had provided more food and an open bar. The party was in full swing when they arrived at about eight. Tom and his wife, Nancy, greeted them and took their coats. Tom immediately took Susannah's arm and steered her to the bar. "What can I get for you?" he asked with a smile. "Welcome to our little team of rivals!"

"A glass of red wine would be lovely, thank you. Why do you refer to your department as the 'team of rivals'?"

"Oh, it's a compliment, really. Lincoln's cabinet was composed of really outstanding people, even though they all wanted his job. There are some parallels to our situation," he said, smiling in a conspiratorial manner. "Let me introduce you around. That's a lovely spring outfit you're wearing, by the way." He put his arm around her waist and moved easily among the guests, introducing her to those colleagues of Will's that she hadn't yet met.

As soon as she could politely do so, she moved out of his grasp to chat with Nancy. Susannah had been admiring the well-maintained colonial house, with its tasteful modern furnishings. "Your home is lovely, Nancy. How long have you been here?"

"Tom's been here for twenty-five years, but I've only lived here for ten—second marriage for him. It's been fun redecorating. It's a great house for parties." As she chatted with Susannah, she watched her husband flirting with one of the department's young administrative assistants.

"What do you do when you're not redecorating?" Susannah asked.

"I do a lot of volunteer work—Children's Hospital, Childhaven, the Seattle Art Museum. It's rewarding and interesting, and I've made a lot of friends. Will you excuse me, Susannah? I need to replenish the ice." She stopped on her way to the kitchen to put her arm around her husband, who was still flirting with the young woman. He moved off to circulate among other guests.

Susannah was watching these interactions with interest when a very handsome man came up to her and introduced himself as the husband of one of the professors. He reminded her of George Clooney, only much bigger—like a pro football player. Before long they were talking and laughing. He had a very sharp wit and interesting ideas, and they were enjoying each other's company.

....

Will was watching all this out of the corner of his eye, trying to pay attention to his conversation with his colleague Leona Devlin. She was a dear, but she'd had a crush on Will for ten years now and couldn't seem to get over it. She always tried to monopolize him at department events. Nancy Bagshot joined them and asked Leona how her poodles were doing; the real love of Leona's life was her poodles.

Will gave Nancy a "thank you" grin and slipped away. He came up beside Susannah and put his arm around her waist. Extending his right hand to the handsome man she was talking with, he said, "Hi, I'm Will Ryan."

"I'm Len Sampson, Fiona's husband. Glad to meet you." Soon Fiona joined them, and they had a conversation about the traffic in Montlake and the difficulty of finding affordable housing in Seattle. Fiona was the newest member of the faculty, and they had just moved to Seattle from Texas. Then another couple joined them, and the talk flowed to politics and got rather animated.

....

They said their good-byes and thank-yous about an hour

later. Their host, three sheets to the wind, kissed Susannah good-bye. She thought it was amusing, but Will didn't look that amused. On the way home they traded stories about their interactions with the other guests. Will was interested in her impressions of people and filled her in on their backgrounds.

"I should have warned you about Tom, but I didn't want you to start out with a negative impression of him. He's a pretty good department chair, but I feel sorry for his wife."

"Yes, it must be very trying," Susannah said.

"You seemed to be enjoying your conversation with Len Sampson," Will observed.

"Yes, I did. He was the most interesting person I talked to. He's really funny." She yawned. "I'm tired! It was a fun party, but it takes a lot of energy to make conversation with a bunch of people you've just met."

"That reminds me. I've been wondering what happens to you when you talk about politics," Will said. "Have you ever thought about that? It's not just you—it seems to happen to everyone. Voices rise. People cut each other off. Poor Fiona kept trying to make her point, and you interrupted her more than once."

There was a loud silence for a few minutes. "I guess you're right, Will—much as I hate to admit it. It sort of spoils the evening to think about it. I know it's a bad habit, this interrupting." She reflected and then added, "I think it goes back to grad school. I was only in my twenties, and it seemed to be so important to make points and win arguments, to show off and look smart. I shouldn't still be doing this."

They were uncharacteristically quiet as they rode home and got ready for bed. Susannah felt Will's admonition was perfectly justified, and she felt chastened and embarrassed; he was right to point out something to her that she needed to correct. But she also sensed that there was something else going on. She went back over the evening in her mind.

Is he jealous? How could that be? Of a lecherous colleague and a guy she'd talked to for fifteen minutes? A lovely evening had ended on a down note. Maybe she was just being defensive by accusing him of jealousy.

....

Will *was* jealous. As he was brushing his teeth, he recognized it, was surprised, and thought it was ridiculous, but he still felt it. What was jealousy, anyway? He thought maybe it was fear of loss. He realized that he wanted to know that Susannah was committed to him. He knew she loved him, but neither of them had made any commitment. *Why is that important?* he wondered. He concluded, after some thought, that it was important because it made things clear between two people. With no commitment, you didn't really know where you stood. He thought he and Susannah had a pretty good chance of being together for a long time. They'd known each other for several months, they'd been friends before they became lovers, they helped each other sort out their issues, and they had a very strong physical attraction to each other. He didn't want to lose her.

The next day was a beautiful spring Sunday, with temperatures in the seventies. Susannah went for a walk and planned to stop for some groceries on her way home. Will was correcting papers and working at the computer on an article. He left at about three for a soccer game while she was making a salad and getting a casserole ready to put in the oven.

He returned at about five thirty, tired and muddy but in a good mood. He went straight to the shower and then came into the kitchen barefoot, in jeans and T-shirt, his hair still wet. She got out a beer for him, and he took a big swallow. "You look cute," he said. "Is that a new skirt?"

"Yes, I just couldn't pass it up—it's so different from anything I have. I got it at that East Indian shop on Broadway." She was wearing a print tank top and a pink gauze skirt with a handkerchief hem and a drawstring waist.

He continued to drink his beer as he told her about their soccer game. All of a sudden, he said, "Susannah! You're not wearing a bra!"

"You noticed!" she giggled. "No underwear today. It's my new regime for Sundays. You haven't finished telling me your story."

"To hell with the story!" He pulled her close and kissed her, his hands finding their way under her tank top and inside her skirt. She tugged his T-shirt over his head and unzipped his jeans. They had never made love so passionately.

Later, when they were lying in each other's arms, drowsy and happy, Will asked Susannah, "What gave you the idea to go without underwear? I think you should permanently give it up, if this is what happens!"

Susannah laughed. "Ever since we had that conversation about body image, I've been thinking about how I've always defined myself sexually," she said. "Inhibited, timid, not attractive enough. That definition came from a lot of influences—how my mother was, my churchy background, the Rainbow Girls' insistence on sitting with your knees together, what 'good girls' did and didn't do, and so on. I realized that all of that was just a story, and that I could have a different story. Not that it's easy to change stories, but I decided I'd start by doing one thing that I'd never done before and see what happened. So I screwed up my courage and bought my new skirt, and . . . here we are! And since that worked so well, I'll have courage to try something else."

"I can hardly wait!" he said. Then, he switched to a more serious tone. "I've been thinking about something for a while. It's not just a spur of the moment thing after the all-time greatest sex I've ever had," he told her. "I love you, Susannah, and I'm committed to being with you, taking care of you, growing old with you. And I want you to be committed to me. I don't want to wonder if some other guy might come along and steal you away." He turned over to face her and ran his fingers through her hair. "Will you marry me?"

A smile spread across her face as she raised herself on one elbow and caressed his face. "Will, every week I think I couldn't be more in love with you, and then the next week, I'm more in love than ever. I just can't believe that I'm so lucky to have found you!" She kissed him. "I'll commit myself to you, Will. For better, for worse, forsaking all others, for the rest of our lives—all those wonderful words apply. I have no hesitation." She stopped talking to kiss him again. "But is marriage the way you want to do it? I mean, is the institution important to you, the legal bit, the social convention? It's the commitment that's important, isn't it, not the convention?"

While he knew she'd said yes to marrying him, he was surprised that she was questioning marriage as an expression of commitment. "I guess I'm not a very modern guy," he said. "I haven't really thought about marriage as an institution for a long time. It's just what you do when you love someone and want to spend the rest of your life with her. But I'm open to talking about it—now that I'm clear about how you feel about me, and us." Will's stomach growled. "Susannah, I know this isn't very romantic—but I'm *starving*. Could we continue this conversation over dinner?"

She laughed and got up to dress. "You'll be happy to know that dinner's ready—if it isn't reduced to ashes after this wonderful delay."

As they sat down to eat, Will restarted the conversation. "Do you think marriage is just a private thing, that people don't need to do anything public about their commitment to each other?"

"No, I don't think it's a private thing," she said. "At least not for me. Some people probably feel that way—like it's nobody's business but theirs. I want the whole world to know how you feel about me and how I feel about you. I don't want to be private about that! I'd like all our friends to celebrate our happiness with us."

She gave him another serving of casserole. "I think it helps to keep your commitments if you've made them in front of people you care about and who care about you. And I like the idea of people writing their own vows. It's an occasion for talking over what matters to you, making things clear that might otherwise not be clear. But I like the old standard marriage vows best—they always make me cry when I hear them. They're so serious, so big. They demand a lot. They set a high standard. You can spend a lifetime living up to those vows."

"I know what you mean," Will said. "I didn't conduct many weddings as a priest, but those vows were always so impressive, so weighty. OK, we've settled on the vows! I want to go back to what you just said, though, about spending a lifetime living up to those vows." He put the last of the salad on his plate. "Isn't that what marriage is—ideally—a lifetime endeavor of growth? What more important thing could people do than grow enough that they could stick with each other for a lifetime? And I don't mean just accepting each other's foibles and giving up some things you care about. There's that, but there's also sticking to your values when there's conflict, and finding a way to make things work for both people."

"I think everything's a potential occasion for growth," Susannah replied, pouring more wine for each of them. "Some of my work experiences were major occasions for growth—I had to really think about what mattered to me, and how much I cared about what people thought about me, and what was the right thing to do. But I agree with you that making things work and helping each other grow and continuing to find meaning after decades with the same person is a major life accomplishment. You don't usually stay with your coworkers for decades."

Will pushed back his plate. "I want to have a fiancée for a

while and a wedding bash. And I think it will be interesting to read about the history of marriage and wedding rituals. Do I sound like an academic?" he asked, grinning. "But if I know you, you're just as bad—you'll have six books from the library in a couple of days, and you'll be telling me about how the institution of marriage has changed in the last hundred years and where the custom of white dresses came from.

"Seriously, Susannah, let's have a good time with this. It's a really big deal for me—the sixty-something bachelor who thought a loving wife was not in the cards for this life. It's like a reprieve, or a huge gift, or something. I love you."

"I love you too. She reached across the table and took his hand. "This will be the best wedding ever! We're not trying to impress anyone, we can do whatever we like, and everyone will be so happy for us—the old fogies getting a second chance at wedded bliss. Aren't we lucky?"

It really wasn't just about bookcases.

CHAPTER FIVE

Unpacking

"Will, how long do you want to have a fiancée as opposed to a wife? I just need to know so I can start looking for a place for the wedding reception." He was grading papers on the sofa, and Susannah had come in from the kitchen where she'd been making rhubarb chutney for Christmas presents.

"We've only been engaged for two months—I haven't had nearly enough time to introduce you to people as my fiancée. I only get to do this once, so I don't want to rush it." He looked up at Susannah and smiled. "How about a fall wedding?"

"Sounds good to me," she answered. "That gives us a few months to find a place and for potential guests to get it on their calendars. How much time can you take off from teaching?"

"Hmm, I could probably work something out to cover my classes for a couple of weeks. But beyond that, I'd probably have to skip teaching for a quarter. I think we'll want at least three weeks, maybe more. I'll talk to the chairman tomorrow and make sure I can skip teaching for the fall term. We can afford the loss of income, and I've never done it, and it's a special occasion, so I think Tom will be amenable."

She moved a stack of papers and sat down beside him. "You do know, don't you, that planning a wedding is often as stressful as getting a divorce? All sorts of stuff comes up that causes tension between families and stresses between the bride and groom." She looked at him in mock seriousness. "We have to be prepared for this."

"Oh, come on," he said dismissively. "We're grown-ups, and our kids are grown-ups—what's the big deal?"

"You said you didn't do many weddings when you were a priest, so you don't have much experience with the phenomenon. How many weddings have you actually been involved in, where you were close to the family, and not just a guest? I'll bet just your sister's."

He thought a moment, head back, looking at the ceiling, then said, "You're right, I've just been the officiant—which is almost like being a guest—except for Allie's wedding, and even then, I just flew in for the wedding, so I wasn't around for the preparations."

"Well, we should expect the unexpected, and watch our reactions as things come up."

"That sounds rather cryptic, but, whatever . . . Now I need to finish these papers. Can we talk about this at dinner?"

"Sure," she said, getting up to return to the kitchen. "I'll have a little list of topics for discussion." She made a mental list as she poured the sauce into the jars and put them into the freezer.

After she finished cleaning up the kitchen, Susannah went to her computer and wrote her list, spreading it out on the page so she could record Will's responses. She smiled to herself, knowing he was clueless about the amount of planning involved in even a simple wedding.

Three hours later they sat down to spaghetti and salad. "OK, I'm ready for your list," he said, taking a sip of wine. "Where do we start?"

"What do you want it to feel like—formal, informal, traditional, what?" she asked him, pencil poised.

"Well, I don't want it to be stuffy, that's for sure. I want people to have a good time. I want the traditional words: 'dearly beloved,' 'for better, for worse,' you know . . . We don't have to have a priest, just someone we both like." Will buttered another piece of bread. "How about your meditation teacher? I like Roger. He can do weddings, can't he?"

"Yes, he can, and I love that idea," Susannah said. "He'd be my first choice. OK, on to the next question. What's the program? Do you want to have a prenuptial dinner for all the out-of-town guests, and what kind of reception—dinner, dancing? Or just cake and coffee in the church basement? If we have it in a church."

He thought a moment and said, "It would be nice to do something with the out-of-town guests besides the reception itself. Let's think about that some more. Maybe we could go ice skating."

"Ice skating! What on earth for?" She was incredulous.

"I'm teasing, Susannah! I just wanted to see how you'd react." He grinned at her and took another drink of wine. "As for the reception, I think a dinner would be nice, and I'd like to do something that would get people acquainted, that would mix them up, because a lot of them won't know each other. Let me think about that."

"Since you're not wild about dancing, I'll assume we won't put that on the program." She sighed inwardly, reminding herself that she couldn't have everything, and then went on. "How many people do we want to invite?"

"Oh, everyone. I'd like a big bash!"

"OK, I suggest you make a list—on the computer, please—and I'll make a list and we'll see how many we're thinking about, and then I can give you an idea of how much that might cost." Will watched her face as she slipped into planning mode.

"It also occurred to me," she said, "that since you have so much family in Boston, we might have a separate event there. That way you could celebrate with more of your family—probably many of them wouldn't be able to fly to Seattle. I'm sure one of your cousins would help us plan something."

"That's a great idea, Susannah! We could have our honeymoon in New England—would you like that?"

"Yes, I'd like that. But let's think about some other options too. I've never been to Hawaii . . . or Iceland."

"Iceland!" he said. It was his turn for incredulity. "Now *you're* teasing!"

"How'd you guess?" she giggled. "One last question for now: who's going to do the planning and arranging, and what has to be agreed on jointly?"

"I don't want to weasel out of all the work, but we both know you're much better at this kind of thing than I am, Susannah. How about you lay out the possibilities and make some recommendations, and then we can discuss them. I won't care about decorations and invitations and stuff like that, but I would like to have a say about the food."

"I'm happy with that approach. You know I love to plan parties," she said. "What fun! I'm going to get together with Allie and Sylvianne. I know they'll want to be involved."

....

The next day Susannah arranged a lunch for the following week with her daughter-in-law, Sylvianne, and with Will's sister, Allie. Allie and Sylvianne had met only once before, at a Thanksgiving dinner hosted by Allie and her husband, Greg.

The women sat outside in the courtyard at the Inn at the Market on a rare warm June day. "Well, ladies," Susannah said, "I'd like to ask your help in planning the wedding. Will and I have had some preliminary discussions—"

"I'm giving the prenuptial dinner," Allie said. "I'm dying to do something really special for my big brother. I still can't believe he's finally getting married!" As a high-powered lawyer, Allie was used to getting her way.

"Hmm," said Sylvianne. "Alex and I just talked about this last night, and we wanted to host the dinner."

"Well, it's usually the groom's family that does the prenuptial dinner," Allie said. "And we're Will's family, so I think we ought to do it. I've already checked into the Yacht Club and the Rainier Club." She looked determined.

Just then the waiter arrived to bring menus and ask if

they'd like something to drink. When he left with their orders, Susannah said, "Thank you both for your offers, but we're not ready to talk about who's doing what yet. What I'd like is your ideas on what we might do, and then we can talk about who's going to do it." She told them what she and Will had discussed.

"One thing we need is some ideas for what to do with the guests from out of town, something Seattle-ish, and something that would get them acquainted with each other. We think we'd like to have a dinner for everyone after the ceremony, but what kind of activity could we do to help people feel more at home with each other, since so many will be unacquainted? Could we brainstorm some ideas? Maybe you've seen something someone else has done that would be fun."

Sylvianne got out a little notebook, ready to jot down ideas. The wine they'd ordered loosened things up, and the three of them had a great time brainstorming through lunch, until it was time for Allie to rush back to her office for a meeting.

"Allie, what about this idea of another reception in Boston—do you think your relatives would like that? And is there someone in particular we could work with?"

"Oh, yes," Allie answered. "Our cousin Kathleen would love to do something for Will. They were great childhood friends before our family moved to Seattle, and they've kept in touch. Why don't I call her and see what she thinks. Are you OK with that, Susannah?"

"Of course, as long as it's clear that we're paying for it. I'd be embarrassed to ask someone to have a party for me. I just need someone to help find a place and suggest what would work best for the family, since I don't know any of them."

"Got it," she called over her shoulder as she sailed out of the courtyard.

....

"See, I told you weddings were occasions for tension," Susannah said as she recounted the tussle over the prenuptial dinner to Will that evening. "I'm sure we can work this out between Allie and Sylvianne, but it'll take some imagination and tact. Allie's just in another universe from us—the Yacht Club or the Rainier Club, for heaven's sake!"

"Is there something wrong with those venues?" asked Will.

"Well, not only are they very expensive places to hold an event, but they seem so exclusive. There's nothing wrong with them, I just wouldn't feel comfortable having my wedding reception in a place like that."

"Why not?"

"Well, isn't it perfectly obvious? We're not those kind of people! I don't want people to think we're pretending to be something we're not."

"Susannah, who cares what people think?"

"*I* care!" she said.

"Honey, have you ever been to a function in a fancy place that you really enjoyed, even though you'd never be a member there?"

"Yes," she replied slowly, realizing that she was about to be caught in some specious thinking. "I've been to some receptions at the Rainier Club and the Women's University Club—way out of my league, but it was fun to be there and see how the other half lives."

"Well then, what's wrong with offering our guests that possibility?"

"I just wouldn't feel comfortable. I'd feel pretentious."

"I still don't see why," he said. "Isn't this *your* hang-up, Susannah? If we can afford it, and one of those places offers everything we want, why shouldn't we have our party there? Allie has tons of money, and if she wants to pay for it and it would make her happy, why not?"

"Those places are very nice, but they don't fit my image of myself—"

"Aha! So this is about your image."

She threw a pillow at him and tacked. "It's not just an

image question. The way you spend your money is a reflection of what you value, and I don't place a high value on having a party in an exclusive joint!"

"OK, I'll go along with that. But I don't think you should be making decisions based on what people will think. How do you know what other people think about the Rainier Club or the Yacht Club, and how do you know whether they really are expensive and exclusive? Have you ever investigated how much it costs to join? Do you even know anyone who belongs, or has been rejected for membership?"

She had to back down. "No, I don't know any of that." She left the room.

A half hour later she came back into the living room, picked up the pillow she'd thrown, and sat down beside him. "You're right, much as I hate to admit it. I have to watch myself with this 'What will people think?' business. It's old baggage. One of the reasons I want to be with you is because you help me see this stuff—you call me on it. Don't stop, even if I throw things at you."

....

A few days after this exchange, Will called his son to tell him about the wedding plans.

"Hey, that's really great, Will—I'm happy for you and Susannah. Congratulations!"

"Thanks, Derek. I wanted you to know so you could put the date on your calendar. We'd love to have you and Trisha with us for the festivities. Also, I wanted to ask if you'd be my best man."

"Wow, that's a surprise. Uh, I don't know what to say." There was an awkward pause.

Will, at first, was surprised at Derek's hesitation. Then he realized that maybe he was pushing the relationship too fast, and that Derek was probably wondering what his mother would think about his being in the wedding of the man who had refused to marry her when she was pregnant with his son.

"Tell you what," he said to Derek. "Why don't you think about it and let me know later—there's no rush. I don't want to push this. I have old friends I could ask, so if you decide you'd rather not, that's fine." They chatted about other things for a few minutes and then said good-bye.

Will realized that Susannah was right; there could be emotional minefields surrounding a wedding.

....

Will was agreeable to almost everything proposed, but when he learned there would be at least thirty minutes of photos before the ceremony started, he balked. "I'm old-fashioned. I don't want to see you before you walk down the aisle. I want the dress and the flowers and the whole bit to be a surprise. It would be such an anticlimax after a photo shoot!"

"But darling, all the guests would have to sit around and wait for us to take photos before the party could start— that's why they do the photos before the ceremony now. It's for the convenience of the guests."

"Well, I don't think they'd mind waiting if they had something to eat and drink. We could even have some entertainment—a slide show of our baby pictures or something. I'm adamant about this."

....

Two weeks before the wedding Susannah announced that she was sleeping in the guest room until after the big day. "I want you to be anticipating the carnal pleasures of your wedding night," she told Will. "A little deprivation will do you good."

"What about you?" Will said, pretending to be indignant. "Don't you have any carnal desires? Is deprivation easier for you than for me?"

She thought a moment. "Well, maybe just one week."

....

The stars were aligned for the wedding. The groom and his son were handsome in their dark suits, the bride was radiant in pale blue, the food was outstanding, the bride's youngest grandson was stopped from eating more than just a bite of frosting from the wedding cake before the cake was cut, and only one intoxicated guest fell into a potted plant. Everyone had a wonderful time. Susannah and Will left the following Thursday for Boston so they would be rested for the Saturday night reception hosted at the home of Allie and Will's cousin Kathleen.

On the flight to Boston, Will explained to Susannah that weddings and funerals were a really big deal for the Irish. And even though his cousins were second- and third-generation Americans, these occasions remained important in their lives. Almost every cousin Will had known growing up would be at the party, with their families. Allie and Will had done the overall planning, and Allie and Kathleen took care of the details.

The reception began at six with a buffet dinner, bottles of Jameson and Bushmills whiskey and a keg of Guinness, among other libations. Everyone was dressed to the teeth, in suits, ties, cocktail dresses—none of the West Coast informality here. Susannah and Will wore their wedding finery. As she and Will circulated among the guests, she carried a glass of Bushmills, which she liked, but she didn't drink for fear of losing track of what was happening. The whiskey and stout were flowing freely, and by the time dinner was over, everyone was loud, jolly, and pink-cheeked.

As usual at a house party, the kitchen was full of guests. Will was laughing with Kathleen, his arm around Susannah's waist, when his cousin Iain, a pint of Guinness in hand, slapped Will on the back and said with false joviality, "Lots of water under the bridge since I saw you last, Will. So, you deserted Mother Church and then the child you bred out of wedlock. What kind of a Catholic are you?"

Susannah was dumbfounded and the nearby guests who had heard the provocation looked uneasy.

"Well, Iain," Will answered, "I see you haven't changed a bit. Still your same old feisty self, ready to pick a fight at the drop of a hat." Will ignored Iain's question and proffered his own. "How's your family?"

"They're fine," was the gruff reply. Iain had probably expected a more defensive response from Will.

"I heard your wife left you and you haven't been on speaking terms with your sons for years," Will said. "That must have been a rumor—you know how things get twisted around when people talk. I'm happy to say that my son and I are on good terms. I've supported him financially since the day he was born, and he was my best man."

"Still the same fast-talker you always were as a kid, aren't you?" huffed Iain. "Never saw anyone as good as you at talking his way out of trouble and blaming somebody else."

"Maybe we should continue this conversation outside," said Will tersely, moving to open the kitchen door.

Just then there was a loud wail from the living room. The piper was tuning up his Irish bagpipes. The kitchen crowd turned away from Iain with relief and pulled Will and Susannah toward the living room, where a young woman was adjusting a fiddle and a cousin twice removed was settling himself on a chair with his tin whistle. The kitchen incident was forgotten as the musicians launched into a string of jigs and laments that had toes tapping and heads nodding. Three of the little girls got up to show off their Irish dancing, to much applause. When the musicians stopped for a break, someone started "Danny Boy" and everyone joined in.

By one in the morning they'd sung everything they knew the words to and the musicians and most of the guests had gone home. Will told Susannah it was fine for her to disappear into a bedroom and lie down. She was overwhelmed and exhausted, but happy, she told Allie and Kathleen, who came in to check on her. "You just rest," Kathleen told her. "This family can be a bit much. We'll take care of the last of the guests."

At brunch with Allie and Kathleen the next day they had a good time comparing notes on the party. Kathleen gave them a flash drive with photos a cousin had taken at the party. Susannah gave Kathleen a potted orchid as a thank-you and promised Allie that a gift for her would be coming from Rome. After many kisses, hugs, thanks, and farewells, Susannah, Will, and Allie left to check out of their hotel and take the subway to Logan Airport. More kisses and thanks, and Allie left for Seattle, while the newlyweds got on a plane to New York City, where they would board their ship.

....

They sat in their deck chairs, swathed in blankets, holding hands and drinking hot chocolate, books in their laps, and journals on the deck beside them. "Whose idea was it go to Europe on an ocean liner?" Susannah asked Will as she snuggled into her blanket. "It was a really good idea."

"Well then, I'm sure it was mine," he joked, kissing her hand. "Hi, wife."

"Hi, husband," she replied, smiling at him. "I was just thinking, this is only our second day on the ship, and we've already talked a lot about the wedding and the party in Boston, but I feel like it's going to take the whole voyage to 'unpack' everything, so to speak." She took another sip of hot chocolate. "I've noticed something." She kissed his hand.

"What's that?"

"After the newness and wildness and euphoria of sleeping together had settled down a bit, and I could be a little more sensitive to you, I felt something in you when we made love. It's very subtle, hard to describe, something like a place of reservation, of holding back. Not from me—I didn't feel you had any reservations about me or us. It felt more like a lack of permission or something."

He held her hand tightly, and looked back and forth at her and the ocean as she spoke.

"But it's gone, Will. It's been gone since our wedding night. You feel completely free now, or unconstrained, or something. I'm not sure what it was, but I think you've let it go, or it's let you go."

He said nothing for several minutes, then he smiled at her and shook his head. "You are really amazing!" he said. "I wasn't aware of that 'reservation,' or whatever it was, but I do feel more free now than when we started sleeping together. My guess is that all my growing-up 'shoulds' have finally been addressed. I've dropped a lot of them, but a few go so deep it's hard to drop them. I committed to you in front of God and everyone, I'm not having sex just for recreation or rebellion, and I'm not going to father a child and desert him. I'm doing what's right and good, and I have no doubts or fears—they've dropped away. Thanks to you." He squeezed her hand. They went back to their books and journals.

Later the stewards came around with more hot chocolate and little plates of sandwiches and cookies. As they munched, Susannah said, "Will, what was all that about with Iain? Were you really going to get into a fistfight at your wedding reception, or did 'stepping outside' mean something different?"

He gazed at the horizon, rising and falling beyond the waves, and the seabirds flying alongside the ship before replying. "I have a terrible temper—"

"What!" she said. "You? I've never met anyone with less of a temper than you! The closest I've ever seen you get to angry is mild irritation."

"That's a real compliment. I've been working on the temper thing a long time. As a kid, I'd fly off the handle pretty easily, especially if it had to do with someone—me or someone else—getting picked on. I got in fights, got sent home from school, fouled out in soccer games. One of my college roommates described me as smart and angry."

"I'm astonished! I never would have guessed. Where did all that anger come from?"

He twisted her wedding ring around her finger, pondering. "I don't know. I've thought about it a lot, trying to figure it out. But it really doesn't matter where it came from. I just had to let it go—not that that was easy. What is anger, anyway? I used to think it was a form of fear. So what was I afraid of? Maybe anger is about life denied—not being able to have what you really care about or being forced to do something you really don't want to do. Anyway, one of the tasks of life is to overcome it, or transform it, or at least stop being limited by it." He leaned back in his chair and studied the pattern on his steamer blanket.

"Of course there were lots of reasons I went into the priesthood, but one was that I thought becoming a priest would help me overcome my anger and turn me into a good man. Well, it helped in some respects, but I still had plenty of issues to work on when I left the church." He continued playing with her ring.

"I've been thinking about that incident with Iain, of course. Being in that house—Kathleen inherited it from her folks, and I'd been there many times for family events—and seeing all those people from my childhood brought back a lot of feelings. And Iain has always been a pain in the butt, an insecure bully. I had lots of run-ins with him when we were kids. So I should have been prepared for something like that. But I just reverted to my childhood reaction—I don't think I would have gone so far as to actually get in a fight, but I really did feel like punching him out!"

"Good grief!" said Susannah in wonder.

"Yeah, it's amazing how stuff comes out of your past and kind of takes you over. It hasn't happened to me for a long time, and it always surprises me when it does happen. I think I've dealt with something, and then there it is again."

He sighed.

"What I really feel bad about, though, is what I said to Iain. I was being just as mean as he was, throwing his estrangement from his family in his face. He's got to be a pretty unhappy guy. He's fouled up all the relationships that matter. I knew that, and I should have been more compassionate, but I wasn't."

....

There were endless things to do on the ship: lessons of all kinds; gambling; a nine-thousand-volume library; lectures by visiting professors; concerts, plays, and musicals with professional musicians and actors; five swimming pools; a gym (Susannah was thrilled that they had a rowing machine); dances; and, of course, all the food. You could eat twenty-four hours a day!

Late on their fourth afternoon they were bundled up in their favorite deck chairs, sipping Irish coffee. They'd done their mile on the promenade deck, gone to the gym, heard a lecture, and eaten breakfast and lunch, and Susannah had gone to a dance lesson (the ship even supplied partners for those who needed them) while Will read in the library and then soaked in one of the hot tubs.

"The last couple of days you've seemed kind of distracted, Susannah. Like you're not here," Will said. "Is something wrong?"

"I don't know what it is. I feel like I'm being smothered in some kind of emotional blanket. Isn't that weird?" She looked over at him. "It's probably a lot of things. It's probably partly a reaction to the stress of the wedding and the reception—even though it all went beautifully, and I couldn't have asked for anything more."

She sighed. "The ship is also kind of overwhelming—I'm not used to all this luxury, and all the activity. I feel like I have to do it all, but it's making me feel strung out. Why do I feel like I have to do it all? It would be fine just to sit in my deck chair all day every day and write stories. That would be just as valuable as all this running around. But at the same time, I'm enjoying doing all these things."

She looked out to sea for a moment. "Have you noticed that two-thirds of the passengers are overweight and over sixty?" she said. "It's kind of depressing to be in such a high concentration of old and unhealthy people—even if they are having a great time, which many of them clearly are. So my hang-ups about getting older are showing up. On the other hand, how could I possibly be concerned about getting old when a handsome sexy man has just married me? It's ridiculous!"

Will was listening intently. He had never experienced this withdrawal before; it seemed so unlike her.

Susannah continued. "You know that quip that goes something like 'Religion cannot confer on a woman the sense of peace that comes with knowing she is perfectly dressed for the occasion'?"

He shook his head, but smiled in acknowledgement of this apparently universal truth.

"Well, that whole thing is going on too. I'm watching myself be obsessed with what I'm wearing and whether my hair is OK, and silly stuff like that. It has something to do with the luxury of the ship, I think. They wait on us hand and foot. They go out of their way to appear 'a cut above' the other cruise lines—four nights of black-tie dinners in a six-day crossing, for heaven's sake—and the merchandise in the gift shops is really high-class and expensive. So you know there are a lot of people with money on this ship. No one is snooty, everyone is perfectly nice, and most people look like us, but for some reason, I just feel insecure. Isn't that stupid? I can rationalize all this. I *know* better, but I don't seem to be able to get away from the feelings. More old baggage."

"Sounds like there's more than the wedding to 'unpack,'" he said, caressing her cheek with the back of his hand. "Aren't we lucky we have the rest of our lives to do it together?"

"*I'm* really lucky!" she said. "Don't forget, you said 'for better, for worse.' You're stuck with me now!"

"I'm really happy to be stuck with you," he said, leaning over to kiss her.

Will sat there reflecting on what Susannah had just told him, and then he said, "Remember when you told me about one of your techniques for dealing with fear? You try to welcome it as a friend, or something like that. Have you tried that approach with this insecurity thing?"

"No, I haven't—I'd forgotten. But now I will. Thank you, darling."

....

They disembarked at Southampton and were whisked away by bus to Heathrow, where they had plenty of time to catch their flight to Rome. When they arrived at Fiumicino—with their luggage, to Susannah's relief—they took the thirty-minute express train to the Termini station, then a taxi to their hotel near the Ponte Umberto. Susannah was drinking everything in, trying to absorb as much as possible.

"Will, this is so exciting! I can't believe I'm here with you. And you speak Italian and know how to get around and all kinds of really neat places. This is going to be such fun!"

When they had talked about their honeymoon, they'd discussed all kinds of possibilities: New England, Hawaii, Mexico, Montreal, Ireland, Greece, France, Italy. They both liked to travel, and they were healthy and could afford a splurge, and they had plenty of time. A warm climate sounded good. She spoke French and had been to France several times. He'd been there but not for many years and didn't speak French. She'd never been to Italy. "Would you like to go to Rome?" he'd asked impulsively.

"Oh, I'd love it! Any place in Italy would be fine. But how would that be for you—would Rome have bad vibes?"

"I don't think so," he'd replied. "I think I've made peace with that difficult period of my life. I've had plenty of time to think about it and sort it out. It would be fun to take you to some of my favorite haunts, and there're a few people I'd like to see again. Rome has so many of those gotta-see places. I know you'd enjoy it."

Their little hotel was perfect—charming, on a quiet street. They emptied their suitcases and went out to wander around, get some exercise, and find a place for dinner. For their first night in Rome, they splurged, starting with roasted vegetable antipasto, then the traditional Roman pasta—pecorino and black pepper, then osso bucco for their entrée. By then they were stuffed and decided to postpone gelato until the next day.

As they were eating dinner, Will mentioned that his throat was getting sore. By the time they were walking back to the hotel, he had a mild headache.

"Susannah, what have you got in your little traveling pharmacy to ward off a cold? I'm feeling the classic symptoms."

She was surprised. He'd been sick only once in the year she'd known him—a two-day case of sniffles after he'd done the two-hundred-mile ride bike ride from Seattle to Portland. But she loaded him up with all her herbs and homeopathic preventatives and gave him a cup of chamomile tea to drink in bed. Then she slipped in beside him and propped herself up on pillows to study her Rome travel guide and decide what to do the next day. She was about to ask him if they should go to the Pantheon first or the Sistine Chapel when she saw that he was fast asleep.

....

The next morning Will felt better and they decided to do the antiquities first. After breakfast, they spent an hour at the Colosseum and then wandered up the Via Sacra through the old Roman Forum, past the Arch of Titus, the main square, the Temple of Vesta and the House of the Vestal Virgins, and the Arch of Septimus Severus. Susannah was still excited about just being in Rome, walking through places she'd only read about and seen in pictures. Will was enjoying showing her the sights, but he felt as if he were seeing things through some kind of haze.

....

They climbed a steep staircase to an overlook with a fountain. Will showed Susannah how to block the spout with her fingers so the water would spurt up for drinking and told her the Romans call this feature "the nose." Then he led her through a back-door entrance to the top of the Monument to Victor Emmanuel, where they had a spectacular view. By then they were hungry, so they made their way down the steps of the monument, wandering around until they found a grocery store that made sandwiches, which they ate in a sunny piazza. Susannah noticed that Will was unusually quiet and asked how he felt. He admitted that the headache and sore throat were back.

"Let's walk to the Pantheon together," she said. "I'll tour it, and you can go on to the hotel for a long nap and some vitamin C. I'm sure I can get back to the hotel by myself. I'll have fun poking around shops you wouldn't enjoy. Maybe I'll find something for your sister."

"I'm sorry I'm such a drag, Susannah," Will said. "Maybe I can avoid getting a full-fledged cold if I rest now—and take all your potions."

They parted at the Pantheon. Susannah sat on the base of one of the porch's gigantic granite columns, near the original bronze doors, and read her guidebook before going in. She was overwhelmed, not just from the beauty of the architecture and the sunlight streaming through the oculus, but also from the realization that this had all been built two thousand years ago. She wondered what had been built in her lifetime that would last two thousand years and couldn't think of anything.

When she'd absorbed all she could of the Pantheon, Susannah went out and strolled in a northerly direction. In a few blocks she came upon the Church of San Luigi dei Francesi, and went in. She found a breathtaking chapel with paintings by Caravaggio, whose work she had only seen in photos. She lost track of time as she meditated and absorbed the beauty of the church and the paintings.

By the time Susannah returned to the hotel, Will was awake. She fixed them some tea, chattering enthusiastically about all she had seen while she sat next to him on the bed. "Are you hungry yet?" he asked her, when she stopped for breath. "Yes! Where shall we go for dinner?"

"I suggest we walk down to the Piazza Navona. It will be lit up, and there are three big fountains and lots of restaurants. Lots going on there at night—just your kind of place. After dinner we can walk around and look at the other lighted monuments and have gelato at the best place in town. How does that sound?"

"Super! I'm so glad you suggested Rome, Will, I'm having a wonderful time—everything is so spectacular!"

They had a delicious candlelight dinner in a romantic restaurant, and then wandered around watching people, appreciating the fountains, and eating gelato.

They planned to go to the Vatican the next day. When they woke up, Will had lost his voice and had a raging headache. He looked miserable. He didn't want her to sit around in the hotel just because he was ill, but was concerned about whether she'd feel comfortable going out on her own. "I'll be fine," she told him. I hate to leave you, but I know you've seen all this, and I don't want you to get worse. I've got my guidebook and it's not that far to Saint Peter's. I just have to see the Sistine Chapel and the *Pietà*, if nothing else."

Will went back to bed, and Susannah had breakfast and then left for the Vatican.

The magnificent artwork and buildings were awe-inspiring; she'd read about them and seen photos of them her whole life. But she felt like she'd need days to appreciate even a small fraction of everything there was to see. Susannah was again overwhelmed. She found a place away from the crowds in Saint Peter's Basilica and sat down to meditate. The thought came to her that they should leave Rome. She went back to her mantra and meditated awhile longer.

On her way back to the hotel she picked up a few slices of pizza, all the while puzzling over the thought that had intruded on her meditation.

It occurred to her that, consciously or unconsciously, perhaps Will didn't want to be in Rome. Perhaps that was why he was sick. He was still asleep when she got back to the room, so she quietly sat down to think and eat her pizza.

When he woke up, he smiled at her weakly and sat up in bed. "I had the strangest dream," he said. "I dreamed we were trying to catch a bus that looked like a lemon. Weird!" He looked around the room. "Do I smell pizza?"

She gave him his now-cold pizza and some napkins and sat down beside him on the bed. "Will, I'm wondering if you're having a reaction to being back in Rome. Maybe it's bringing up some stressful stuff for you, and that's why you're getting sick. What do you think?"

He considered her question. "Well, you could be right, but it's buried pretty deep if that's what's going on. I haven't had any conscious thoughts about it. Still, a lot of the emotional turmoil that led to my leaving the priesthood did happen here." He stared off into the distance as he ate his pizza.

"Let's go somewhere else," Susannah said. "How about the Amalfi Coast? I have a friend who got married there, and from her photos it looks like a very scenic place. Couldn't we go there by train? Would that be easy?"

"Sure, it would only take a few hours, and I'm sure we could find a room because it's not high season," Will said. "But there's so much you haven't seen in Rome."

"I know," she replied. "But I'm here to be with you. Being

a tourist is secondary. Let's go someplace that's beautiful and low-key—this is our honeymoon, after all. Rome is amazing and exciting, but it's also kind of over-the-top. Shall we think about it a while longer, or shall I go downstairs and tell Signor Cardini that we'll be leaving earlier than planned?"

"Let's decide after dinner. I'm well enough to go out for pasta and a stroll—and some more gelato. Didn't someone tell us that gelato has antiviral properties?"

....

The next morning they checked out. Signor Cardini made a train reservation for them and a reservation at a hotel in Sorrento that he recommended. Susannah promised to send all her friends to his hotel when they came to Rome and blew him a kiss as they went out the door to their taxi. They changed trains in Naples, and by midafternoon were rolling their suitcases through sunny Sorrento on the fifteen-minute walk to their hotel. Their room had a balcony facing the Bay of Naples.

"Oh, how romantic," Susannah said. "I'm so glad we decided to do this! Besides, I think you've looked better and better as we got farther from Rome."

"I do feel better. But we'd better play it safe and not visit any churches!" They laughed as Will gave her a big hug. After they put their things away, they went up to the hotel's rooftop garden, where they had been invited for a welcoming aperitif. There was a gazebo to protect against too much sun. White wrought-iron furniture and large planters filled with little lemon trees, bougainvillea, and jasmine were scattered around the black-and-white marble-tiled floor. In the center a little fountain splashed and burbled. Sipping their Limoncello, they admired the view of the bay, the town, and Naples in the distance. Their hotel, and a good deal of Sorrento, was high above the sea on a cliff. They could walk or take an elevator down to a tiny beach belonging to the hotel, an excursion they planned for the next day.

The seafood restaurant recommended by their concierge was in a little marina in town, at the bottom of the hill. "We can have all the calories we want for dinner, since we'll work them off walking back up," Susannah said. "I want calamari and scallops, and something obscenely rich for dessert!"

After they had ordered and their prosecco had been poured, Will said, "I've never told you anything about why I left the priesthood, have I? I've been thinking about that. We've known each other for a year, and lived together for almost half that time, and now we're married, and I've never talked with you about that part of my life."

"Yes, I've wondered about that. But I haven't felt that you were trying to hide anything. It's just never seemed to matter that much. There're lots of things in our lives that we haven't shared with each other yet."

"But it's curious, isn't it," Will said, "what we choose to talk about and what we leave out? We must have some kind of unconscious criteria that we use to filter all the possible topics for discussion. For example, I didn't consciously think 'I'm not going to tell Susannah about leaving the priesthood because . . .' It was a big deal, it was a big influence on who I am now, but I've never talked to you about it."

"How we decide what intimate details of our lives to talk about or not to talk about is an interesting question. But as far as this intimate detail of your life is concerned, do you *want* to talk about it?"

"Seems like the right time, doesn't it?" he replied. "We're in the country where I spent some important years of my life, the topic's come up, and maybe I got sick because of some related emotional stuff. I'd say it's time to fill you in."

Susannah gave him all her attention as he talked, taking in his body language and expressions, smiling or nodding when she felt some response was called for.

"It all sounds very rational," she said when he seemed talked out, "and like you've been over it and over it very thoroughly. Knowing you, that's what I'd expect. But it's not just a rational matter, is it? You can look back at yourself as a young man, with all your idealism and your blind spots about yourself and what you were getting into. You can analyze the pros and cons of doing God's work in a religious setting and a secular setting. You can make a very good case for the decision you made—and that many other men and women have made. But it seems to me, as I listen between the lines of what you've said, that you still have some kind of attachment—regret or guilt or something." She stopped as the waiter came by and refilled their wineglasses.

"You said once that part of the reason you wanted to become a priest was to please your parents," Susannah said. "Not that they pressured you, but you knew they'd approve. Your very Catholic extended family would also approve, certainly. And you told me about Father Timothy, for whom you had enormous respect. And then there was the challenge of being a priest. Like getting old, it isn't for sissies. Maybe you were giving up the usual macho things that men do, but for a macho reason—to be better than the other guys."

"You're saying I decided to become a priest because of my ego?"

"Sure, but that's normal. Isn't ego what causes most of us to do everything in life? I think of ego as our 'operating system,' the mechanism that we use to run our lives. Egos are different because people's life experiences are different, but we all have them. The trouble is, they're limiting, because of our life experience, and usually we're not conscious of how they're influencing our decisions, our reactions, our emotions. But you know all this. You're really good at pointing out my ego stuff to me." She leaned back in her chair and started fiddling with her coffee spoon.

"All I'm saying," Susannah said, "is that maybe there were factors you weren't conscious of that were influencing your decision to be a priest and then not to be a priest anymore—in spite of all the thought and soul-searching and discernment that you went through. Maybe it would be helpful to know what they were. Maybe not. Maybe it's just a matter of self-forgiveness."

"What do you think needs forgiving?" he asked, absently folding and refolding his napkin.

"*I* don't think anything needs forgiving, but *you* might. You've talked about feeling guilty about conceiving a child and then not being in his life. Maybe you've got some guilt about joining the priesthood and then leaving it. In either case, guilt is just an ego trip, though, isn't it? It's what you feel when you think you didn't do what you should have done to be loved and accepted. She reached across the table and took his hand.

"But enough! I know you've really searched your soul about these questions, Will. I don't pretend to have some special insight. I'm not trying to 'fix' you. I love you just the way you are."

They decided to forgo the obscenely rich dessert. There wasn't much conversation as they puffed up the steep, winding street to the top of the cliff and back to their hotel, glad for their jackets in the cool evening air.

They got in bed, but neither of them went to sleep. Susannah was raging at herself, questioning what she'd gotten them into: She'd suggested they leave Rome. She'd suggested that Will might be having emotional problems about decisions made years ago. She was playing amateur psychologist. She was ruining their honeymoon just because he got a cold! She tried not to toss and turn, and finally dropped off to sleep.

....

Will watched long-forgotten thoughts and emotions reappear and swirl around in his mind and body. Had he really let go of all that stuff, or was it still influencing him subconsciously? Had he deprived himself for years of a son and a wife, and maybe other children, because of guilt? Did he become a priest to score points? Did he leave for good reasons, or just cover up bad reasons with ones that seemed justifiable? He felt unsettled.

And why was this coming up at all? Were he and Susannah overreacting to his cold? After all, he'd just got married and was on a long trip; that much stress, even good stress, could easily bring on a cold.

He got out of bed carefully, not wanting to wake his wife, put on a robe, and stood in front of the French doors, looking out at the starry night and the moonlit bay.

....

Susannah woke when he got up; she lay in bed watching him, wondering if she should say something. But she feared making things worse.

He finally came back to bed and they both slept fitfully the rest of the night.

Following breakfast the next morning they walked downtown to the bus station to find out about trips along the coast. After picking up a schedule, they wandered around town, where shops were slowly opening. They bought sandwiches, some Pellegrino, and some amaretto cookies for their lunch. By the time they got back to their hotel, the sun had reached the beach, so they took their picnic down to the water. The waves and pebble beach had polished shards of broken glass, and Susannah gathered a handful of various colors to take home, intending to make earrings from them. When the sun moved around the cliff and their little beach came into the shadows, they went back to their room, gathered their books and journals, and went up to the roof garden to sit in what was left of the afternoon sun.

Susannah felt that Will was . . . not withdrawn, exactly, but perhaps preoccupied. He didn't comment on things he noticed, as he usually did, though he was his usual good-natured self. She felt for the first time since she had known him that she was struggling to make conversation.

At dinner they debated whether to rent bikes the next day. Both of them were looking forward to a more strenuous workout than walking around town. But Will was concerned about the traffic; Susannah wasn't used to cycling in traffic, and it was downright manic in Sorrento, especially the Vespas.

They decided on a bus ride to Marina del Cantone, at the end of the Sorrento Peninsula, and from there a four-mile loop hike to Punta Penna, which was reported to have good views. The weather was iffy, but they put their rain parkas and hats in Will's backpack, along with a lunch, and got on the bus. Not long after they left Sorrento, Susannah pointed out to Will that their bus was driving past fields of lemon trees. "Your dream was prophetic—we were supposed to come here!"

About an hour later they arrived at the little town where the hike began. The sun was in and out of the clouds as they walked through fields of basil and olive orchards and up and down hills with stupendous views they frequently stopped to enjoy. Their luck ran out about an hour before they expected to be back. It started to rain, and the dry, dusty path turned to slippery mud. Coming down a steep section, Susannah slid and fell, scraping her hands on the rocks in the path. "Uh-oh. I've turned my ankle—it hurts!"

Will was quickly there to help her up, but when she tried to stand, she found that her ankle hurt enough to make her slightly dizzy.

"I'm so sorry, Will. What a bother!"

"I just hope it's only twisted and not sprained or broken! But right now let's think about how we're going to get you out of here. It should be easier to walk once the path levels out—that's only twenty or thirty yards," he said, looking up the trail. "I'll see if I can find a stick we could use to take some of your weight. Can you stand alone for a few minutes?"

"I think it would be better to sit," she said. "Have we got anything in the pack that I could sit on to keep from getting even more muddy?" They rummaged in the backpack and found an old plastic poncho, which she put on; then Susannah eased herself to the ground while Will went searching for a makeshift cane. While he was gone, she rinsed the dirt off her scraped hands with the remains of a bottle of water.

He was back in five minutes with a branch from an olive tree. "We're lucky we're near some orchards. I hope this isn't too old and brittle."

They made their way very carefully down the rest of the slope and continued slowly along the path. "Will, I don't know if I can keep walking for another hour. Do we have any other options?"

"Your face is as white as a sheet, honey. Let me see what I can figure out." He took a map out of the pack. "The map shows that we should come to a little road very soon. Maybe I can jog down the road and find someone with a car who can either come pick you up, or take me to town so I can get a taxi and come back. Do you think you can go a little farther?"

She thought she could, so they continued slowly down the path, arms around each other's waists, with Susannah leaning as much as possible on the makeshift cane. In ten minutes they reached the narrow road and found a place for her to wait under a tree, out of most of the rain.

"I'll leave the backpack with you, honey. Maybe you should drink the rest of the wine we didn't drink for lunch," he said with a tense smile. "I'll be back as soon as I can, but it might be an hour or more." He kissed her and jogged down the road.

Susannah made herself as comfortable as she could, trying to elevate her leg as much as possible. She loosened her shoelace to accommodate the swelling and leaned back against the tree trunk. She was soaking wet and worrying: about catching a cold, about how this accident would affect their trip, about Will's preoccupation with the old life issues that had come up again. She tried to let it all go, to trust that things would be fine.

About twenty minutes later she was startled from her meditation when she heard a car coming up the road. An ancient green Fiat chugged into view and pulled up near her. Will got out, as did the driver, a tall, lean woman, probably in her seventies, with gray hair in a chignon.

"Susannah, this is Signora Bulgari. She stopped to offer help when she saw me running down the road. She's offered to drive us to Sorrento to a doctor she recommends."

"Mille grazie, Signora Bulgari." Susannah smiled at the woman and attempted to stand.

"Let us assist you, my dear," said Signora Bulgari in perfect Oxford English as she and Will helped Susannah to the car.

"I'm very muddy—do you have some newspapers or something that we can use to protect the seat?" asked Susannah anxiously.

"Do not worry about the car. It is not difficult to wipe off the seat." They helped her into the backseat, where she sat sideways, to elevate her ankle. Will and Signora Bulgari got in the car, which she turned around and drove back down the road, turning off in an almost-hidden driveway. "I will return shortly," she said. "I am just going to get a blanket for the signora, and I will telephone the doctor to make sure we should go to her office, rather than the hospital." She parked beside an old cottage with a small terrace surrounded by flowerpots and gardens.

She returned in five minutes and tucked a blanket around Susannah, and they started off to Sorrento.

"Dottoressa Verdi says that we should come directly to her office. She will determine if the ankle is sprained or broken and what to do next. It will take about forty-five minutes for us to get there." Signora Bulgari then skillfully plied them with questions about themselves and their trip—nothing too personal, but enough to distract them from Susannah's accident and make the time pass. She also told them about herself. By the time they reached the doctor's office she must have had a good sense of who they were. They in turn knew that she ran a yoga studio in Sorrento and had traveled and lived all over the world.

....

Signora Bulgari insisted on waiting until they knew the results of the doctor's examination, so that she could drive them to the hospital or back to their hotel. Will protested that they had taken enough of her time and could take a taxi, but she was adamant. So as they were waiting for the doctor to finish with Susannah, they chatted about her yoga studio. Will asked how many of her clients were interested in the spiritual side of yoga and how many just did it for exercise.

"I make them all do the breathing exercises and a little chanting, but I don't speak about the spiritual side of it unless someone asks. I would say that a quarter of them, or perhaps fewer, are seriously interested in yoga as a spiritual practice. Are you interested, Signor Ryan?"

"Yes, I am. I've studied a bit about yoga, the various types, how they developed, and so on. Just enough that I can explain it to my students when I'm teaching Hinduism, but I've only actually done it once or twice, not enough to really appreciate it. It's been on my list of things to do for a long time, but I haven't gotten to it yet." He glanced at her apologetically.

Dottoressa Verdi emerged from the inner office with Susannah, who looked tired, but no longer anxious. "We were lucky, Will. It's just a sprain, and I need to elevate and ice, and stay off it for a while. I have a walking cast that will take some of the weight off my ankle and keep me from turning it again. Look at this—plastic and Velcro, it just zips off and on, and hardly weighs a thing!"

She turned to the doctor. "Thank you so much, Dottoressa Verdi. I'm very relieved, and I appreciate your seeing me on such short notice."

"You must remind her to take the arnica I gave her, Signor Ryan, and don't let her walk too much too soon." She smiled at them both and went to attend to her next patient.

"This is going to be so boring for you, Will. I don't want you to sit around with me." The strain was back in Susannah's face.

Signora Bulgari smiled at them. "If Signor Ryan should find himself with time on his hands," she said, "he is invited to visit my yoga studio. I'd be happy to work with him, whether in a class or not. Your husband tells me that he's interested in practicing yoga but hasn't had much opportunity."

"Well, I'd love for him to do it, if he'd like to," Susannah said. "I always feel so much better when I'm doing yoga, and I'm pretty sure he'd really get a lot out of it."

Will paid the bill, and they walked slowly to the car.

As Signora Bulgari was driving them back to their hotel, Will asked her if they could take her to dinner as a thank-you. She accepted their dinner invitation for the following evening. "And you must call me Amadea. *Arrivederci!*" she called, waving as she drove away.

The hotel staff made a fuss over Susannah as she limped in, muddy and disheveled. While she was showering, their maid brought ice packs. The bartender followed with a pot of tea and two glasses of cognac. Will asked him to make a reservation at the restaurant next door to the hotel for dinner that evening.

When Susannah was robed, with her ankle elevated and packed with ice, Will flopped down on the bed beside her. "Tea or cognac?" he asked, smiling at her.

"I think I'll have tea, before it gets cold, thanks. I'll save the cognac till later."

"I'm having mine now. What a relief that your ankle isn't hurt too badly!" He sipped his drink. "I think Amadea is a special woman—more than just a helpful passerby."

"Yes, I think so too," said Susannah. "I was pretty preoccupied with my ankle, but even so I could feel something. It's hard to put my finger on it, but I felt like I was in the company of wisdom and strength. I don't know how it's possible to think that, having had so little contact with her. But that's how she comes across." Susannah set down her tea and picked up her cognac. "I hope you'll take up her invitation to do yoga. I can find things to do here tomorrow. The hotel has a big library of English paperbacks and lots of DVDs, so I can entertain myself. Maybe the day after tomorrow my ankle will be improved enough that we could take the bus down the coast."

Will put his half-drunk cognac on the bedside table and pulled the duvet up. "I'm going to have a nap," he said. "Wake me up in time to get ready for dinner, will you?"

....

At dinner Will was again more quiet, or preoccupied, than usual. Susannah could watch part of herself becoming anxious: *He's never been like this. What if we really didn't know each other well enough to get married? What if he decides he made a mistake?* Another part of her was more rational: *We'll spend the rest of our years together discovering things we didn't know about each other and ourselves. I know we love each other—trust love.*

The next morning after Will left to check out the yoga class, Susannah hobbled into the hotel foyer to look at the selection of paperbacks. Marco, the concierge, offered to carry the books and DVDs she'd selected to her room. But he also invited her to stay and use the foyer, which had very comfortable furniture, lovely views, and a selection of games. She decided to stay. She picked out a book, sat down, and propped up her ankle while Marco asked one of the maids to bring some ice packs. Susannah was soon comfortably ensconced, deep in a thriller. An hour later, coffee appeared, as well as fresh ice packs. She drank her coffee and got up to move around a bit.

"Marco, you all are taking such good care of me. Thank you so much!"

"It is our pleasure. This accident was so unfortunate, and we'd like to help reduce the impact on you and your husband. And if you get tired of reading, just let me know. I confess, Signora Ryan, that I have a passion for backgammon. Since it's very quiet here now, we could play unless the phone rings or someone comes in."

"I've played before," she said. "But it's been so long that I've forgotten the rules. Would you mind playing with a novice?"

"Oh, no," Marco replied. "I would be happy to explain the rules and the strategy. It's just a game, just for fun—it's popular in the casinos—and it might make the time pass more quickly for you."

Susannah was amused at his enthusiasm. He got out a backgammon set that came in a leather-like case and set it up on a coffee table between them, explaining the rules as he arranged the checkers. Susannah got the hang of it fairly quickly. Occasionally, Marco had to stop to answer the phone, or give instructions to the staff or attend to another guest, but they were able to play fairly steadily.

....

While his wife was learning to gamble, Will was pushing his physical limits in Amadea Bulgari's yoga class. He found the studio easily from her directions. She welcomed him quietly and introduced him to the other participants—five women and a man somewhat older than Will. This gentleman, Alberto, showed Will where to change his clothes and where to get his mat, strap, and foam block.

They began with breathing exercises and a short chant—three "om" sounds. The chant filled the room, and Will could feel the sound vibrating in his body. It brought back memories of chanting as a priest, which he had always deeply enjoyed. As Amadea led them through the poses, she moved among the students, suggesting adjustments verbally or with a light touch. She told Will to do what he could, rest frequently, and not hold the pose as long as the others if it was difficult. This was not a beginner's class.

Their teacher was limber beyond belief. Will couldn't imagine ever being supple enough to attain many of the poses she was demonstrating. He found the exercise to be very challenging physically, and at the same time exhilarating—which he wasn't expecting. Maybe it was the endorphins, he thought. At the end of the session as they lay in savasana, he felt completely exhausted, but it was a good kind of exhaustion.

Dressed again, he paid her assistant for the session and confirmed dinner plans for the evening. Will asked Amadea to choose a restaurant that she especially liked. She insisted on picking them up. "Until this evening, then," she said. "I look forward to hearing about your yoga experience, Will."

Will stopped on the way back to the hotel for sandwiches, beer, and biscotti. He was famished. In the hotel lobby he found two of the maids, the bartender, and the gardener whooping and hollering as they stood around Marco and Susannah.

"Signor Ryan, your wife should be at Monte-Carlo!" laughed Marco.

"Will, I've discovered a new skill," Susannah said, "if that's what you call it. Apparently, I can play backgammon really well! Look at how much I've won." A large bowl of beach glass normally decorated the enormous coffee table. Most of it was now piled in front of Susannah, with a much smaller pile in front of Marco.

"I hope you've brought lunch," she said, eyeing his paper bag. "Gambling makes me hungry!"

The staff returned to work, and Will and Susannah took the elevator and their sack lunch up to the rooftop to enjoy the midday sunshine. They sat on the white wrought-iron chairs, among the potted plants, and compared notes on their morning. Susannah told Will about learning backgammon, how competitive Marco was, which staff members were cheering for whom, and her speculation about why that might be. She also told him what Marco had told her about Amadea. "He was just gossiping. He only knows her by name and has hardly ever spoken to her, but it was interesting. She seems to have a gift for healing—physical ailments, relationships, emotional problems. Marco's cousin had back pain for years, and it was finally healed after some yoga sessions. There was a woman who had emotional difficulties, which drugs and therapy didn't seem to help, but Amadea managed some kind of breakthrough. She seems to be enormously respected by the locals. I'm looking forward to talking with her this evening." She got up awkwardly to adjust the sun umbrella. Tell me about yoga."

"I really like it," he replied, as enthusiastic as he was tired. "I'm going to keep doing it when we get home. I'm exhausted, of course—it'll be nap time after lunch. You've done it, so you know how physically challenging it is. But now I know what you mean when you say you feel better after doing yoga. It's not quite the 'feeling better' that I feel after soccer or riding my bike. It's a little different—not sure I can put my finger on it.

"You would've enjoyed the people-watching," he said. "There wasn't much time for it, but I couldn't help noticing that everyone in the class looked wealthy—lots of diamonds and spandex couture. Still, very pleasant folks. It's pretty obvious that they have a lot of admiration and affection for Amadea. I'm looking forward to this evening too."

Will was asleep as soon as his head touched the pillow. Susannah snuggled in beside him, propping herself up to meditate and then read. Her meditation was filled with more thoughts than usual, and she was aware that her sense of unease was still present.

Amadea Bulgari arrived thirty minutes later than they had agreed to meet, but Will had explained to Susannah the Italian sense of what "on time" means, so neither was bothered. The maître d' at the restaurant she had chosen greeted her warmly and seated them at his best table. A complimentary bottle of prosecco appeared.

"You have an admirer," Will teased her. "Is he one of your students?"

"We have been friends for a long time," she replied with a smile. "His wife was my student for many years."

Over an excellent dinner, Will and Susannah found themselves telling Amadea about the major life issues that had arisen for them.

She told them something of her background—coming from a poor family, not fitting in, wanting something different from what was expected for girls in her small town. "I was fortunate to meet people who helped me at significant times in my life—a job, an experience, advice, resources. I discovered yoga on a trip to India in my twenties, and have managed to make my living from it for many years."

She asked Will about his experience in class that morning. He mentioned the effect of the chant, and how he had felt when the class was over—something more than a good tiredness. Will asked Amadea to recommend some books so that he could read more about yoga from her perspective. She gave him some titles, and they also agreed that he would have a private session with her early the next morning. That would still leave plenty of time for Susannah and Will to take a bus down the Amalfi Coast, and to return to Sorrento by boat in the afternoon.

As Susannah and Will were getting ready for bed, they talked about their dinner conversation with Amadea. "I was amazed to hear myself talking about leaving the church," said Will, "and about Derek—with someone I've only known for a couple of days. And I don't have any regrets. I don't feel it was inappropriate. She's one of those people with whom you immediately feel comfortable, like you've known her forever."

"I feel the same way," said Susannah. "She's such a good listener. I felt accepted, without a hint of judgment. It was worthwhile, turning my ankle—we got to meet Amadea!"

....

Will's yoga session began with five minutes of chanting. Amadea suggested a "va" sound for the in breath and the "om" sound for the out breath. Very soon after they started chanting, Will felt himself getting very warm, especially in his solar plexus. As they proceeded through the poses, Amadea encouraged him to work hard, but not to struggle. "You must not feel frustrated or disappointed if you cannot do the pose as I do it," she told him. "In time, it will come, if you keep up your practice. Meanwhile, give yourself credit for doing something that is good for your body and your soul."

Will was in very good shape for a man his age, but his legs were shaking by the time they'd finished only three poses. Amadea frequently reminded him how to breathe. She was doing the poses alongside him, stopping now and then to show him how to adjust his body.

After thirty minutes, Will told her he was beginning to feel light-headed.

"That's not uncommon," she replied. "You might also find your muscles flex as a release occurs, so don't be startled. Are you willing to keep going?"

"Yes, but I feel like I'm in . . . some kind of bifurcated reality or something. I've never experienced this before, and it makes me kind of anxious."

She told him to stop for a moment, breathe deeply, and focus on various places in the room to restore his sense of physical place; above all, he should not struggle against any feelings or emotions that might come up. Then they went on.

"Now, when you finish," she told him when they were in the last pose, "you might have some physical and emotional reactions that you didn't anticipate. Whatever happens or doesn't happen is all right. There is nothing to worry about. We will remain in corpse pose for ten minutes."

As he lay in savasana, his mind empty, his body exhausted, he suddenly felt very angry. His hands clenched involuntarily, and both his arms twitched. In a few minutes he felt the anger turning to sadness. Tears filled his eyes and ran down his face.

Amadea's hand covered his. "Breathe deeply," she reminded him softly.

Gradually, the sadness disappeared, and Will experienced a release, a deep relaxation that left him feeling as though he were physically and emotionally lighter.

"Are you all right?" she asked him.

He nodded.

"Very well. Turn over on your side, and sit up slowly, and we'll chant three oms."

He followed her instructions, and she directed him to put on his clothes, get a big drink of water, and join her in the lobby, where there were comfortable chairs.

She smiled at him when he came in and sat down in a chair beside her. "How are you?"

"A little shaky, but OK, I think. What happened?"

"What do you think happened?" she replied.

"I'm not sure," Will said. "I think it will take me a while to 'unpack' this, as we say."

"Yes, you are correct. But I also think that you will notice a good feeling, even before you sort it all out intellectually.

I recommend that you have a quiet day, take a nap, drink lots of water, and forgo alcohol until tomorrow. I don't expect you will have any negative effects, but if you want to call me about anything, here is my phone number." She handed him a card.

"We're planning to leave Sorrento the day after tomorrow, but I'll be sure to stop in or call you to say good-bye." They stood and kissed cheeks.

Still weak in the knees, Will wandered absently up the main street of Sorrento, which was just beginning to wake up. Sidewalks were being swept, and shops were being aired. He looked idly in the windows and noticed some dishes he thought Allie would like. He'd tell Susannah about them. *Will she be disappointed if we don't go on our planned bus trip? What will she think about this experience I've just had? What do I think about it?* He still felt a little disoriented when he arrived back at the hotel and joined Susannah in the breakfast room.

She took one look at him and got up to give him a big hug. She smiled and kissed him lightly. "How about some breakfast?" she said. "Sit down. Lucia will be back in a minute with fruit and yogurt and croissants. We'll order some tea for you."

Will dropped into a chair opposite her and smiled weakly. "Well! I've got quite a lot to tell you, but I'm not sure what, and right now I'm too tired to know where to start. Would you mind if we postponed our trip down the coast until tomorrow? I think I should kind of lie low for a while."

"No problem," Susannah said. "My ankle is much improved, but I'm sure it wouldn't mind another day of minimal walking. And I can always challenge Marco to another game of backgammon—that's good for half a day, at least."

Will ordered his herbal tea and began on the croissants, slathering them with butter and jam. When Lucia came back with his tea, Susannah ordered another basket of bread and asked for some eggs for Will. He was ravenous.

"Oh, I saw some little bowls in a store window," he said. "They have the local designs, and I thought Allie might like them. You can always use little bowls, can't you?"

"That's a good idea," Susannah replied. I was thinking of a set of bowls for dipping bread in olive oil, or maybe some little Limoncello glasses. Or both. Maybe I'll walk downtown and look around a little, later on. You can come if you want."

Will decided to have his nap before lunch, rather than after. "I'm going to crash for a while. Sorry to desert you, but I really need to sleep."

"Sleep well, darling. I'm going to the foyer to read in my favorite chair. I'm at an exciting place in my thriller."

When she returned to their room about noon, Will was up, splashing water on his face. "Are you hungry? Once I have some lunch, I think I'll be in the realm of the living again. Can you walk downtown?"

They ambled down the hill to the main part of town, holding hands and inspecting menus as they went, until they found a little restaurant that looked good. They ordered, and Will began telling Susannah about his yoga session—the physical strain, the anger, the tears, Amadea's reaction. "Then during my nap I dreamed about my parents and Derek. When I woke up, I remembered that in the Native American tradition, healing work is meant to have a generational effect—as if you're healing your ancestors and your descendants, or maybe your relationships with them.

"I could spend hours analyzing all this stuff," he said, "looking at it from this perspective and that perspective—doing my left-brain thing. But intuitively I feel like 'Why bother?' I think I know what it was about: unrecognized guilt. It feels like I've just emptied out a truckload of shit!" He looked around, hoping no one overheard him. "I'll have things to work on as long as I'm alive. But I feel like *this* old stuff isn't going to hold me back anymore." He leaned back in his chair and drank the last of his beer "You know,

Susannah, I think I was numb, all those years. I was living in my head. And then you came along and the numbness started to wear off, or something. Anyway, I feel really good—I think I could even go shopping with you."

After lunch they went to look at the bowls Will had seen. Susannah agreed they would be a perfect gift for Allie, so they bought six and had them wrapped for packing in a suitcase. They then had some gelato, and stopped to admire the sexy underwear in a shop window. "It's so expensive," Susannah said. "And there's only about two square inches of fabric and a bit of lace! Who'd pay so much for that?"

"Evidently someone would," replied Will, laughing, "or these people would be out of business. Besides you're not paying for the fabric. You're paying for what you feel like when you wear it—or what your partner feels like. *Non è vero?* That's Italian for *n'est-ce pas*, by the way."

"When did you get to be such an expert on women's underwear?" Susannah asked, with eyebrows raised.

"Oh, this is a great story—you'll love it. A few years ago some of my students thought I should have the Victoria's Secret catalogue, so they signed me up. It came to my office, and I got razzed a lot. It took months to get them to take me off the list. Every time one came, I had to bury it in the wastebasket so my students didn't see it when they came in to talk to me."

"So you had to look at pictures of pretty women in sexy lingerie for months. Too bad! I'll bet you hated it."

"Yeah, it was awful. Then I had an idea. I thought I could get a few other catalogues, maybe from different countries, and compare them. You know, do some research and write a paper. That's what professors do, after all. My colleagues thought it was a terrific idea—they were willing to help out with the research. We joked about that for weeks, coming up with screwy ideas to make it sound very academic."

By the time he finished his story, both of them were laughing. "Let's go sit in our roof garden," Susannah said.

"I'm ready for my Limoncello."

They meandered back to the hotel, got their hats and books, and went up to the roof garden. The bartender appeared with her liqueur and Will's lemonade, and then left them to enjoy the sun and the view and each other's company.

"Well, wife, here we are again, sitting in our deck chairs, drinking good things and looking at the sea."

"There's no place I'd rather be," she said, leaning across to kiss him.

They read for a while, chatting now and then.

Suddenly, Will stood up, set Susannah's book aside, and pulled her up into his arms. "I just thought of someplace I'd rather be—in bed," he said pulling her close and nuzzling her neck.

"You've figured out just what to do, haven't you? It's like flipping a switch when you do that nuzzling thing. I'm instantly turned on!"

"I want to undress you."

"So," she said, pressing her body closer to him and whispering in his ear, "do you like the ripping sound of unfastening Velcro on a walking cast? Is that what turns you on?"

He laughed. "It's OK, but what I really like is the sound you make when I unfasten your bra. C'mon, let's go. I'll come get this stuff later."

They left their books and hats scattered on the deserted roof, and hurried, as fast as she could hobble, to their honeymoon bed.

CHAPTER SIX

Commencement

Derek and Trisha were aware of a tension between them that hadn't been there in the year and a half they had been together. They didn't talk about it, each assuming that the other probably didn't feel it, and vaguely afraid that bringing it up might be worse than just letting things ride. There was a lot going on emotionally—they were graduating in two weeks, they had summer jobs in different places, Trisha had been accepted to med school at Johns Hopkins, and Derek didn't know what he wanted to do after his summer job ended. He'd been accepted into two grad school programs, but he wasn't excited about either prospect.

"Want to go to a movie tonight?" asked Derek as they walked to the cafeteria for dinner. "It's Friday, after all, and they're showing *Mrs. Doubtfire*. That should lighten things up a bit."

"It's tempting," Trisha said, "but I'd spend all the time between now and then and after the movie worrying about finishing my microbiology experiment. I think I'd rather finish it first, and then take a break."

"Trisha, I know you. You won't take a break," he said crossly. "You'll just move on to the next book or paper or task." He put his arm around her as they walked. "You know it's better if you take a break. All the studies—which *you* showed *me*—prove that you need to take breaks, and sleep before tests, and so on. Besides, we haven't slept together for ages—that would be good for you too," he said, grinning down at her.

"Not to mention good for *you!*" she said, but she smiled as she said it. "It's only been a week—quit complaining. But I miss you too. It's just that I can't forget all the stuff I have to do. It just keeps piling up. Did I tell you Professor Simonson asked me to give him a few quotes about our research so he could include them in an article he has to submit by Monday? Anyway, I'd rather deal with the anxiety by getting things done than by putting them off."

As he held the door open for her, he said, "I don't think that's the solution. You've done a million things and you're still anxious." They went in for dinner, after which Derek went to the movie alone.

....

The family dynamics surrounding graduation were Byzantine. Trisha's rancorously divorced parents were coming from San Diego, her father with his new spouse, Faye, and her mother with Trisha's two younger brothers. Betsy and Steve Bailey, Derek's parents were coming from Ashland, along with Will and Susannah.

Aware that interactions among this group could be unpredictable and awkward, Susannah and Will had been thinking about how they could be there to celebrate Derek, without adding to the stress. They had talked with Derek on the phone and agreed that they would not sit with his family during the ceremony but would show up at the reception in the cafeteria to shake his hand and say hello to everyone. Then they'd leave, so Derek would have more time with his folks and Trisha's family. Will and Susannah would take him out for brunch the next morning, and then his folks would help him pack up the stuff that was going home to Ashland. He had arranged to live in the basement apartment of one of his professors in Portland for the summer, working on her research project, and would need very little of the stuff that he'd accumulated over four years at Reed.

As they were driving to Portland on the morning of graduation, Susannah asked if Derek had any idea how his parents felt about Will's being there. "I asked him that when we talked a couple of weeks ago," Will said. "I told him we wouldn't come if he thought it would be awkward. He'd already asked Betsy, and she said we were welcome to come."

....

Betsy didn't tell anyone, but she was nervous about seeing Will again. Derek and Trisha had gone to Will's wedding, and Derek had sent Betsy a link to the wedding photos. Betsy thought, a little jealously as she perused the photos, that Will's wife looked pretty good for a woman her age. There was a photo of Trisha and Derek clowning for the photographer, and a good candid photo of Will and Derek talking at the reception. Will was as handsome as ever, and Derek looked just like him.

....

The sun shone down on the graduates, seated on the soccer field, and on the guests and families in the bleachers. A light breeze fluttered the banners and flags and the graduates' robes, and kept everyone from getting too warm. Reading the program, Will said, "Look, Susannah. Derek's graduating *cum laude*. He didn't tell me that!" After the usual platitudes and speeches, and the awarding of diplomas, the crowd streamed toward the cafeteria for the reception. Beverages, cookies, and light hors d'oeuvres were being served.

As they waited in the slow-moving line, Susannah and Will looked around for Derek or Trisha in the milling crowd. They had just collected their punch and cookies when they saw Derek waving to them from across the room. He was standing next to a woman of about fifty and a man considerably older, perhaps seventy. Susannah and Will worked their way through the press of people. Derek, flushed from the sun and excitement, was surrounded by his and Trisha's families.

"Susannah, Will—this is my dad, Steve, and my mom, Betsy."

"I'd love to shake hands with everyone, but it looks like the cups and plates have foiled us," said Will, smiling. Everyone's hands *were* full—of refreshments, garments, handbags, programs, and cameras. "I'm very pleased to meet you, Steve," he said, "and to see you again, Betsy. You've done a fine job with this young man. You must be very proud."

"He's got good genes," Steve quipped magnanimously.

Betsy blushed. She wished she hadn't put on quite so many pounds in the past few years, and was glad that she had a new dress and a fresh haircut for the occasion.

"Well, I'm proud too," Will said, "even though I haven't contributed anything but genes." Susannah snapped a quick photo as he put his arm around Derek's shoulder and gave him a hug.

"I'd say paying for half my college expenses and providing a getaway for Trisha and me counts for quite a bit," said Derek. "It was really great coming to Seattle and hanging out with you two."

Most of the graduates had unzipped their hot robes, revealing a wide variety of clothing. Betsy noticed that Derek and Will were both wearing dress shoes, chinos, and a white shirt, though Derek's was a muscle tee and Will's was a button-down dress shirt.

Betsy turned to Susannah and said somewhat formally, "Thank you very much for being so hospitable to Derek and Trisha. Derek's told us how much he's enjoyed visiting you." She noted Susannah's gray hair with vestiges of blonde, and the little crow's feet at the edge of her eyes. She also noticed her stylish haircut and dress, and her distinctly unflabby upper arms.

"It was our pleasure, Betsy," Susannah replied. "I'm just so pleased that Derek and Will have had a chance to get acquainted—it means a lot to Will. Besides, they're lots of fun to be around. Trisha and I both row, and Derek and Will play soccer, and we've had lots of interesting conversations about a variety of things. It's really stimulating talking to young people, isn't it?"

"Yes, it is," Betsy said, thinking that Derek and Trisha never talked to her about anything and wondering how this woman could row a shell—she was at least ten years older than Betsy.

Susannah asked if she could get a photo of Derek and his parents, and the next few minutes were consumed with various combinations of people photographed with various cameras.

As they were finishing their photo shoot, a pretty woman with disheveled hair and an expensive but rumpled dress came up to them. "Hi, Betsy." Turning to Susannah, she said, "You must be Derek's stepmother. I'm Trisha's mom, Gretchen. She's told me so much about you—you two seem to have a lot in common. And it was really nice of you to give Trisha and Derek a place to stay when they needed to get away from school for a break. They couldn't really come home to San Diego for a weekend!" Gretchen rambled on about how busy she was taking care of her two sons who were still at home, how the older son was planning to attend UCLA in the fall, how hard it was to get them to come to graduation with her, and she showed no sign of stopping until Trisha came up and interrupted her.

"Hi, Betsy. Hi, Susannah. Mom, I'm going to take everyone on a quick tour of the campus. Derek's coming too. Do you want to come along?"

"Oh, no thanks, dear, I'll just talk with Susannah and Betsy. I haven't met Derek's father yet, either. You go ahead. Shall we meet again in an hour out in front of this building?" Trisha agreed, looking relieved, and left to lead her tour.

"You have a very accomplished daughter, Gretchen," said Susannah. "*Magna cum laude* and Phi Beta Kappa—you must be very proud."

"Yes, nice, isn't it? She didn't get all those brains from me, that's for sure. Her dad's very smart, as well as being a smart-mouth. I'm so glad to be rid of him! Excuse me, I'm just going to get a few more cookies. I'll be right back."

....

"Oh dear," Susannah said to Betsy. "It sounds like that wasn't an amicable parting. Do you know Trisha's parents very well?"

"No, not well at all. I've never met him. I understand from Derek that he's never been to campus to visit Trisha. I've met Gretchen a couple of times at school events. Derek hasn't said much about them, but I gather her mom is struggling with the divorce. She has plenty of money, but she and Bill don't get along well, and she's doing most of the parenting by herself. And I know from experience that's not an easy job."

Susannah wondered if that was a jab at Will, or just an expression of sympathy for Gretchen.

Just then, Steve and Will joined them, along with Gretchen, who had returned with a heaping plate of cookies.
"I brought some to share," she said, offering the plate to everyone.

"You must be Will," she said, turning to him. "Derek looks just like you. I'm Gretchen, Trisha's mom. She's just taken the rest of the family for a campus tour. Hi, Steve," she added belatedly, and then returned her attention to Will.

"What does it feel like to meet your son after twenty-some years?" she asked, taking another bite of cookie. Susannah was a bit taken aback at her gaucherie, but Will responded graciously.

"I wish it had happened sooner. But I can't change that, so I'm just glad we can be friends now. He's a fine young man—Betsy and Steve have done a great job of parenting." He then deftly changed the subject. "Trisha's a lovely young woman, Gretchen. I guess we won't get to see her much now that she's going to the East Coast. That'll be much harder for you, I'm sure."

"Yes, it's so far away. But you know, after she started high school, she was so busy that she was never around much anyway. Oh well. I'll get to explore Washington, DC, and Baltimore when I go to visit her. I haven't been there very much." Her eyes were scanning the room as she talked. "Oh, there's my youngest wandering around. I thought he went on the tour. Guess I'd better go gather him up. Nice to meet you." She moved off through the crowd.

"We need to be going too," Will said to Betsy. "Susannah and I have a dinner reservation in Dayton, and I want to allow plenty of time to get lost. We've agreed to meet Derek right here at noon tomorrow, and we'll take him out for brunch and then bring him back to finish the packing ordeal. It's been really good to meet you," he said, extending his hand to Steve and then to Betsy.

"I'm glad to finally meet Derek's folks in person," said Susannah, also shaking hands with both of them. "I'm sure we'll stay in touch through Derek. Congratulations on his graduation. It's such a bittersweet moment, isn't it? My son's graduation was for me."

After a few more parting pleasantries, Susannah and Will walked through the thinning crowd into the late afternoon sunshine, and back to their car.

....

Betsy and Steve watched them go. "Nice people," Steve said. "I don't feel the least bit threatened or disappointed or anything. I'm glad Derek's got an extra set of parents."

"Well, I wouldn't call them parents, exactly," Betsy replied. "He took his own sweet time showing up, didn't he?"

"Yes, but Derek told me you told Will that Derek wasn't interested in knowing him. Why did you tell Will that if you thought he should be in Derek's life?"

"If he'd really cared about knowing his son, he'd have

made more of an effort, even if Derek wasn't interested. He should at least have tried."

"Apparently, Will agrees with you," Steve said as they moved out of the reception room and turned toward Derek's dorm. "Derek told me Will said he felt guilty and afraid that Derek would reject him. But that he should have tried anyway. Well, he finally did—that's what matters. And I think Derek's glad about that. By the way, is Derek coming to dinner with us tonight?"

"No, he's going with Trisha tonight and with us tomorrow night."

....

Derek and Trisha stood in front of her dorm, waving at the black Mercedes rental car carrying her dad and his wife away to their hotel. She didn't know when she would see them again, since they were leaving fairly early the next morning.

"God, I'm glad *that's* over!" Trisha said to Derek. They had just returned from a dinner "celebration" with her family at an expensive restaurant. It had been a rather tense affair, with her mother drinking too much, Faye barely participating in the conversation, and Trisha's brothers acting up.

"I'm glad you were there to help me get through it," she said to Derek, putting her arms around his waist and leaning her head on his chest.

"Why did your parents ever get married in the first place?" Derek asked her as they went inside and up to her dorm room. "They sure don't get along!"

"Oh, I don't know. It wasn't always like this, but I guess it was slowly deteriorating," Trisha said. "I don't know why. You've probably noticed that Mom's not exactly the analytical type, so asking her probably wouldn't shed much light on the question. And Dad just doesn't want to talk about it."

"How are you supposed to learn anything from your parents if they don't even know what happened, and won't talk to you about it? Aren't they supposed to have some wisdom or something? Don't they have anything worthwhile to pass on?" Derek was often angry at her parents; he thought they were making her life difficult, instead of being supportive of her and proud of her for working so hard.

"What good advice have you got from your parents, Derek?" she asked acidly. "You don't talk to them about your life and your issues, and I've never heard anything from them but platitudes. I was watching your mother watch Susannah. She looked green with envy."

Derek sat down on her bed. "Why are we talking like this?" he said after a while. "Why are we bad-mouthing each other's parents? What's going on?"

"Oh, I don't know, Derek. I don't want to think about it. I'm exhausted. I just want to go to sleep."

"Is that code for 'I don't want to sleep with you tonight'?"

"It's not code for anything," she said. "I'm just worn out. Let's just call it a night and start over tomorrow."

He got up and left, shutting the door quietly. She crumpled up on her bed and cried. She'd sent away the best person to comfort her.

....

Derek's thoughts were not happy ones as he walked back to his dorm. *She wouldn't even let me take care of her. We didn't have to make love—I'd have been happy just to hold her and try to make things better for her. She's determined to do everything on her own. And she never wants to think about anything emotional. Is this the woman I want to be with all my life?*

....

Susannah and Will had a fine dinner at a wine-country restaurant they'd read about in *Sunset* magazine. It had lived up to its reputation, and they were walking back to their B&B after dinner, holding hands, each reflecting on the events of the day and their related feelings. "I hope this was a happy day for Derek and Trisha," Susannah said, with some doubt in her voice. "These big events can sometimes be more trying than happy."

"Yes, I've been thinking the same thing," Will said. "I think Derek was doing OK, but I wondered about Trisha. From what we've heard about her family, it could have been a difficult day for her. Which would have made things harder for him, too."

"How was it for you, seeing Betsy again after all these years?"

Will didn't answer immediately. The streetlights dappled shadows through the big old trees they passed beneath. "Seeing her reminded me of having done something I was ashamed of. It kind of brought back all the feelings from that time—the guilt, the anguish about whether I was doing the right thing, if I was making the best of a bad situation. That didn't feel so good. But I'm not wallowing around in all that—just remembering it. I can't even wish it didn't happen, because then I wouldn't have Derek. And maybe I wouldn't have you. There's no way to know what might have happened, is there?"

Will got out his key as they reached the front door of the B&B. They tiptoed down the hall to their room. Susannah threw her wrap on a chair and sat down on the bed to take off her shoes. Will sat down beside her, kicked off his shoes, and flopped back on the bed. He pulled her down on top of him. "What is it about being in another bedroom than your own that's so sexy?" he said, running his fingers through her hair.

"I don't know," she said, kissing him. "Maybe you should write a paper on this topic, Professor Ryan." Another kiss. "We could do some research." Another kiss. "We'll probably need to do *a lot* of research."

"We'd better start right away," he said, turning off the light.

....

They had a light breakfast early, knowing that they'd have brunch with Derek and Trisha if she could make it. Then they drove around wine country before heading back to Portland. Derek was waiting for them alone. "Good morning, graduate! How's it going?" Will said as Derek got in the backseat of the car.

"Oh, it's going, but I'm pretty wiped out. I'll tell you about it when we get settled at the restaurant."

"We thought we'd go to that restaurant on the river," Susannah said, smiling at him. "We heard they have a good brunch."

"I've heard it's a really nice place," Derek said. "Never been there—it's a little out of the student price range. Trisha sends her regrets. She couldn't come with all the family and packing and whatnot. She'll be sorry she missed it."

In about twenty minutes they were seated at a table near the window, with a view of the Willamette River. The hostess explained how the buffet worked, how to order eggs, waffles, and pancakes, and that mimosas were included. "Well, shall we start?" asked Susannah when the hostess had left.

It was an amazing buffet. A vast array of fruits, pastries and breads, cold and hot cereals, meats, salmon, vegetables, cheeses, and crepes, waffles, pancakes, and eggs any way your heart desired. "Wow, I won't have to eat dinner tonight," Derek said enthusiastically.

"I won't have to eat for two days!" said Susannah. They filled their plates and returned to their table, where mimosas were waiting. "Oh, this crepe is heavenly! How are your eggs Benedict, Will?"

"Fantastic! I just have to concentrate really hard to eat slowly, to keep myself from rushing back for the salmon and asparagus and strawberry shortcake."

"Everything is *really* good," said Derek, intent on his prime rib, biscuits and gravy, and vegetables.

"One mimosa will be enough for me," Will said, "so I'll

drive us home. You can get high as a kite, if you want to, honey."

"I'll try not to do my kite routine," Susannah said, "but I might have just a little more."

"I definitely feel like doing a kite routine!" said Derek. "Tell them to fill my glass up again. I'll be right back." He went to the buffet table for round two.

When he sat down again, he began telling them what had been going on over the past couple of weeks. "These last few days have been an emotional roller coaster. It's the end of a really big part of my life . . . I don't know what I want to do next . . . Trisha does know, and I don't know if I want to go where she's going or if she wants me to come . . . Her family's a mess, and that's been an ongoing burden for her, and it really peaked yesterday . . . I was a little uptight about you meeting my folks, but as soon as you were introduced, I could see it was going to be just fine." He sighed, put down his fork, and had another sip of mimosa.

"Hmm," said Will, after a moment. "You've got a lot on your plate, literally and figuratively. Sorry, couldn't pass that up!"

Derek grinned. "Guess I should lighten up a little."

"How big a deal is it that you don't know what you want to do next?" Will asked him. "Who cares? Is somebody bugging you about it?"

"No, I guess not," Derek said. "I think it's mainly got to do with what happens between Trisha and me. If I knew what I wanted to do and it didn't fit with what she's going to do, we'd know where we stand. It would probably be over between us. But if I'm just going to float around until I figure something out, I could get a job to pay the rent and be with her until I do make up my mind."

"You'll probably do lots of different things in your life," Susannah said. "You don't have to choose one thing for all time, you know. Don't you think it's OK to float around for a while and try different things?"

"Yeah," Derek said. "I'm all right with that, and my folks are too. They're not pushing me to get a job or make a career choice or go to grad school or anything. I know sooner or later I'm going to have to decide something, so there's this big unknown kind of looming out there. But I'm OK with that for a while."

"So it's the Trisha question that's really the big one? Is that right?" Will asked. Then he put up his hand, signaling Derek not to say anything. "Sorry, Derek. We don't want to pry. If that's too personal, just forget it."

"No, no. I feel like you're just trying to help me unscramble everything. I appreciate it—I've kind of been going in circles. I can't quite sort things out." He went back to eating, and they were all quiet for a few minutes.

"Well, why don't you tell us what you do know for sure and what you're not clear about," Will said.

"OK. Let's see," Derek said. "I love Trisha, and I don't want to break up with her. But I'm not sure I want to spend my life with her either. I think she feels the same way, but we haven't talked about it. Breaking up would hurt like hell, though." He took a bite of his bagel with cream cheese and lox. "Since you and my folks have paid for my education, I don't have a lot of debt, like a lot of my friends. I'm not dying to earn a lot of money right away, so I'm happy to live cheap and do something worthwhile, try different things, see what I like and don't like." He paused for another bite. "I like Portland, and I have a lot of friends from this area. So I don't mind staying here for a while. I'd like to travel at some point, but I'm not sure where or when. So I guess that's it."

"You're always welcome to hang out with us, Derek," Will said. "I hope you'll be close enough to Seattle that we can get together more often than we have in the past eighteen months. And if there's anything you need help with, you know you can call on us."

"Thanks, Will. That means a lot to me," Derek said. Then he added, a little shyly, "I like being with both of you."

They had their final round of brunch and coffee, chatted some more, and the check arrived. While it was being processed, Will drew an envelope out of his jacket pocket and handed it to Derek. "Congratulations, son. I'm very glad to be in your life, finally, and I'm very proud of you."

Derek read the graduation card and smiled at them, and then pulled the check out of its little compartment. He looked stunned. "Are you sure there's not one zero too many?" he asked.

Susannah and Will laughed and said, no, it was the right amount of zeros. "Put it in the bank for your travel fund," Will said.

It was time for them to take Derek back so he could finish his packing and move the few things he needed to his new apartment. When they arrived at his dorm, they all got out and Susannah and Will each gave him a big hug. Just then Trisha came out of the dorm. She ran up to get her hugs too.

"What good luck," Susannah said. "I've got something for you." Susannah pulled a little silver box with a silver ribbon out of her handbag. "I'm glad we could give it to you in person. Congratulations, Trisha."

She opened it immediately. It was a sterling silver serpentine bracelet with matching earrings. "Oh, they're beautiful!" she said. "And they're so classic, I'll be able to wear them forever. I'll think of you two every time I wear them. Thank you so much!"

"You're very welcome, Trisha. You're also welcome to come visit us in Seattle. We'd love to see you whenever you can make it."

More hugs, and then Will and Susannah drove away.

....

"I just came over to see how your packing was coming,"

Trisha said. "Your folks are up in your room, putting stuff in boxes. Steve looks a little red in the face from carrying them out to the car, but Betsy says she thinks they'll be finished in time for dinner."

"Yeah, the plan is that we'll go out for dinner and then they'll stay one more night in the hotel and drive back to Ashland with all the stuff tomorrow," Derek said. "I'm staying in my new digs tonight. Want to join me?"

"Yes, I do want to join you. Mom said I could stay with them in the hotel. But this is my last night with you for a while, until we figure out when we can see each other again." Trisha looked in the direction of her dorm. "I've got to go help her finish packing. I'll call you around eight to let you know if she's going to drop me off or if you should come pick me up. Love you." She walked quickly down the sidewalk, turning once to wave to him.

After his parents took the last load down to their car, Derek spent a moment in his empty room. This room had been his home for the past two years—where he'd had all-night philosophical discussions, counseled younger students as their resident assistant, listened to his friends' troubles, made love with Trisha. He couldn't believe all that was behind him. He took one last look, then he quietly closed the door and ran down the stairs and out to his parents.

"I'll get my car and pull in here," Derek said, "and then you can follow me to Professor Lundberg's so you can see where I'll be living for the summer." He jogged to the lot where his aged Honda was parked and drove around to meet them.

Professor Lundberg lived only five minutes away, in a pleasant Portland suburb. The daylight basement had been remodeled to create a guest bedroom/sitting room. The bathroom also contained a washer and dryer. There was a tiny refrigerator, a small microwave, and an electric teakettle. Very homey for three months' accommodation. His parents looked pleased.

After all that packing and running up and down stairs, Derek found he could eat a full dinner after all, despite his big brunch. At the restaurant, he and his parents talked about the events of the day, the research project he'd be working on, Trisha's family, and when he might get to Ashland for a visit. As they were finishing dessert, Derek said, "Mom and Dad, you know I appreciate all you've done for me, but I just want to say thank you again, for the record. I'm really lucky not to have the huge college debt a lot of my friends have. But I also appreciate all the support you gave me growing up—Boy Scouts and soccer and putting up with my high school antics. And thanks for not being weird, like Trisha's parents!"

"We're very proud of you, Derek," said Steve. "I was lucky to find your mother and you. You've turned into a fine young man. I know you'll do a lot of good in the world. By the way, this might be the time to mention that there's a newer Honda waiting for you when you get home. Happy graduation!" Steve was the biggest Honda dealer in the southwest part of Oregon.

"Wow, thanks, Dad! I'm blown away!"

Betsy had tears in her eyes as she hugged him good-bye. "I love you so much! Come see us soon."

He waved as they left the parking lot, then he drove to his new home. He lay down on the bed and closed his eyes, scenes from today and the day before flooding through his mind: Trisha walking across the stage to receive her diploma; Will shaking hands with his dad and mom; Trisha's preoccupied father and nutty mother; the brunch with Will and Susannah and their gift; dinner with his folks. It felt good to be alone for a while, and just breathe.

Thirty minutes later his cell phone rang. "I think you'd better pick me up, Derek, if that's OK," Trisha said. "I know I could find your apartment, but I'm not sure Mom could find her way back to the hotel. Oh, and can you bring me back to her hotel around eight tomorrow morning? That would give me time to have breakfast and help get everyone to the airport. The plane leaves at noon, but we have to return the car first."

"Sure, that's fine. I'll pick you up in a half hour, right in front of the hotel. The Heathman right?"

"Right," she said. "Thanks, Derek. I can hardly wait to be with you."

....

They didn't say much during the drive back from the hotel, content just to be together. Trisha wandered around the apartment, taking in details she'd missed on her hurried visit the first time she'd stopped by. "This is a really nice place, for a short-term stay. I think you're going to be very comfortable here."

"Yeah, I think so too," Derek said. "Professor Lundberg left me a few tea bags. Would you like some chamomile?"

"Yes, please. That sounds really good. I could use some calming."

"So catch me up," he said. "Besides the big dinner last night, what happened yesterday and today? How are you feeling?"

"Oh, I'm all over the place. Both glad and sorry it's over," Trisha said. "Graduation, I mean. I'm glad my parents at least get it that they're supposed to go out of their way when their firstborn graduates. But they're so self-centered I just take what emotional crumbs I can get. She continued her wandering, opening and closing the doors on the kitchen cabinets.

"Dad got me a new laptop," she said. "And—get this— Mom gave me a two-hundred-fifty-dollar gift certificate from Victoria's Secret. She thought I should have pretty lingerie to start med school. It's supposed to keep my spirits up when I'm working too hard. The thought was nice." She sounded dubious. "And I guess I could buy enough underwear that I wouldn't have to do laundry for a month—that might be a help." They both laughed.

"By the way, I'm sorry I said what I said about your mother looking envious—that was really out of line. Forgive me?"

He put his arms around her and kissed her. "I'll forgive you if you give me a back rub."

"Ask and you shall receive," she said, pulling his T-shirt over his head. "Take off your shoes and lie down. And then tell me how the weekend was for you. Did it go OK with your folks and Will and Susannah?"

Facedown on the bed, he began telling her how he felt before he introduced Susannah and Will to his parents, and how quickly he felt at ease. His story was interrupted with grunts and groans of pleasure, as Trisha massaged the tight muscles in his back and shoulders.

"It's funny," Derek said. "You'd think that maybe Will would be ill at ease because he sort of left Mom and me, and was showing up late in the game. But he had just the right manner or tone, or something—I don't know what to call it. It's not like he was trying to pretend that nothing ever happened, but he put us at ease. Dad was cool too. Not that I expected him to be uptight anyway. He and Will seemed to hit it off. Mom seemed a little uncomfortable, though."

"I can imagine why," said Trisha. "Here's the guy she was madly in love with, who rejected her and left her in a tough situation, and he's still as handsome and charming as ever. *And* he's got a new wife who's maybe ten years older than your mom but who's twenty pounds slimmer. That'd be a pretty loaded situation for any woman!"

"Well, Susannah was her usual gracious self, and I think Mom got over her nervousness, or whatever it was, pretty quick. She seemed fine today and at dinner tonight," he said.

"Oh, and I forgot to tell you—Will and Susannah gave me a check for a thousand dollars, and Dad and Mom are giving me a new car—or a newer car. I'm not quite sure what it is yet. I'll get it when I go home the next time. Pretty nice, huh? I can't quite take it all in, really. Guess I got lucky when they handed out parents."

"You sure did!" she said. "OK, my turn. You can make it up to me for having such good parents by giving me a foot rub. Prop yourself against the wall with pillows, and I'll put my feet in your lap."

He followed orders, and it was her turn to sigh and moan with pleasure for a few minutes. Then she got her tea, took one of his pillows, and sat back down on the bed beside him.

"Trisha, are you really sure you want to be a *lifeguard* this summer?" Derek asked. "Couldn't you get a better-paying job than that with all your credentials and your dad's influence?"

"I decided this was my last chance for a no-stress job. It'll be years before I get out of the stress business, so I thought I'd just take a mindless job and work on my tan. Besides, I'll earn more at Dad's club than I would at a parks department job in Portland—I know you were about to ask why I couldn't stay here and be a lifeguard, right?"

"Yeah, I was. And I suppose you won't be paying rent, living at your mom's."

"You suppose correctly."

"Trisha, what's going to happen next?" Derek asked, his voice tense.

She put her cup down on the floor and, turning back to him, put her arms around his neck and kissed him. "What happens next is we're going to make love," she said.

They were slow and gentle with each other, enjoying their privacy in the quiet apartment. No dorm noise, no one knocking at the door, no tests or papers on their minds—just the knowledge that they weren't going to be together as they had been.

As they lay in each other's arms afterward, Derek felt physically satisfied but emotionally burdened. "Trisha, I love you so much—I'm going to be miserable when you're gone."

"I love you too, Derek," she said, running her fingers through his hair. "Hey, would you set your alarm for seven o'clock, so I can get back to Mom's hotel in time? I've set mine, but I thought we should have a backup."

Efficient Trisha, he thought. He took his cell phone off the bedside table, set the alarm, and put it back.

"Thanks, babe. You are such a good guy," she said. "I don't know how I got so lucky to be with you for almost two years. You may have good luck in the parent department, but I have good luck in the boyfriend department." She smiled up at him. "But Derek, I think it's time for the words every couple dreads: 'We have to talk.' We've been putting this off, but I don't think we can put it off any longer." Her head was on his shoulder, and she was absently running her hand over his bare chest. "A long time ago, we talked about the right time to settle down, or get married or whatever. We both thought late twenties, early thirties was about right. Remember?"

He nodded.

"That's eight to ten years from now," she said, smoothing the sheet across their bodies. "We've both got a lot of stuff to do in those years—a lot of people to meet, some to love, a lot of things to figure out. Like whether we want to get married, or have kids, what we want to do with our lives."

She looked up at him. Tears had begun to run down his face.

"Machiavelli apparently said something like 'Spread out your good stuff, but dump your bad stuff on people all at once.' I'm trying to do that as gently as possible, Derek. It's going to be painful no matter what, but I don't think we should get together this summer and I don't think we should think about living together next fall. Trisha's expression was strained.

"I'm doing all the talking—I'm sorry. What do you think, Derek?" she asked softly.

There was a long silence.

He wiped his face with the sheet and took a deep breath. "You know that Robert Frost poem, 'Reluctance,' that I like so much?" She nodded. "It's been running through my mind the past few weeks. It does feel treasonous . . . to accept the loss of . . . us, Trisha, but I guess I do yield to reason. I hate it, but I know you're right. It's just so Goddamn painful!" He buried his face in her hair.

"This has taken every ounce of energy I have," she said. "Maybe I sound reasonable, but I don't feel reasonable. Hold me close, Derek. I love you so much."

....

One evening the week following graduation, Will got a call from Derek. "Will . . . uh . . . I need to . . . mmm . . . ask you a favor. This is kind of . . . uh . . . hard." Will thought his voice sounded very strange.

"Derek, are you all right? If you need something, just let me know, son."

"Yeah, I think I'm going to need some help, Will. I got a call from the Jackson County Sheriff's Office about an hour ago. My parents were killed this afternoon when their car went off the road over an embankment. I was wondering if maybe you could come down here and help me deal with all this. I don't know what to do first."

"Where are you now, Derek?" Will asked, putting him on speakerphone so Susannah could hear the conversation.

"I'm in my apartment in Portland."

"Do you have any other family close-by?"

"No, I really don't have any other family. Dad just has an elderly sister in Minneapolis, and Mom's parents are pretty old too. I don't think they can be much help, and I haven't called them yet. They live in Medford."

"OK, how about this, Derek. Have you got some paper and a pencil handy?" He waited until Derek said he was ready. "You don't have to write all this down, but you're probably in shock, so you might want to try to take some notes. Susannah and I will leave early in the morning. We'll drive down to Portland and pick you up at about eight. Then we can all drive to Ashland together, and on the way we can talk about what needs to be done. We can probably get there by the early afternoon—but I guess you know how long it'll take. You can call the sheriff's office either tonight or tomorrow morning and tell them when we'll be there. You can also ask them if there's anything you should be doing, what kind of questions will need to be answered, that kind of thing. OK? How does that sound?" There was a pause. Will assumed Derek was writing things down.

"That sounds like a good plan," he said, his voice still shaky but a little stronger. "I'm sorry to bother you, but I really appreciate this, Will. I don't know how I would have figured out what to do on my own."

"This is what family's for, Derek. You don't need to apologize for asking for help. Now tell me your address. I'll look it up on Google Maps. If we get lost, we'll just call you for directions, but Susannah's a pretty good navigator. Oh, also, you might not be back to Portland for a while, so you should probably pack whatever you'll need that you don't have in Ashland. Now, let me think a moment, and see if Susannah has any other immediate thoughts." He put the phone on mute and looked at Susannah.

"He should tell his grandparents right away. Otherwise, they might hear it from someone else, or maybe even read it in the newspaper. I don't know exactly where Medford is, but this is sure to be in the local paper. I think he can wait on the aunt."

Will took the phone off mute. "Derek, Susannah and I think you should call your grandparents tonight. It's best they hear from you, rather than someone else, or worse yet, read it in the paper. I know this will be a hard call to make—probably the hardest thing you'll have to face in this ordeal. But I think you'd better do it."

"OK, I'm sure you're right. I'll try to think how to say it, and I'll call them tonight."

After getting Derek's address, Will told him to call back if he had any questions or wanted to talk about anything. "I'm sorry we can't be there with you right now, Derek, but I think this plan is the next-best thing. We'll see you around eight tomorrow. But remember, it's fine to call again tonight."

After Will hung up, Susannah slid over on the couch next to him and put her arms around his waist. "I'm so sorry for Derek. I wish he weren't so far away."

"Yes, I'm thinking the same thing. It's going to be a long night for him."

....

Derek sat on the bed holding the phone, hands dangling between his knees, staring at the wall. He'd planned to go to Ashland in three weeks. His mom had promised to make his favorite lasagna and peach pie, and his dad was looking forward to giving him the new (to Derek) car. How could they not be there all of a sudden?

His mind jumped from memory to memory: the wading pool he loved to play in at a nearby park; painting his room with his dad at age fourteen; driving lessons; his mom making costumes for the fifth-grade play; arguments about undesirable friends and tattoos; music lessons and soccer camp.

Looking at the to-do list lying on the bed, he tried to think how to break the news to his grandparents. Then he realized that there was no one else to take care of *them*; from now on, he'd have to do what his mom had been doing for the last couple of years: taking care of their finances, getting them into assisted living, dealing with doctors and hospitals.

He made the call. They were as shocked as he was, and the conversation rambled around as they tried to take it in. But they understood that Will and Susannah were coming to help, and they were glad for that news. He told them he'd call them back when he got to Ashland and knew more.

In no particular order he began writing down everything that came to him that needed to be done: Call Trisha. Find the wills and call the lawyer. Get someone to take care of the house until he could decide what to do with it. Plan a memorial service. Pack all his stuff and clean the apartment. Write an obituary. Find out what to do about banks and bills, et cetera.

He was exhausted just thinking about all of it, and most of it had to be done in Ashland. But he could write the obituary here. He sat on the bed with his laptop.

Where do I start? All English majors should have obituary writing as an assignment—everyone has to do it sooner or later. What's a good one, and what's a bad one? Or isn't there much difference? Should it be long, or just have the "high points": birthplace, career, activities, survivors? Who's it for, anyway. Maybe he could Google "obituaries" and get some tips, or read some for famous people. Maybe he should Google his parents—he'd never done that. Maybe there was something out there on the Internet that he didn't know about them. Instead, he just sat there, staring at the blank screen. Nothing came. *OK, forget the obit for now. Do laundry and pack.*

He put clothes in the washer and then got his suitcases out from under the bed and started filling them. There would just be room for the clean clothes. He put his laptop in its case and put it by the door, along with his soccer ball, tennis balls, and racket. He washed the dishes. He vacuumed the floors, washed the windows and mirrors, dusted the furniture, and took out the trash, and it was still only one in the morning. Every so often he found himself staring at the floor, or wondering what was in his hands, or thinking about the accident. He couldn't help wondering if his parents had suffered as they died.

Professor Lundberg and her husband were away for the weekend. He got his laptop out again and sent her an e-mail explaining the situation, telling her he'd be back in touch to let her know if and when he could return to work on the research project. Then he set his alarm for six a.m., so that he'd have time to do one more load of laundry before Will and Susannah arrived. He thrashed around most of the night, but he finally fell asleep about four.

When the alarm went off, he made himself a cup of coffee and put a couple of Pop-Tarts in the toaster. It would be another hour until Will and Susannah arrived. He wanted to call Trisha, but was afraid he'd break down. And what could she do anyway? He sat on the bed with his cup of coffee and cried.

Finally, everything was done. He carried the suitcases and bags out to the street just as Susannah and Will drove up. There were hugs all around, and then they loaded the trunk. Derek took one last look around the apartment, left the keys on the desk, and shut the door. "I'm ready," he said.

Susannah motioned him to sit in front with Will, Derek gave Will directions to the freeway, and they left Portland.

"Will and I have already eaten, but I've got some cut-up fruit, and some bagels and cream cheese, if you'd like something to eat," Susannah told Derek. "We also got a latte for you. You should try to keep your strength up."

"Sure, that sounds good. I'll have some fruit and a bagel." She handed him a container with bananas, strawberries, peaches, and grapes in it, a plastic spoon, and a bagel wrapped in a napkin.

"Thanks again for coming," he said while eating some fruit. "I'm really glad to see you. Last night was the loneliest night of my life—no girlfriend, no parents, no friends around."

"I'm so sorry we couldn't be here, Derek," Will said, glancing over at his son. "What would help you the most? Do you want to talk, or not talk? Whatever works best for you is fine."

"I'll try to talk with you about things I need to do, but I'll probably be a little incoherent. I keep finding that I just blank out every now and then." He took a few bites of bagel.

"Susannah's the world's greatest list maker, and she's got a good list for us to start on. She's been through some deaths more recently than I have, so she knows a lot of the things that need to be done. Just let her know when you're ready."

Derek nodded his head and ate some more. "If you still have that latte," he said, "the caffeine might help clear my head." Susannah gave him an insulated mug.

By the time they stopped in Eugene for a break, they had gotten through both Susannah's and Derek's lists, prioritizing the tasks and deciding who should do what. Derek made some calls on his cell phone to get answers to some questions and make appointments with people he needed to see.

In Ashland they went straight to his parents' home. His mother's car was in the driveway. The newspaper was on the kitchen table, along with a mug of coffee. The answering machine was blinking. Derek looked around, bewildered. *Where are they?* he thought.

"Derek," Susannah said, "we appreciate the offer of your guest room, but are you sure it won't be awkward having us in your parents' home and cooking in your mom's kitchen?"

"No, I'd like you to be here. I don't want to be alone," he said. "I'm sure it will be a little weird at times, having you here, but that's OK. It's way better than being alone." He wandered through the familiar rooms, stopping in his dad's office. On his desk were a set of car keys and the title for Derek's new car. He picked up the keys and went to the garage, where he found a spotless late-model Honda with only twenty thousand miles on it. Will found him in the car thirty minutes later, sobbing, his arms and head resting on the steering wheel, his shoulders shaking.

Derek held it together over the next difficult days: making cremation arrangements, planning the memorial service, seeing his grandparents, meeting with the realtor who arranged to take care of the house for him, paying bills, closing accounts, greeting friends and neighbors who came with food and condolences, and the endless other tasks associated with death. He felt strangely detached, as if he were at a movie—watching himself going through the motions and getting things done. But writing the obituary was like hitting a wall.

He sat at the desk in his room, laptop in front of him, staring at the photos on his bulletin board: a picture of him in the Halloween costume his mom made when he was six; the three of them after high school graduation; his dad handing him the keys to his first car; his parents at an anniversary celebration. His parents had always been there; how could they not be here now? He poked his finger with a sharp pencil to see if he could feel anything. Yes, physically. No, otherwise. Just blankness.

"How are you feeling, Derek?" Will stood in the doorway.

"Kind of numb, I guess." Derek paused, fiddling with the pencil. "What keeps coming up for me is the big question about death. In one way, it's so natural—we have to have death or there'd be too many people. But when it's personal, it doesn't seem to make sense. Why didn't my parents die of old age? Well, because Dad had a massive heart attack and drove off the road. But why did he have a massive heart attack and not someone else. And why was Mom with him?"

Will gazed at the ceiling for a while and then said, "Those are really big questions, Derek. I can't give you any quick answers. You'll be thinking about this for a long time. But maybe the death of your parents will open up possibilities that you never could have imagined."

After the memorial service on Thursday, they collapsed in the kitchen, surrounded by cakes, pies, cookies, and casseroles. Derek got out his dad's Crown Royal and poured them each a glass.

"I think I'll write a short story called 'Death by Casserole,'" Derek said. It was just the right remark to break the tension and lighten things up. They had a good laugh.

....

They had an appointment with the Baileys' lawyer the next morning. Harry Hughes had been a friend of Derek's father for thirty years. He handled Steve's business affairs as well as the family affairs. He had already advised Derek on several matters, and had asked to meet with them after the memorial service to wrap things up.

Harry ushered them into his well-appointed office and provided coffee and tea. They sat around a walnut conference table.

"Before we go into the wills, I want to tell you something that Steve said to me when we were playing golf a few days after your graduation, Derek. He was telling me about meeting Will and Susannah, and he said that he had a good feeling about Will, about both of them. He was glad that Will was in your life and hoped that you two would become close over time." He smiled at all three of them.

"Now, let's finish our business," Harry said. "In short, both your parent's wills leave everything to you, Derek, except for a few charitable donations, which I've taken care of. I will give you a check for fifty thousand dollars before you leave today." Derek dropped his pen. "In addition, you'll receive ten thousand a year for the next six years. You will also receive as much as you need to cover educational expenses if you decide to go to graduate school or do some other kind of training in that time period. When you're thirty, the balance of the estate will be yours. I doubt that there will be any federal estate taxes, and Oregon's estate taxes are modest." Harry paused to make sure they were following.

"Your father and mother wanted you to be able to travel, to get more education—if that's what you decide to do, to support or engage in things that you believe in. They wanted you to work hard, enjoy life, and do good things in the world. But they didn't want you to sit around on *their* laurels.

"One more thing," he said. "Your grandparents are well provided for. They have assets and income that will cover them until they die. They won't need any money from you, but they will need you to be involved in their lives as they become increasingly unable to care for themselves.

"So! There you have it, in a nutshell. I'm sure this is all rather bewildering. I have several files for you to take home and read. They'll explain a lot. Of course, I wish the circumstances were different, I must say it makes me very happy to be delivering such good financial news. More often than not, the news is not good for bereaved families. Questions?"

Everyone looked at Derek. "Could I have some more coffee?" he said.

They all laughed, and Harry poured more coffee for everyone.

"Maybe it's covered in the papers," Derek said after taking a sip, "but could you tell me what happens to Dad's business?"

"I guess he hadn't told you yet, but he sold it about six months ago. It's a complicated transaction, but the proceeds will be going into your estate over the next few years. He was going to stay on as the general manager, because he wasn't quite used to the idea of retirement." Harry handed each of them a business card. "Feel free to call me anytime, Derek, or arrange an appointment to come in and talk. Are you going to stay in Ashland, or have you decided yet?"

"I haven't decided yet. I'll be here while I deal with the house and all the stuff, but I don't know beyond that."

"Selfishly, we're hoping that he'll come to Seattle eventually," Susannah said. "But he'll have to sort that out himself." She smiled at Derek.

They stood up, readying to leave. Harry handed Derek a two-inch accordion-pleated file, closed with a tie. "There's a check in there, and I suggest you take it straight to the bank. And I know it seems hard to imagine right now, but try to have some fun with some of it! It was a pleasure to meet you, Susannah and Will. Good luck to you, Derek. Stay in touch."

"I'm totally flabbergasted!" said Derek as they stood on the sunny street in front of Harry's office, all looking slightly dazed,

"I'm sure you'd rather have your parents than the money," said Will. "But what a tremendous gift they've given you—so many possibilities for your life."

....

A year later Derek sat outside a cantina in a little Mexican town where he had been volunteering for several months in a grade school. He was lonely. People were friendly. They appreciated his help, and the children liked to play soccer with him. He didn't think about Trisha so often; that was one advantage of being immersed in another culture and speaking another language. But he still couldn't quite believe his parents were gone.

In college, he didn't think of them when he went to the ATM, though they supplied the money he took out of the machine. But now he thought of them every time he replenished his cash, appreciating their generosity but wishing they were still alive. He called Will and Susannah every week, when he was in a place where his cell phone worked. When they flew to Oaxaca to visit him, he'd enjoyed showing off his Spanish and showing them around, but at the same time he'd noticed a feeling of relief. It was good to be with people he knew cared for him and would do whatever they could for him.

Six months later he was in Shanghai, having found himself a job teaching English through a classmate from Reed. It was challenging, but not in the same way as Mexico. The culture and language were so different he found himself questioning the most basic things he'd believed all his life. There were a lot of expats around, so he had friends to hang out with, even a girlfriend from Romania for a short romance. But he still felt disconnected—like he didn't belong anywhere. Will came over for a two-week visit, and they did some traveling in the countryside. Derek felt even more alone leaving the airport after seeing Will off.

A year later, on his way to Turkey, he met Will in India for a three-week trek to many of the sacred sites Will had always wanted to visit. They talked a lot about philosophy and religion and how they were applied or ignored in people's lives, including their own. In their conversation, they both got a sense for what had been happening for Derek internally, and what he was making of all this intense experience.

Then he was in Ankara learning Turkish and coaching soccer in an international school where English was the primary language. He fell in love with a young Muslim woman who taught at the school, but the cultural gap was too large for them to cross. He flew home for six weeks when his grandfather died and spent three weeks with Will and Susannah in Seattle, then returned to Turkey.

After a year there, he took off again with a friend from Moscow, the son of a wealthy Russian businessman. They'd met in Ankara at a party and found they had a lot in common. Mikhail was in no hurry to return home, so they worked their way through Greece and up through the Balkans.

At last, he'd had enough. He realized he was ready to stay in one place and figure out what he wanted to do with his life.

....

Derek sat at a sidewalk café on Seattle's Capitol Hill, eating dinner with a slender young woman in a yellow sundress; her name was Bridget. They had met a couple of weeks earlier in a coed soccer league and since then had been to a party and a movie together. She wouldn't be described as pretty, but she had smiley blue eyes and Scandinavian blonde hair, and she was very fast and agile on the soccer field. They liked each other a lot.

"So, is it time for the exchange of life stories?" she asked, smiling at him over her salad.

"Yeah, I think it's time. You get to start."

"OK. Born in Portland. Pacific Lutheran University, sociology. MA in nonprofit administration. Various low-paying jobs. Some travel. And I've been the assistant director at Planned Parenthood for the past two years. Oh, and I just moved into a new apartment. And you?"

"Are you sure you didn't use too many words?" he said, laughing. "That was pretty . . . succinct. I'm sure the life-story gods will allow you a few more lines!"

"I'm just really curious to hear your story. From a few things you've said here and there, it seems like you've been to some really interesting places."

"OK, my turn. But I'm not going to try to compete with you on brevity! Born in Ashland. Reed, English—I'm even with you so far! Not long after I graduated, my parents died in a car accident. My inheritance was enough for me to travel and go to school. So I did a Spanish immersion course in Mexico, and traveled around there, got a job as a volunteer in an orphanage. I was in Mexico for about a year. While I was there I ran across this little school up in the mountains. Do you know anything about Waldorf schools?"

"Mm-hmm, my sister has two kids at the Portland Waldorf School. So I know a little about it."

"Cool! I'm really glad you know something about Waldorf, because I'm really into it. But back to my chronology. I traveled in the Far East, taught English in China for a while, moved on to Turkey, Greece, and the Balkans. I spent another two years or so just traveling around. And I kept running into these Waldorf schools. My stepbrother's wife is a Waldorf teacher and runs a little tutoring program out of her home. Anyway, I got interested in that, took the three-year training program in Eugene while I was working as a soccer coach, and then I got a teaching job in Seattle. My dad and I help coach my nephews' soccer team. There you have it!"

"Wait. I thought you said your dad died in a car accident."

"That was my adoptive father. I grew up with him. My biological father, Will, came into my life about seven or eight years ago. I'd like you to meet him sometime—and his wife, Susannah. I'm sure you'd like them. But that's a long story I'll save for another time."

"What was it like, traveling all that time, living abroad for so long?"

He finished the last of his beer and considered her question, turning his spoon end over end. "Exciting . . . lonely . . . thought-provoking. I learned a lot. One thing that really stands out is how much people care about education for their kids. No matter what country you're in, or what the income level is, parents really want that for their children. So that got me thinking about education. And then I realized that I really like working with kids. It takes a huge amount of energy, but you also get energy back. It's really rewarding."

They spent the remaining daylight hours at the restaurant, eating and filling in the blanks in their respective stories. When the bill was paid, Bridget asked Derek if he'd like to see her new apartment. He would.

....

The next night Derek was at Susannah and Will's for dinner. They were having a belated thirtieth birthday party for him. Susannah put only one candle for each decade on the cake, so it was no problem for him to blow them out. 'Yay—you'll get your wish!" she said.

"I'm going to bring my wish to meet you pretty soon," he said, smiling. "Her name is Bridget. Meanwhile, I want to tell you about my conversation with Harry Hughes last week. Remember, he was Mom and Dad's lawyer? He's mostly retired, but he could still handle this bit of business. In a nutshell, to use Harry's phrase, I'm a millionaire. Actually, I'm a three-millionaire."

There was silence while they took in this piece of information. "Goodness!" said Susannah finally.

"Wow," said Will. "I thought it would be substantial—otherwise, your folks wouldn't have kept the amount secret and put off giving it to you for so long—but I had no idea it would be that much!"

"I suppose it's too soon for you to know what you're going to do with it," said Susannah, "but I'm sure you've started thinking about it."

"Actually, I've been thinking about it for a long time. I had no idea it would be that much money either, but it doesn't change what I plan to do," said Derek. "For the last couple of years, I've been researching socially responsible investments, and I've discovered an outfit that I really like. They don't pay a lot of interest, but I really like what they do with their money, they've been around long enough to have a good track record, and I could have some say in what my money gets invested in. So I'm going to put the bulk of the inheritance in this foundation. I've got a car and a job, and a house paid for by my grandparents, so I'm set." He grinned, twirling his knife around on the table. "Well, almost set. Now all I need is a wife or partner or whatever, and some kids."

"You know," Derek said later as they were cleaning up the kitchen," "Or maybe you don't know—it's meant so much to me to have you two in my life. I know I haven't been around much since I graduated, but just the knowledge that you were here, and our frequent phone calls while I was doing all that wandering and searching—that was an anchor. I didn't feel totally disconnected. And I've really appreciated your wisdom, and your being a family for me."

Will couldn't speak. He just gave Derek a big hug, followed by Susannah, who said, "Derek, you couldn't have said anything that would make us happier. We're so glad to be your family, and that you're here where we can spend more time with you—and many happy birthdays!"

CHAPTER SEVEN

Soccer Dad

As he prepared for the Saturday game, Alex was going over in his mind how he happened to end up as the coach for his twelve-year-old son's soccer team. He got the job because his work schedule was more flexible than most parents, and because he was willing to do it, though with reservations. He hadn't played a lot of soccer, so they weren't getting someone who could teach the kids very much. But he didn't want to hear any complaints about his coaching, since no one else was even willing to take on the job. He wished they could find a real coach.

Alex really depended on his assistant coaches—his stepfather, Will, and Alex's much-younger stepbrother, Derek—both of whom had played a lot of soccer. Since he was a teacher, Derek could usually get to practice after school, and between the three of them they were almost always able to make sure the boys had two coaches for each practice and game.

It was starting to rain as Alex began rounding up his sons. "I can't find my soccer jacket, Dad," Paul announced with a worried expression on his face.

"Think about where you last wore it and go look there," his father instructed patiently. "Where's Andrew?"

"He's down in the basement," Paul said over his shoulder as he ran off to find his jacket. "Building a model race car."

"Andrew," Alex called down the stairs. "If you want to go to the soccer game, you need to get your stuff together right now. You can finish your project after dinner."

No answer.

"Andrew, are you down there?"

"Dad, I just need to glue this last piece. Come see my model."

"Andrew, it will be there when we get back, and I'll look at it then. I told you fifteen minutes ago that we were getting ready. You have to decide—do you want to go to the soccer game or work on your model? If you want to go, get your stuff right now. We're leaving in five minutes."

Ten minutes later, Alex checked the boys' gear and clothes and herded them out the door to the car.

"You're the world's best dad," Sylvianne told Alex, kissing him on the cheek. "I hope the other parents appreciate how much time you take off from work to coach their kids. I think they do, but still." She waved out the window as they drove away.

As they drove to the soccer field, Alex wished some of the parents, especially the dads, weren't so focused on winning. They could get rather trying at times.

The Emorys parked in the lot adjacent to the field thirty minutes before game time. Before Paul could run off to join his teammates, Alex reminded him to keep his jacket on until the game started and to take his duffel bag and put it on the bleachers. Helping his father tote equipment, ten-year-old Andrew shuffled down the path to the bleachers, dragging a bag of balls. Will couldn't make it today, but Derek arrived a few minutes after Alex and the boys. Other players and their families gradually filled up the parking lot and bleachers, the latter a riot of brightly colored umbrellas and rain jackets. The coaches got their teams organized and began their warm-up drills.

Paul came running up to tell Alex that their "star forward," Matthew Raymond, hadn't arrived yet. "It's OK, Paul—don't worry. I'm sure he'll get here."

Sure enough, Matthew and his mother, Audrey, came running down the path from the parking lot about two minutes before the game was to start. Matthew dropped his bag, pulled off his jacket, shoved it into his mother's arms, and ran out onto the field.

"Sorry to be late," Audrey said breathlessly to Alex and Derek. "I couldn't find my car keys, and then the parking lot was full. But it looks like we made it."

Inwardly annoyed at her persistent lateness, Alex replied, "No problem, Audrey. You're here, so all's well."

The whistle blew, and the other team kicked off. One of the dads, Simon Martinson, came to stand by Alex on the sidelines. "I heard there's a rule in kids' soccer that everyone is supposed to play at least half of the game. Is that the case?"

"Well," Alex responded, irritated but trying not to let it show. "It's not a rule. It's a guideline—Oscar, keep your position! Nels, remember to pass!" he shouted to two of the boys on the field. "Sorry, Simon, got to do the coaching thing. We try to let all the kids play as much as possible. But it partly depends on their attendance and skill. If Eric had attended more of the practices, he could play more. But I can't in good conscience have him playing as much as kids who've attended every practice and who play better than he does. I think he's only been to half the practices this season. Can you get him there more often?"

Martinson went off, muttering, "We'll see what we can do."

Ten minutes of play made it apparent that the two teams were fairly well matched. Most of the boys on Paul's team had played together for only a year. Derek focused on defense. Alex was concentrating on the offensive play, shouting encouragement to his players, or correcting errors. Derek came running up the sidelines to him, splashing through the deepening puddles, about five minutes before the end of the first half. The score was three to three.

"Alex, we've got a problem down at my end of the field. Matthew's dad is down there yelling from the sidelines, and he's really out of line. He's dumping on the kids when they make mistakes. Especially Matthew—he's getting upset and starting to really mess up. I've spoken to the dad—his name is Mitch, as I remember, but he just keeps doing it."

Alex and Derek loped back down the field just as the whistle blew, signaling the end of the first half. Alex remembered that Matthew's parents had separate addresses on the team roster. They slowed to a walk as they approached Matthew's father, who was smoking and pacing back and forth, watching the boys leave the field.

"You're Matthew's dad, aren't you?" Alex extended his hand so the other man would have to be rude not to take it. "I'm Alex Emory, the coach, and this is Derek Bailey, the assistant coach."

"Mitch Raymond," he said, giving Alex's and Derek's hands a perfunctory shake. He was a big man, a head taller than Alex and slightly taller than Derek, with a heavy frame and a thickening middle.

"Can't say that I approve of your style of coaching, Emory. These kids are just playing around. They aren't hungry to win."

"Well, it sounds like we have different philosophies, Mitch. My philosophy is that at this stage, it's most important for the kids to learn the game and have a good time. They've got plenty of time to get into the winning thing later on, when they've played more. I just don't want them to get turned off now because of too much pressure. So I'd appreciate it if you wouldn't yell at the kids from the sidelines—unless it's something supportive."

"Sure, sure," Raymond responded. "I don't think they'll ever get anywhere with that kind of philosophy, but you're the coach."

"Why don't you come down and join the rest of the parents?" Derek asked.

"No, thanks," he said. "Nobody likes a smoker."

Derek and Alex went back to the other end of the field, where the boys were eating orange slices, drinking water, and mopping the mud off their faces. Some parents had managed to get their boys to put their jackets back on until halftime was over. Everyone was excited about the tied score.

Derek and Alex reminded the boys of some of the mistakes they'd been making, encouraged each of them to work on his particular weakness, and reminded them that the important thing was to try to improve and have a good time. "Don't pay attention to anything from the sidelines unless it's from me or Derek. Ignore anything else. OK? OK, go play your best!"

The boys ran onto the field, and the second half began. Alex moved down to the other end of the field to his team's goal, as did several of the parents. As he walked, he saw Mitch pull a flask from his raincoat pocket and take a swallow.

Mitch apparently had no intention of complying with Alex's request for positive comments only. When one of their forwards was offside, he yelled, "Hey, number three, don't you know the rules?" A few minutes later: "Pass you little wimp, pass!"

The play shifted to the other end of the field, and Alex took the opportunity to remind Mitch a little more sharply about being positive.

"Look, Mitch, you're upsetting the kids. They've been playing worse since you started yelling at them. They're not used to belittling and name-calling."

Mitch didn't respond.

The other team scored, and play moved back to Alex's end of the field.

Alex could see the boys looking over at Mitch, instead of concentrating on the game. They must have known grown-ups weren't supposed to act like this, and it was probably making them uneasy, as they wondered who Matthew's dad would yell at next.

"Run, Matthew, run! You're playing like a girl," Mitch

shouted at his son. "You can do better than that!" Matthew missed his pass, the ball was stolen from him, and play moved back down the field in the other direction.

"Jesus Christ, Matthew!" his father yelled.

Alex was angry. He'd never seen such inappropriate and disrespectful behavior from a parent. He needed to get this guy out of here.

"Look, Raymond, I'll be blunt. You're having a bad effect on the team. I'm asking you to leave before they fall apart altogether. I'll meet you somewhere later if you want to talk about this, but right now I'd like you to leave."

"You've got no right to ask me to leave my own son's soccer game! Who do you think you are?" he said, taking another swig from his flask.

Alex decided to change the subject. "I'll bet you played football, right?"

The startled father replied immediately. "Yeah, I even played in the Rose Bowl."

"Well then, you know that what the coach says goes. And I'm the coach here. I'd like you to respect my role and do what I'm asking. I'm asking you to leave."

By now Alex's team was back at his end of the field, well set up to score. Both men turned their attention to the field. Matthew passed to Paul, and Paul kicked a goal, so the score was tied again. Matthew, Paul, and their teammates were high-fiving and jumping up and down in excitement.

Matthew's mother had been anxiously watching her ex-husband's interactions with Alex from about ten yards down the field, where many of the other parents were standing. When Alex was called to talk with the referee about a possible foul, Audrey moved to Mitch's side. "Mitch, please, either stop shouting at the kids or leave. Matthew's wanted you to come to a game for weeks, and now you finally show up and act like a jackass—this isn't the kind of impression you want to make on your son. Would you please just go?"

"Oh, you'd like me to go, so you could flirt with the coach, or maybe the assistant coach, is that it? Is that why you take Matthew to soccer, so you can ogle the coaches? Now that you've ditched me, you're free to sleep around, right?"

Audrey looked mortified. Derek was standing nearby and heard the whole exchange, as did a couple of other parents. She tried to maintain her composure.

"Mitch, this is no time to rehash our marital problems—we've done that a thousand times. You need to move on. And you need to stay away from Matthew if you can't be civil. If you keep behaving like this, he won't want to be with you."

Play had resumed, but neither of Matthew's parents noticed.

"I'm sure you're bad-mouthing me night and day, Audrey. Nothing I could say would make a difference to him." He took another pull on his flask.

"Goddamn it, Mitch! It would make a difference to him if you'd stop yelling at him and his teammates, and not show up drunk at his soccer game!"

"I'm not drunk, bitch, leave me alone!" He shoved her shoulder, and she staggered into the linesman, who was just moving up the sideline with his flag and chain. He caught her before she fell.

"OK, that's it—leave!" shouted Alex, who saw this exchange as he returned to his place on the sidelines. He came up behind Mitch, grabbed his coat sleeve, and pulled him around. "You're harassing people—get out of here!"

"Who's going to make me?" snarled Mitch, shoving Alex hard.

Alex, taken off guard, fell on his side in the mud. But he was up instantly. Play had stopped on the field, and everyone was watching, stunned into immobility. Alex, standing about ten feet from Mitch, calmly pulled his cell phone out of his pocket, punched in 911, and said, "I'd like to report an assault in progress at Nineteenth and John on the south side of the soccer field. Could you—?"

Mitch charged like an offensive tackle. Alex, who had anticipated this, moved out of his way, tripped him, and had his arm twisted behind his back in a wristlock and his face in the mud before anyone knew what had happened. Mitch struggled, but then he seemed to deflate, and he just lay there in the puddles.

Derek asked everyone to move away to give Alex and Mitch some space. He fished Alex's cell phone out of the mud and asked a couple of the dads to stand ready at a discreet distance, just in case. One of the moms had her arm around Audrey, who was crying, and the two of them walked slowly down the field to the bleachers.

Derek ran out onto the field with the boys, who were standing shocked and bedraggled in the rain. He and the referee and the other coach were conferring about what to do. They decided to call the game a draw, and Derek and the other coach slogged through the mud to their respective parents to let them know.

Two police cars arrived, sirens wailing. The officers came running onto the field, and the parents nearest them pointed toward Alex and Mitch. By then, Alex was helping Mitch up. There was a conversation of about five minutes, after which the officers returned to their cars, and Mitch left alone.

Alex walked up the field toward the gathered parents and boys, who were milling around and wondering what to do. Derek jogged back across the field to ask the other coach to join their group.

When everyone was gathered, Alex said, "First, I want to talk to the team. Boys, sometimes parents do stuff they shouldn't do. Everyone does things they shouldn't do, right? Even *you* have done things you wish you hadn't, right?"

The boys nodded solemnly.

"Well, Mr. Raymond has some problems, and they caused

him to do some things he wishes he hadn't done. He's sorry. So let's just put all this behind us, OK? He ruffled the wet hair of the boys on either side of him.

"The last thing I want to say is that there was some mighty fine soccer being played today. You guys were really doing well—you've improved so much since the beginning of the season. Keep it up!

"Parents, I'll send you an e-mail about my conversation with Mr. Raymond and the police. If you want to talk about this after you get the e-mail, feel free to call. I think the best thing for the kids right now is a hot shower, something special to eat, and some attention from their folks. See you next week at practice."

....

Alex helped Sylvianne get the muddy clothes off the boys and into the laundry, and then he and the boys took showers. When they appeared in the kitchen, Sylvianne gave the boys some cheese and crackers to tide them over until dinner, and they went down to the basement to work on their Lego robot and model car.

Alex filled his wife in on the afternoon "incident." Underneath his composed exterior, Alex had been steaming. "I've about had it, Sylvie," he said with disgust. "The parents are more childish than the kids! They can't get to practice on time. They want their kids to play even when they only get them there for half the practices. They're fixated on winning. Now this jerk with his flask! It really pisses me off when parents embarrass their kids. You can just see the hurt go into them, and you know it's going to be there a long time, if not forever."

Taking a glass of scotch with him, Alex went to the computer. He started a new e-mail message, tapped his soccer group into the "To" line, and sat there wondering what to say. He tried to let go of his annoyance, so that he didn't say something that would come back to haunt him or make the situation worse. Then he started typing.

>Dear Fellow Soccer Parents,
>
>   For those of you who weren't at the game this afternoon, I want to describe an incident that happened, so that you'll be getting it straight from the source, rather than a perhaps garbled version from your son.
>
>   Matthew Raymond's father, Mitch, came to the game this afternoon. He was drinking, and he was shouting inappropriately at the players of both teams. Both Derek and I asked him to refrain. When he didn't, I asked him to leave, as did Matthew's mother. (Some of you may not know they are divorced.) They had words, and he pushed her. I interfered, and he pushed me over, so I got up and called 911. In the midst of that call, he charged me and, given his condition, I prevailed. (All those years of aikido and wrestling came in handy!)
>
>   By the time the police arrived, Mitch had seen the error of his ways. I told him I would not press charges if he would write a letter to the parents apologizing for his actions and if he would not attend games for the rest of this season. He agreed.
>
>   I would like the best possible outcome from this event for our sons. This is what I'm going to tell mine:
>- I don't excuse bad behavior, but I try to understand where it comes from.
>- Just because people make mistakes doesn't mean they're bad people.
>- One way or another, there are consequences for wrongdoing, even though we may not always know what those consequences are. We don't necessarily have to deliver the consequences or be the judge of someone else's bad behavior.
>
>   All kids love their parents, even when those parents make mistakes. It's not going to do Matthew any good

to hear people berating his dad. So please be careful what you say about all this in front of your children.
If you feel you need to talk about this in person, please call. But not tonight—we're having guests for dinner!

Sincerely,
Alex Emory

Sylvianne came in to read the letter. She rubbed his shoulders and told him she thought it looked good. He gave a big sigh and pressed "Send."

"I'm glad you haven't had much of your scotch," she said. "Sally Preston invited the boys over for pizza and a sleepover. Can you run them over to her house?"

"Sure," he said in a tired voice. "I'll gather up their pj's and toothbrushes and take them over. That was a nice offer on her part."

While Alex was driving to Montlake with the boys, Will, Susannah, Derek, and his girlfriend, Bridget, arrived, bringing contributions for dinner. They settled in the kitchen with their drinks, and Derek related all the details of the afternoon's event.

"What do you know about this Mitch guy, Derek?" Susannah asked, cutting up an avocado and tossing the salad.

"I overheard the conversation between him and his wife," Derek replied. "It must have been a pretty unfriendly divorce. He was accusing her of being on the make. He sounded deliberately nasty, to me. She was trying to reason with him, but she lost her temper. Understandable, but it didn't help the situation. That's when he shoved her. Luckily, someone caught her before she ended up in the mud too." Derek stopped to dip a tortilla chip in salsa. "Otherwise, I don't know anything about him at all. I've never heard the kids talk about him, or any of the parents. Matthew's mom, Audrey, is a nice lady but seems kind of scattered. They're always late to practice and games. She does her part, but it seems like a major effort for her—like she's juggling seven balls or something."

Alex came in the back door. He greeted everyone, was introduced to Bridget, hung up his coat, got his scotch, and sat down in the breakfast nook opposite Derek and Bridget.

"Well, my son," said Susannah, "sounds like you've had quite the day. Congratulations on maintaining your cool. Are you still 'processing' or are you sick of all this?"

"I guess I'm still 'processing,'" Alex replied. "I sent an e-mail to the parents about the whole episode, and I hope they handle it well with the boys, so we can at least get some positive lessons out of it. No crisis should be wasted, and all that."

"I feel sorry for Matthew," said Derek. "He must be so embarrassed. And his mother. It must be pretty awkward for them."

"Could I interrupt this conversation while we get dinner on the table?" asked Sylvianne. After a teasing toast to the head coach and team bouncer, they sat down to eat.

"Why do people play soccer, anyway?" Susannah asked.

Will, Alex, and Derek looked at each other as if to say "Is she serious?"

"That's a pretty good intro for a dinner conversation topic, Mom," Alex said, laughing.

"Not just soccer," Susannah said. "I mean any team sport, but especially the really competitive ones. I *get* 'playing,' but most sports seem to go beyond just 'playing.' There's the need to be better than someone else—to win. I've always wondered if that's really good for children. Why can't they just play, period?"

"Setting aside the question of the right age for kids to start, I think they're lots of good reasons for playing team sports," Will said. "You learn how to cooperate. You learn about things you do well and things you don't do well. You learn that you can get better at something if you practice.

You learn how to lose—that life isn't always fun. You learn to value people for different qualities, not just their physical prowess, but their social qualities, like cheering each other up, or being positive."

"Yeah," Derek said. "Those are all really good reasons. And then when kids are older and they can be more sophisticated about strategy, and more proficient physically, they can start to appreciate the . . . um . . . Zen of it, for lack of a better word. Or maybe you'd call it 'transcendence.' What do you think, Will? Sometimes everyone is on the same wavelength, and a play happens that is just magic. It's not planned—it's just a combination of a bunch of things, and it's just beautiful."

"But doesn't the same thing happen with music or dance?" asked Sylvianne.

"Sure, it happens there, but I don't do music or dance," answered Will. "Or at least you wouldn't want to see it or hear it if I did! But I can play soccer, and I know what Derek means when he talks about that special thing that happens, the Zen of it."

"I don't disagree with what you're saying," Susannah said. "But I see precious little transcendence going on at most of the soccer games I've attended. Or any other athletic events, for that matter. So much of the time it's all about winning, and the losing team is dejected, and sometimes reviled. And there's all this analysis of who made what mistakes."

"Not to mention the idolatry of pro sports figures," Sylvianne put in. "Why do those people get paid so much money? And why do so many people watch them?"

"Lots of reasons," answered Alex. "People who play a sport like to watch people who are really good at it—they can appreciate what's going on. But even if you don't play the sport you're watching, you can still appreciate it when it's done well. Or you can enjoy being part of a group that's all doing something together. It's a bonding thing, like doing the 'wave' in the stands. Then there's the distraction of it, something to occupy your time if you don't want to think about what's going on in your life."

Sylvianne passed the roast and vegetables around the table again, and Derek refilled the wineglasses. The soft light from the candles and the chandelier cast shadows on the dining room walls and sparkled off the glassware and silver.

"But back to my original question," Susannah said. "What's all the competitive stuff about, the emphasis on winning? I know plenty of women are competitive, but in the big picture, it seems like a guy kind of thing. The vast majority of competitive events involve men, and of course it's mostly men who do the war stuff."

"Hey, wait a minute!" said Will. "Are you equating war and soccer?"

Everyone laughed.

"Well, for the sake of the conversation, yes," Susannah said. "I think there's something in sports, some aspect of sporting events that's like war: 'We want your turf,' 'We're better than you are,' 'We can beat you,' et cetera. There's something in men that gets expressed in these ways. Come on, Sylvianne. Come on, Bridget. I need some help here."

"I think we need to look underneath the war and the ultracompetitive sports," Sylvianne said. "From an evolutionary perspective, men were suited physically to protect women and children, which had to be done for the species to survive. And they had to have courage to hunt wild animals so everyone could eat. Maybe they're 'hardwired' to do challenging physical things. And then it gets twisted when there aren't any mastodons or saber-toothed tigers to fight off—the energy goes into sports and war."

"Don't forget the showing off to attract mates," Will added. "That's a fairly common biological behavior, and there's certainly that aspect to sports and war. The captain of the football team and the conquering warrior get their pick of the women."

"So how does all this relate to Mitch Raymond?" asked

Derek. "Is it like he's got some fear that equates to the fear of fighting off tigers thousands of years ago, and since there aren't any tigers now, he picks a fight with his son's soccer coach? I'd say that's pretty twisted all right. Looks like I'm going to have to know a lot more about biology and evolution if I'm going to be a soccer coach!"

"Sorry, Bridget, we've hardly let you get a word in edgewise," Susannah said. We're quite a bunch of talkers. Sometimes we get carried away."

"That's OK. I'm just trying to keep up with the conversation!" said Bridget. "Maybe I'll have something to add around midnight, after I've absorbed all this."

"You'll get used to us pretty fast," Derek told her. To the others he said, "She has lots of thoughtful opinions. She's just kind of shy with people she doesn't know yet." His hand rested on her knee under the table.

Alex checked his e-mail one last time before bed. There was a message from Mitch Raymond, asking Alex to pass along an attached letter to the team families.

> *Dear Parents and Team Members,*
>
> *I would like to apologize for my behavior at the game, especially to Matthew, his mother, and Coach Emory. There were reasons, but none of them good enough to excuse what I did. Team sports were a big part of my life as a young person, and I think good sportsmanship is very important. So I feel really bad that I was not a good sport.*
>
> *You have a good coach, and if you all follow his lead, you'll have a fine team and lots of fun.*
>
> *Sincerely,*
> *Mitchell Raymond*

Alex forwarded the message to the team e-mail list and then got ready for bed.

He was lying in bed reading the latest issue of the *Economist* when Sylvianne climbed in beside him, propped up her pillows, and settled down with her stack of reading.

It wasn't long before she rearranged her pillows, turned out her light, and snuggled up to Alex. "Can you let go of progress—or lack of it—in the capitalist world for a while? I'm just wondering how you're feeling about the day's events."

He dropped his magazine on the floor and gathered her in his arms. "I'm three issues behind," he grumbled. "But I really wasn't reading, I kept thinking about the job of being the coach. You know I had mixed feelings about taking it on. I was annoyed that no one else volunteered, and I felt a little imposed on just because my work schedule is more flexible than others'. That's not how you should choose a coach—because of his work schedule, for Pete's sake!" He shifted to get more comfortable.

"As far as what happened today, I'm fine, I guess. But I'm kind of wondering if I should be fine, given what happened. In one respect, it's OK to act like it was no big deal—I don't want the kids to be upset. But what kind of world is it when people have so little self-control and so much stress that they do stuff like that?" Sylvianne sighed and gave his hand a supportive squeeze.

"I've been thinking about my reaction to all the things that happened today—I was impatient, irritated, angry. But you know how my mom's always talking about trying not to be reactive when something difficult happens, but to act out of another place? I was just thinking that these parents are pretty good people, all in all. They do annoying things sometimes, but so do I. They have lots of stresses and busy lives. I'd like them to cut me some slack when I don't act perfectly, so I ought to treat them the same way. So, yeah, I guess I'm not angry anymore." He turned toward her and plumped up his pillow.

"There's something more fundamental, though. I realize

that I've been more uptight than I thought I was about how little I know about soccer. I didn't want the kids to suffer because of my inexperience. But the real issue was that I didn't want to look bad as a coach. That just bubbled up to my consciousness tonight. It's a stupid ego trip, and I think that's where all my complaining and annoyance about the parents was coming from. If I try to be objective, it seems to me the kids are having a good time, and they're getting better. Will and Derek more than compensate for my inexperience. So I should just try to let go of this ego thing."

He kissed his wife and turned out his light.

CHAPTER EIGHT

Winning and Losing

Sylvianne reminded herself of what a good role model Alex had been when Paul and Andrew were little and Alex was their soccer coach. He'd overcome his insecurities about his lack of soccer knowledge to become a fine coach. Now the boys were in college, and she found herself increasingly frustrated and angry with her husband of twenty-five years. Successful in business, devoted to family and friends, witty and fun to be with, he could also be overly sarcastic and overbearing, given his verbal and intellectual skills. Sylvianne kept telling herself that she had her own weaknesses and their marriage was strong. But somehow that wasn't enough; she was still angry and frustrated. Was that about him, or about her, or about both of them?

Like most couples who'd been married a long time, they'd had their share of difficulties, but they had always been able to talk their way through problems. She had prided herself on their emotional maturity and problem-solving skills as they had weathered the storms over the years. *But,* she thought, *pride goeth before a fall.*

They met when Alex was thirty and she was twenty-eight, moved in together within three months, and were married three months later. Their two sons were born within the next two years, and she and Alex had agreed to compromise their career paths in favor of shared child-rearing responsibilities. It had worked. Once both boys were in school, Sylvianne had developed a practice as a reading and math tutor, based on her training as a Waldorf teacher.

She enjoyed working with children. So many of them were anxious, nervous, and depressed—even the little ones—and she loved seeing them progress and feel good about themselves. She even enjoyed the challenge of dealing with their parents—also anxious, nervous, and depressed, not to mention worried about their grade schoolers' readiness for Harvard. She was soon in the enviable position of having more demand for her services than she could meet, so she could choose her clients and adjust her hours as she wished.

Sylvianne was one of those rare and lucky women who had always been happy with her parenting and career roles. She was quick to admit that Alex's attitude and willingness to share the parenting had eliminated a lot of the dissatisfactions that many women experience trying to negotiate career and child-care responsibilities. She had heard a piece on NPR about the significant progress that had been made in allowing women access to jobs traditionally held by men, but there had not been nearly as much progress in men being willing to take on roles traditionally held by women. She had been fortunate, and she knew it.

So what was the problem? She couldn't put her finger on it; she just knew that she was increasingly irritated by everything Alex did. Last night at a cocktail party given by one of his business associates, he had talked animatedly and longer than she thought seemly with an attractive young woman, a new member of the friend's firm. And he did his usual thing of repeatedly restating his points in a discussion in different words, rather than stating them once and letting people respond. Why couldn't he just be articulate in the first place instead of monopolizing the conversation?

This morning when she got in her car to go get groceries, she was annoyed at the dirty floors. Alex had volunteered to vacuum the car for her a couple of weeks ago, and it still wasn't done. Now she'd either have to do it herself or have dirty floors when she picked up her friends at the airport.

Sean and Olivia were waiting outside the Delta baggage claim when she drove into the loading lane. She jumped out of the car and hugged Olivia.

"Oh, it's so good to see you," Sylvianne said to both of them. "I hope you haven't been waiting long."

"Perfect timing," replied Sean, giving her a hug. "We just walked out the door. I was kind of looking forward to trying the light rail into town, but with all this gear, I'm relieved to have a ride." He looked doubtfully at the several pieces of luggage that contained clothes, camera gear, and scuba equipment. They were doing a piece for *National Geographic* on a new underwater park in Puget Sound, and were staying with Alex and Sylvianne for a couple of nights before renting a car and driving north to the site of the park for the photo shoot.

They loaded everything into the car and joined the heavy stream of traffic heading toward downtown Seattle. "How long has it been since you were last here?" Sylvianne asked. "I remember your visit when the boys were in middle school, but I'm drawing a blank on anything more recent. I've just given up pretending that I remember things—life's too fast, and the brain cells are overloaded and wearing out."

"Welcome to the club," Olivia said, laughing. We feel the same way. Sean is always playing this word game with me—trying to guess the noun on the tip of my tongue that just doesn't seem to come out. Usually something really difficult like 'mustard' or 'headphones.' He's getting pretty good at it."

"Yeah, it's a thing she does to keep me mentally alert. You know—to avoid Alzheimer's." From the backseat, Sean winked at Sylvianne in the rearview mirror and tousled his wife's short curly hair. "To answer your question," he said, "I came through Seattle a couple of years ago, but I was only here on a layover, and I had a meeting, so I didn't even contact you. We did have a really nice visit to Portland last year, though. Olivia took me out to Lewis and Clark, and showed me the dorm where you two were roommates. Gorgeous campus."

"I've only been back two or three times since we graduated—let's see, was that thirty years ago?" Sylvianne said, her eyes on the traffic. "But each time I was surprised at my emotional reaction. It was almost like I was twenty again—I was excited just to be on campus, and amazed that I could be in such a beautiful setting with such interesting classes and professors. All those feelings came flooding back every time I visited. I guess the place really made an impression on me!"

At the Emorys' Capitol Hill home, Alex took time out from his lawn-mowing to help move Sean and Olivia's luggage into the guest room. Then he asked what they would like to drink after their thirst-inducing travel. "I've only got two more passes with the mower, and the backyard will be ready for us. I'll finish up and put the lawn chairs back and bring the drinks while you're getting settled."

Soon they were comfortably ensconced in Adirondack chairs around a table of cheese, crackers, crudités, and dip, sipping their drinks and catching up.

"You're looking very fit, Alex," remarked Sean. "How do you manage to keep the physique of a high school wrestler?"

"It's a lot of work," Alex admitted, "and getting harder every year. I go to the gym three times a week, and Sylvie beats me at tennis weekly, so between that and watching what I eat, I'm holding my own. She, on the other hand, seems to eat anything and still manages to stay svelte." He smiled at her affectionately. She smiled back.

"Would you like to go for a walk and stretch your legs?" Sylvianne asked.

The travelers were instantly ready—except that Olivia had to get her camera, which she always carried with her. They walked around Lake View Cemetery and Volunteer Park for about an hour, and changed walking partners frequently. As the men were engrossed in a conversation about airline security, Sylvianne and Olivia lagged a bit behind.

"I don't know what's wrong between us, Olivia. Alex acts as though everything is fine, but I feel so far away from him, and annoyed by little things that shouldn't bother me. Even the fact that he doesn't seem to notice that I'm annoyed annoys me. Have you ever felt like that with Sean?"

"No," Olivia replied, "but we've only been married for ten years, both after unsuccessful first marriages. I know you appreciate all the good things about your marriage and about Alex, but maybe it's an intellectual appreciation. You haven't had a marriage fall apart and gone through a divorce. And then known the joy and relief of finally finding someone you feel pretty confident you'd like to spend the rest of your life with. We've gone through all that, so we both feel blessed to have what we have. Not that we don't have the little differences and annoyances with each other that everyone has, but it's all minor."

Sylvianne smiled at her good friend, putting an arm around her shoulders. "Are you telling me to stop whining and be glad for what I've got?"

"No, I don't want to belittle what you're feeling, Sylvie. But I'm at a loss as to what it's about."

"That makes two of us!" was the response Olivia got as they caught up with the men, who were now discussing whether they should go home and barbecue steaks, or go out to dinner and do steaks the next night.

"It doesn't matter to me," Sylvianne said. "The salad and dessert are ready, but they'll keep till tomorrow."

Olivia noted that it was only six, and a weeknight, so they should be able to get into most restaurants on the spur of the moment, but that would also be true the next night.

"We've got good weather for being outdoors tonight," Sean said. "Is it expected to hold for tomorrow?"

"At this rate we'll be here all night deciding," Alex said

with a touch of good-natured impatience. "Unless someone has strong feelings otherwise, I'm going to make a unilateral decision that we barbecue tonight."

"Spoken like a true leader, Alex," laughed Sean. "Take the troops home."

Olivia must have noted Sylvianne's slight frown, because she shrugged at her, as if to say "Let it go."

That evening as they were getting ready for bed, Alex asked her, "Is something bothering you, hon? You seem a little preoccupied or something lately."

"Oh, I don't know," she said. "I just feel restless or dissatisfied or something—I don't know what I feel."

"Well, let me know if there's something I can do when you figure it out," he said, kissing her on the cheek and climbing into bed.

She thought his response was perfectly reasonable, but it annoyed the hell out of her.

....

Sylvianne stopped in at her mother-in-law's to get a recipe for a chard-and-goat-cheese quiche Susannah had made for a recent family dinner. She was always looking for good vegetarian dishes. "Hi, anybody home?" she called as she went in.

"I'm in the library, Sylvie, come on in," Susannah answered. She was sitting on the floor in front of one of three walls of bookcases, with a half-filled box of books beside her. Their second bedroom had become Will's office and their library, and it was overflowing.

"I didn't know I was marrying a book addict!" she said crossly. "I keep telling him he can't buy more books unless he gets rid of some, but he just ignores me." She looked around at the stacks of books on the floor, the desk, the chairs. "It's not the money— it's the clutter! He says I'm a neat freak, and I am, but it's about aesthetics, not about control. There's just something so peaceful about a room with everything in its place." She sighed. "So I'm going through the books, trying to find some we could both agree to get rid of—or at least cart off to storage. I'm afraid this is an irreconcilable difference."

Sylvianne looked at her sharply.

"Not that kind of irreconcilable, Sylvie," Susannah laughed. "Just one of those that will probably be a perennial issue for Will and me. I knew there were bound to be some, but I just didn't know what they would be."

They sat at Susannah's kitchen counter over mugs of tea. "I feel like Alex and I need some 'spaces in our togetherness,'" Sylvianne told Susannah, who looked encouraging but didn't reply, probably waiting for more information. "You know, like Khalil Gibran said. Anyway, Maybe I'm having a midlife crisis or something. I don't know what's wrong, but I just seem to be negative about everything. Especially Alex."

"I'd be the first to admit my son can be trying at times, but I'm wondering if it's really Alex, or if you're projecting your dissatisfactions with your own life onto him. Or maybe both."

"Yes, I've wondered the same thing," Sylvianne replied.

"Perhaps you've arrived at a place in your marriage where you're taking each other for granted. Or maybe you need to do some soul-searching about what's going on in your life. Your boys are in college, your career has been chugging along for fifteen years or so, and maybe it's time to think again about what really matters to you now." Susannah sipped her tea and then went on.

"Maybe it's a coincidence—though I don't believe in them—but I've been thinking lately about how good it would be for you to take up some kind of creative activity. You could blow glass, or make pots, or paint or write, or whatever. You'd be amazed at the unexpected ways that can shake things up in your life—truly. I'm speaking from my own experience, you know."

"Yes, I know how much your writing means to you, how it's enriched your life. But I'm not an artistic person."

"Artistic isn't the point, Sylvie—creative is the point. Get lost in something new. Try various things until you find something you like. Don't think about whether what you do is 'artistic' or 'literary' or good enough to win prizes. Just do it and see what happens. I've got some books on the creative process. I'll go dig them out for you."

Susannah left to rummage around in the library and came back with three books. "Another thing you might consider is taking a trip by yourself," she said.

"These are all good ideas, Susannah—thanks for getting me out of my box. I've just been going around and around."

"You and Alex have been blessed with a wonderful marriage and family and careers. I know you love each other deeply, Sylvie. But people change, and need to change. It's often not easy, but it may still need to happen. Sorry—I don't mean to sound like a therapist or a self-help book. I feel like I'm mouthing platitudes. But I think platitudes sometimes have a bit of truth in them."

They hugged, and Sylvianne left for the grocery store, considering what Susannah had said.

The next day, Sylvianne's brother, Guillaume, called from Paris, asking if they'd like to meet him and his wife, Laurence, in Provence. A friend had offered the use of his *gîte* for a week but the vacation cottage was only available for a particular date. She told her brother she'd come, whether or not Alex could come or not. She could practically hear his raised eyebrows, but he discreetly said he'd look forward to seeing one or both of them. She told him she'd check into flights and call him back.

About an hour's worth of online research turned up a reasonably priced flight from Seattle to London, with a connection to Nice. They could meet there and rent a car for the three-hour drive to the gîte, in the Rhône river valley. She even had frequent-flyer miles that could be applied. In her mind, that clinched it—the trip was meant to happen.

At dinner she told Alex about the invitation.

"Damn," he said. "That's the week I have that big meeting to review the test results from the new robot. There's no way I can miss that meeting. What a shame we can't go."

"I'm sorry *you* can't go, but there's no reason I can't go. It's too good a chance to pass up. I haven't been back in a long time, and I haven't seen Guy and Laurie for two years."

Alex looked surprised, but he said, "Well, that will be fun for you. You haven't traveled alone lately, but I'm sure it will go just fine."

"Of course it will go fine," she said tartly, then immediately regretted her tone.

Alex just looked puzzled.

....

Before she knew it, Alex was taking her to the airport. He stopped in front of the British Airways ticket area, got out her bags, and put them on the curb. He pulled her close and gave her a big hug. "I'm going to miss you, contessa," he said, using his private nickname for her. "Have a wonderful time."

She smiled and kissed him. "I will. I promise. And I'll be back before you get used to my being gone."

Sylvianne was an inveterate people-watcher, a pastime she immediately fell into as she moved slowly through the line to check her luggage. She let her preconceived notions categorize people, and then tried to make up little stories that put people outside the mold she'd instantaneously placed them in:

- Twenty-five-year-old with two toddlers: *Looking anxiously for the nanny who's going with them to France, where they will meet her husband.*
- Distinguished-looking pilot: *Likes to make jam from the berries in his yard*

- Fifty-something woman with dyed red hair in a leopard coat: *Another Erin Brockovich*

She was stereotypically Parisian in appearance: petite with dark hair and eyes, an aquiline nose, and elegant clothes in which she looked totally comfortable. Her mother was French and her father American, and she had lived in both countries long enough to be bilingual without any trace of accent.

In the airport bookstore, Sylvianne found the third volume of a thriller trilogy she'd been looking forward to reading. It would take up several hours of time on the plane. The salesclerk raved about it, and they compared notes on what they'd liked in the first two books. Finally, it was time to board.

After the first meal had been cleared away and she had chatted with the young woman sitting next to her, a student on her way to a semester in Greece, she closed her eyes to think about what she was doing and why. Aside from a few domestic flights to conferences and get-togethers with old friends, Sylvianne hadn't traveled without Alex since they were married. They had traveled a lot—Mexico, Greece, Finland, Egypt, France—so she wasn't too worried about the travel logistics. And since she spoke fluent French, there'd be no problem with language on this trip. But it would feel good to figure out the little travel glitches on her own, to find her way around, to be independent. It wasn't that she was dependent on Alex when they traveled; it was just that there had always been two of them to deal with whatever came up. She was enjoying being alone, not having another person's likes and dislikes to consider.

Remembering how they had met, a little smile came to her lips. It was a Mardi Gras party. She and her date, whose name she'd now forgotten, went as eighteenth-century French aristocrats. Sylvianne was wearing a powdered wig and a hoopskirt. Alex had come as a cowboy, complete with spurs, chaps, and ten-gallon hat. It was crowded and noisy, and his spurs kept getting tangled up in her skirt while everyone was dancing. When he leaned over to shout apologies in her ear, his hat and her wig collided. After collecting their headgear, they found a semi-quiet place to get acquainted. It was then that he'd started calling her "contessa." They had been together ever since.

....

The nine-hour flight brought her and her fellow travelers uneventfully to London. She got her bag, went through customs, and transferred to another terminal for her next flight. She had time for a salad and a walk around the terminal before boarding. When she landed in Nice, she headed straight to baggage claim. Guy and Laurie were scheduled to arrive thirty minutes before she did, and there they were—*les voilà!*

Hugs, kisses, and happy exclamations filled the next few minutes as they gathered up their baggage and Guy led them to the rental agency where their car, a little blue Renault, was waiting. Very shortly they were on the freeway driving toward Aix-en-Provence.

"I can't believe I'm really here," Sylvianne said from the backseat. "It's amazing! You just press some keys in front of a screen, go to the airport and press some more keys, swipe plastic through a gizmo, fly through the air in a silver tube, and, presto, you're in Southern France!"

"It'll seem more realistic when you're wide awake at three a.m.," Guy reminded her.

The rest of the two-hour trip passed quickly as they caught up on family news. They stopped in Carpentras to buy some basics in a supermarket, and then found their way to the gîte. It had once been a barn; the walls were a foot thick, and it had a red tile roof. But it had been very tastefully converted into an apartment with tile floors, big windows with wooden shutters, high ceilings, and all the modern conveniences, including a laundry, dishwasher, and fully equipped kitchen.

"I think we can find happiness here," joked Laurie.

"It's beautiful, said Sylvianne. "So thoughtfully done."

Their host had left them a bottle of the local rosé, which they immediately put in the fridge to chill. Then they unpacked and regrouped for an early lunch of pâté, cheese, olives, hard boiled-eggs, and bread. By the time they finished eating, Sylvianne's head was drooping. It was three in the morning her time but only noon local time. Guy suggested a walk before she took a nap, so they rambled down the gravel road in the sunshine, through fields and olive orchards. .

When they returned from their walk, they put on their swimsuits and rolled back the pool cover. Sylvianne was trying to stay awake as long as possible, in the hopes that she could take a nap, get up in time for dinner, and then stay awake until it was dark, getting back into a natural rhythm. When she dove into the pool, the chilly water banished her sleepiness.

They lined their lounge chairs up in a row so they could talk, applied their sunscreen, and took in the surroundings.

The hillside above their gîte was covered with vineyards. A road wound along the side of the property and switched back and forth up the hill. At the top they could see more orchards, but different from the olive orchards they had passed through earlier. The landscaping around the "barn" was primarily bougainvillea, now in full flower, and other decorative plants suited to a location of frequent wind and hot summers.

As they lay there admiring the view, they heard the noise of an engine, and a tractor appeared at the end of a row of grapevines about twenty yards from the pool. The rider, wearing a battered straw hat, cut the engine, climbed down and walked toward them. Guy jumped up to meet him.

"Etienne! How good to see you again. How goes it?" he said, extending his hand. He called back to Laurie and Sylvianne, "This is our host, Etienne Trudeau. Pull up another chair, Laurie. A glass of something, Etienne?"

"I do not want to disturb your vacation. I just wanted to welcome you and ask you to let me know if there is anything you need—just come over to the house and knock. I won't stay now. I have more pruning to do before I quit for the day."

"At least let me introduce you to my wife, Laurence, and my sister, Sylvianne."

Their host took off his hat and shook hands gravely with both women.

"Will you join us for aperitif this evening?" Guy asked. "Surely you'll be finished pruning by then."

"I regret that I have a previous engagement this evening," Etienne said, "but would tomorrow evening be free for you?"

"Of course! We'll look forward to seeing you about six."

Etienne returned to his tractor and began working his way down the next row of vines.

"What an imposing man!" observed Laurie. "Sort of a cross between Edward R. Murrow and Humphrey Bogart."

"Yes, I agree," Sylvianne said. "But he's not that old. Why are we thinking of people who were in their prime in the 1940s?"

"He has a kind of gravitas that we don't see much anymore, don't you think?" said Laurie. "How many people can you think of you'd describe as dignified?"

"Not many!" replied Sylvianne. "But it's also the dark eyes and dark hair—and the way he wears it. Maybe Antonio Banderas. What do you think, Laurie? Is he married, Guy?"

Guy was looking at them in amazement. "Where do you women get this stuff? Humphrey Bogart in a straw hat? I don't know if he's married or not. Why don't you ask him tomorrow night?" he teased.

They went back to their sunbathing, and Sylvianne promptly fell asleep under the umbrella.

When she woke, the sun was low in the sky and Laurie

was reading in the chair beside her. Guy had gone to town to buy something for dinner. Sylvianne jumped in the pool and swam a few laps, then went in to shower and dress. She came back out to ask Laurie for the Wi-Fi password so she could send a message to Alex. "I keep forgetting—and I don't want him to worry."

They sat on the patio at the picnic table for their dinner. A soft warm breeze rustled the leaves of the old olive tree near the door. When they had finished and cleared away the dishes, they moved to the loungers beside the pool and gazed at the stars.

"I know I've already said this, but I still can't believe I'm here," Sylvianne said. "It's marvelous—especially to be here with you two."

"I'm going to pry," said her brother. "Why did you come without Alex? Are you two having problems?"

"I don't think he's having problems, but I am. The trouble is, I don't know what they are. All I know is that I'm always irritated with him. He's no different than he ever was, and he didn't used to irritate me, so I guess I'm the one with the problem." They waited and after a moment she continued. "I think my mother-in-law is right—I'm unhappy with my life or myself, and I'm projecting it on Alex as the cause. But what is there to be unhappy about? I have a lovely home, two fine sons, a fulfilling career. I'm married to a man I like and respect and who's been a wonderful partner. Most women would think they'd died and gone to heaven to have a husband like Alex."

"You sound bored, Sylvie," said Laurie. "Where's the enthusiasm, the excitement, the challenge?"

Sylvianne looked very serious for a moment, and then she said, "I've got it—I'll become a flamenco dancer and compete all over the world!" She jumped up and launched into a faux flamenco routine with arms raised, snapping her fingers, clapping her hands, stomping her feet, flinging her hair around, and scowling fiercely.

They had a good laugh, and Guy said, "You can start tomorrow night—I'm sure they'd welcome you at the brasserie in town. Those old guys will never know what hit 'em!"

None of them noticed Etienne passing in the shadows. He'd returned from dinner at his neighbors' and was just walking up the road as Sylvianne launched into her routine. He watched with amusement and then went in to bed.

"Good morning! How did you sleep, Sylvie?" asked Guy, as she came out to the patio with a cup of coffee.

"I got a good eight hours," she said, sitting down and picking up a croissant. "Unfortunately, it was only two hours at a stretch. But I'm resigned to jet lag—it gets worse the older you get, and you just have to live with it. What are we doing today?"

"I'd like to go into town and poke around, look in the shops," said Laurie. "Guy wants to try a couple of wineries, and there's a picturesque little village nearby where we could have lunch. How does that sound?"

"Perfect! I see you've already been in the pool. I'll swim a few laps and get ready to go."

An hour later the women took the five-minute drive into town, while Guy walked down the road about a mile in the other direction to a winery they had seen the day before.

Laurie and Sylvianne parked in a public lot at the edge of town and walked down the main street, looking into a number of little shops. There was the usual tourist fare: table linens and serving dishes in Provence designs, herbs, soaps, lotions, and potions. Tucked away on a side street they found a pottery, where the wares were made and sold. They chatted with the proprietor, Aron Agustyn, an immigrant from Poland. He was a big man, very outgoing and genial. On a whim, Sylvianne asked him if he gave pottery classes. He did, but usually in the winter when the trade was slow. However, if she was interested, he offered to find some time in the evenings. Would she like to come tonight at about eight o'clock for an hour or so? he asked. She agreed to return at eight.

"When did you get interested in pottery?" asked Laurie as they left the shop.

"I don't know if I really am interested," Sylvianne said. "But Susannah suggested I try something creative, so I thought I might as well try this since the opportunity presented itself. Maybe I won't enjoy it, but at least I'll try it out."

They bought groceries for aperitifs and dinner, and drove back to the gîte to pick up Guy. Then they drove to Le Crestet, parked in a lot at the edge of the village, and climbed up the narrow cobbled lanes to a restaurant that had a view of the valley below. They enjoyed lunch in the sunshine on the patio. Then it was back to the barn for swimming and reading by the pool.

"Goodness," Sylvianne said. "Etienne will be here in an hour, and we haven't got anything ready! I'll go get dressed and start setting things out."

"I've done my part," said Guy. "I've chilled the wine." He continued to read the thriller his sister had finished.

Etienne arrived at the appointed hour, and they all sat down around the patio table. Guy poured some of the local rosé and they sampled cheese, bread, and olives from the area.

"Tell us about your property, Etienne," Laurie said. "Have you been here long?"

"It's been in my family for over three hundred years," he said. "We lost some of it during the revolution, and then it's been divided up among heirs over the years, so there isn't as much as there was originally. My sister and I own this large parcel. Besides the vineyards, we have olive orchards and cherry orchards. You're welcome to pick the cherries that are left." He waved his hand in the direction of the cherry trees. "Most have already been harvested, but there are some on the trees at the top of the hill. We sell olive oil made from our olives. And the grapes go to a cooperative that sells them to vintners."

"It sounds like a lot of work. Do you have helpers?" asked Sylvianne.

"Yes, it is a lot of work at some times of the year, and I do have help. There is an immigrant family, from Algeria, who lives in a house on the property, and they help with all the farm work," he said. "But even with the pro-agriculture policies of the French government, it's not possible to make ends meet from farming. That's why I renovated the barn to make a rental unit. I have plans to build two more units. It's not easy—there are all kinds of rules about how new structures must look—they have to 'fit in' with the existing architecture, so that the area maintains its 'look' and appeal to tourists."

"Renting vacation units is very different from farming," Laurie said. "Do you enjoy it?"

"I'm getting used to it," he replied. "I expect to be more selective in my tenants as time goes on and I build up a clientele. And I do enjoy meeting some very interesting people. Like yourselves," he added graciously. "But my first love is farming. I like being close to the land, changing tasks with the seasons, trying new approaches to improve production." Laurie refilled his glass as he spoke. "It *is* hard work. You can't just take off when you might want to. But it's very rewarding."

They chatted for about an hour, covering such topics as local politics, how olives are pressed for oil, and why French men seem to be so taken with bicycling. Sylvianne asked about the tennis court behind the barn. Etienne replied that he played but didn't often have anyone to play with. Did she play? he asked. As a matter of fact she did. A date was made for a game at ten the next day, which would give him time to attend to some morning tasks, and would avoid the hot afternoon. He could loan her a racket.

After he left, they prepared a light dinner, and then Sylvianne drove to town for her pottery lesson.

"First, we must talk—or I must talk," Aron said. "I always start by telling my students that pottery is not just about producing something. It's about creativity and discipline. If you want something worthwhile, you must understand your materials and you must be committed to following through, to working hard. You must be aware of yourself, open to finding something new with the aid of this material, this clay. One teacher said, 'To find one's way with clay is to integrate one's inner search with one's outer practice.' You could develop very good technique, but what you produce will be dead if there is no 'you' in it. So! This may sound very philosophical right now, but as you progress, you will see what I mean. We'll start with pinching."

Soon Sylvianne was totally engrossed in taking her apple-sized ball of clay and turning it into a pot.

"Well, how was it?" asked Guy when she got back to the gîte. "Do you like getting all muddy?"

"I *did* like it," Sylvianne replied enthusiastically. "In fact, I'm surprised at how much I like it. First, it takes total concentration. You don't think about anything else. That's such a breath of fresh air—not to think about things that are habitually on your mind. Then there's the newness, all these things to learn. And once you've learned about something, you have a whole new appreciation of it. So now when I look at pottery, I'll have a better sense of what was involved and how challenging it was to make. And then there's the whole artistic element. I don't consider myself 'artistic,' but I can learn some of the basics. Susannah was right—doing something creative is really exciting! And Aron's an encouraging teacher. He's offered to let me practice in his studio during his working hours. I'm going back tomorrow night for another lesson. But right now I'm going to swim a few laps before bed."

While she slept better that night, Sylvianne was still awake at five the next morning. She dressed and made herself a big mug of coffee to take on a walk up the hill, stopping to watch the early morning sun spread over the valley, a patchwork of fields and orchards intersected by little one-lane roads, with the low mountains in the distance. Beautiful and quiet. The hill was steep, and she was warm from exertion by the time she reached the top and found the cherry orchard. She wandered among the trees, finding plenty of plump, sweet unpicked cherries. She ate some, and filled her empty coffee mug with as many as it would hold. Tomorrow, she thought, she'd bring a bowl.

As she walked back down the hill, she saw Etienne, apparently working on some machinery, perhaps some irrigation equipment, in what looked like a pump house. They waved to each other, and she continued back to the barn with her cherries. She had her yogurt-and-croissant breakfast at the patio table and wondered what she should wear to play tennis. She had plenty of tennis clothes at home, since she played at least twice a week, but she hadn't thought about the possibility of playing on this trip and so hadn't brought anything special. Shorts and a T-shirt would have to do. She did have a couple of terry-cloth visors, which she had brought as sun hats. She and Laurie wore the same size shoe, and Laurie had brought running shoes, so she could make do.

Around seven, Laurie came out in her swimsuit, yawning and carrying a mug of coffee. "Good morning, Sylvie. We'll have the pool to ourselves. Guy is still sleeping, since he stayed up late reading that book you gave him. Guess I'm going to have to read it too. Think I'll swim before breakfast."

They both swam and sat in the sun until Sylvianne went in to shower and dress for tennis. She appeared at the court at ten, dressed in white shorts, a pink T-shirt, white visor, sunglasses, and Laurie's shoes. Etienne showed up wearing faded Bermuda shorts and a white T-shirt, carrying his racket and a lightweight racket that was just right for her.

"How did you happen to have a racket of this size?" she asked. "It's far too light for you."

"I used to give lessons," he said. "So I have a few extras for new students to use until they decide if they want to buy their own."

"You lured me out here on false pretenses—giving me the impression you just played for fun. That's not fair!" she said with a smile. "I probably won't be able to keep up with you."

In fact, her years of lessons and regular practice made her a formidable opponent for someone who was good but out of practice. He won the first set—barely, and she won the second set—barely.

"I must stop now, or you'll win again!" he said. "You play tennis as well as you dance flamenco!"

"You weren't supposed to see that! I was just being silly," she laughed, but she was glad she had the excuse of the exertion of their game to cover her blush.

He smiled, but didn't tease her further, and they agreed to play again the day after tomorrow. "What are you doing with your time, besides reading and swimming?" he asked as they walked back toward the barn.

She told him enthusiastically about her pottery classes. "I haven't ever done anything like this before, and it's fascinating. I'm really looking forward to my next lesson.

....

Finally, a good night's sleep! After tennis and lots of swimming and ambling around the narrow local roads that ran through the fields, she had slept through the night and at last felt rested and energetic. As she lay by the pool, Sylvianne thought about her second pottery lesson the night before. Aron said that normally he would have a student pinch pots for several sessions before moving on to the wheel, but since she didn't have much time, she could start working on the wheel at her next lesson. Even pinching pots was very challenging, and she had to start over many times just to make a simple little four-inch pot. She was looking forward to learning about glazes, in hopes of having something that she could take home with her.

That afternoon Laurie and Guy took a tour of the wineries on the loop through Gigondas, Suzette, and Beaumes-de-Venise. Sylvianne stayed at the barn to swim, read, and think. She noticed that she didn't miss Alex at all. Did that mean that she didn't care about him anymore, or just that it was good to have the "spaces in their togetherness"? Probably the latter. Maybe he wasn't missing her either. Her thoughts wandered around, and then she noticed that she was thinking about Etienne—his tan arms and legs, his craggy weather-beaten face, his look of intense concentration during their tennis match.

Sylvianne found him attractive. She realized that she didn't usually notice that about men anymore. It might cross her mind that a man she passed was good-looking, but she didn't feel attraction. She missed that sexual energy, the electricity, the sense of aliveness. Where did it go? And wasn't it interesting that she didn't feel that way at all about Aron? Attraction was a mysterious thing.

She swam a few more laps and went in to shower. There was no hot water. She tried the kitchen sink and Laurie and Guy's shower—none there either. She'd have to go over to Etienne's and leave him a note, if he wasn't in. Hopefully, he could fix it, whatever it was. He wasn't in, so she left a note in the door where she thought he'd see it and went back to the barn. She'd had enough sun, so she put on one of the jazz CDs she'd brought and sat down to read. When that CD was over, she put on another. She was listening to "The Lady in Red" and dancing around the room, trying to remember how to do the nightclub two-step, when she noticed Etienne leaning against the doorframe, his toolbox in hand.

"Is there any kind of dance you don't do?" he asked, grinning at her. Before she could answer, he apologized about the hot water situation and said he thought he knew what the problem was. The water heater was in the laundry, and he set to work immediately. He came back into the living room about fifteen minutes later and said he thought it was fixed, but they'd have to wait for a while to see if the water actually heated up. She offered him a glass of wine while they waited.

They settled into their chairs, and he asked her if this was her CD. "Yes, I brought several with me, and a portable CD player. Jazz is my favorite kind of music, but I like the old rock and roll too."

"I like jazz too," he said. "Who are your favorites?"

"Oh, Dave Brubeck, Oscar Peterson, Ramsey Lewis, Jessica Williams—I obviously favor piano jazz. But I like other things too—Stéphane Grappelli, Pearl Django, really just about anything. Who are your favorites?"

"Miles Davis, John Coltrane, Monk—the classics." He paused and then said, "There's a concert in Avignon tomorrow night. It's a young pianist and his trio, very much in the style of Michel Petrucciani. Would you and Laurie and Guy like to go?"

"What a wonderful idea! I'd certainly like to go, and I think they'd enjoy it too. Is it too late to get tickets?"

"I'll call and find out if there are tickets and what time it starts," he said. "I'll come back later this evening to let you know. And now I must check the hot water." He went to the sink and turned on the hot water faucet.

"Good—my repair has worked, and your hot water will soon be back to normal. Again, my apologies for the inconvenience."

When Laurie and Guy returned, bearing a case of wine from various wineries, Sylvianne told them about Etienne's suggestion. As she expected, they were definitely interested. They had dinner and adjourned to the patio to try the newly bought Beaumes-de-Venise after-dinner wine.

Etienne was invited to join them when he came to bring the concert news. "Alas, only two tickets left. I reserved them. So we have various possibilities. Two of us can go to the concert, and two forgo the trip to Avignon. Or all four of us can go to Avignon and two go to the concert and two go out for dinner or a movie. What do you think?"

There was much discussion. Finally, Laurie said "This is way too complicated! Sylvie and Etienne should go to the concert, since they're the jazz buffs. We can hear good jazz in Paris anytime."

So it was settled. Etienne looked pleased with the outcome.

....

The next day when they met for their tennis game, Etienne said, "If I win, you must be my guest for dinner tomorrow night."

"And if I win, you have to let me pay," she responded. It was all she could think of on the spur of the moment. Something was going on here, something more than a tennis game. One way or another she was going to be alone two evenings in a row with a man she found very attractive, and who might feel the same way about her.

They had played hard during their first match, but not like this. She hadn't felt that he was holding back before, but now he was definitely determined to win. Still, she kept up with him. When they reached the third set, they had each won one of the previous two. "Prepare to lose!" he taunted with a grin and a wicked serve. She lost—just barely.

"My God, you don't have to *kill* me to pay for my dinner!" she panted.

"I was taking no chances," he laughed. "Thank you for a very challenging match. I'll come for you at seven this evening." They shook hands and she walked back to the barn, aware that he was standing on the court, watching her leave.

....

Etienne had not been so attracted to a woman for years. He liked her ability to be silly, her directness, her competitiveness. Yet she wasn't pushy. She seemed very balanced. And, of course, very beautiful. It had taken all his concentration to win the tennis match and not be distracted by her fit and sweaty body in shorts and a sleeveless shirt.

He'd had a few short affairs, and some one-night stands, but no one had come along that he could think about spending a long time with—until now. And she was married. But, he reasoned, she wouldn't be here alone if there wasn't something wrong in the marriage. So maybe there was a chance.

....

Sylvianne kicked off Laurie's shoes and dropped right into the pool in her tennis clothes, she was so hot and tired. "Looks like Etienne wore you out," laughed her brother from his pool chair.

"Oh, this feels so good! I'm never going to get out," she announced, grabbing a blow-up lounge chair that was resting against the side of the pool. She bobbed around the pool, looking at the clouds and bougainvillea and grapevines, wondering what she was getting herself into.

Later she and Laurie drove into town to buy groceries. Hands on the steering wheel, Laurie glanced at Sylvianne and said, "You know he's after you, don't you?"

Sylvianne sighed. "Yes, I guess so," she said. "I don't know what to do. I don't want to appear prudish, but I *am* a married woman who loves her husband."

"I think it would be good for you, and indirectly good for Alex, if you had a fling, Sylvie. It doesn't mean you don't love Alex, it just means that you find other men attractive and they find you attractive. So why not?"

"Laurie, are you encouraging me to be an adulteress?"

"Well, I wouldn't use that word. Don't you feel more alive now than you've felt in years? Tell me the truth!"

"Yes, I have to confess I do," Sylvianne replied. "Is that just because some guy thinks I'm cute? I feel so stupid about all this."

"It's the contrast between the French and American mores, I think," said Laurie. "You're more American than French now." After a moment, she went on. "Sylvie, Guy and I have both had little affairs now and then over our twenty years together. But they haven't threatened our marriage. We have fun together, we care about each other and have the same values, we're committed to the children's welfare—none of that changes because we've slept with someone else occasionally. In fact, these little affairs make life spicier in a way. Each of us knows that the other is attractive to other people. It kind of keeps us from taking each other for granted. If we were insecure about our relationship, these affairs would probably break us up."

"Do you think I'm insecure about my relationship with Alex?"

"I don't know. Only you can answer that for sure. I think you're bored and you need to rethink what matters to you. That's what you're doing here, isn't it? And if so, then Etienne will help you sort that out."

"I don't know," Sylvianne responded. "Being around Etienne doesn't encourage clear thinking on my part. And I don't think what he's interested in is clear thinking."

"Neither do I," laughed Laurie. "But whatever you decide, have a good time, Sylvie. Get something valuable out of this experience."

....

As she was swimming her afternoon laps, Sylvianne dithered about what to wear that evening. Should she dress down or up? She only had two dresses, so she'd have to wear one tonight and the other for dinner tomorrow—unless she wore pants one night. Or she could buy something new in town tomorrow to wear to dinner. This was ridiculous—she was just going to a jazz performance. It was no big deal!

Etienne looked both casual and elegant in navy cotton slacks and a polo shirt when he came to get her. She thought she would be OK in her white cropped pants, scoop-neck yellow top, wedge espadrilles, and dangling earrings. Off they went, waving good-bye to Guy and Laurie, who were on their way to town for dinner.

"So, you had a difficult day today—tennis, pottery, and swimming," he said as they pulled out of the driveway. "How is the pottery going?"

"I like it more than I thought I would," she said. "Who would have thought getting dirty would be so much fun." She went on to tell him about the stimulation of doing something new, something creative, something requiring concentration. "Today I was experimenting with glazes and exterior finishes. I was paralyzed!" she laughed. "There're all these choices. What should I use? What would look good? Aron said just do something, anything, and then something would happen. So I did. I was pressing leaves into the little tiles I made to experiment with—and seed pods, rope, whatever was at hand. Most of it I wadded up and set aside to reuse. But gradually, I found some things I liked, and then some other ideas came to me, and I tried those, and before I knew it, two hours had gone by."

She asked Etienne about his day.

"I was also having fun getting dirty. Ahmed and I worked on the irrigation system for the landscaping. Not as creative as pottery, I'm afraid. But it was satisfying to figure out the problem and get it repaired."

They chatted during the hour's drive about how he'd figured out that it could be financially worthwhile to get into the rental business, and what she liked about tutoring, the differences in the French and American educational approaches, and soon they were in Avignon. As they were walking into the cabaret, she felt more comfortable; she realized she had been worrying for no reason.

The trio was very good, playing a mix of jazz standards and their own tunes, written mostly by the pianist. As they sipped the champagne Etienne had ordered and enjoyed the music, Sylvianne felt more and more relaxed. It was a small club with a small dance floor, and about half the people were dancing. If he asked her to dance, she thought she could manage it—though it had been a long time since she'd been out dancing. He did ask her, and they did a kind of swing thing to an upbeat tune on the crowded floor. Then the band switched to a slow ballad, "When I Fall in Love." A piece that slow can't be danced to, she thought; people just kind of ooze around the floor. It was a perfect excuse to hold someone close, which Etienne did. Sylvianne was feeling all sorts of things: desired, worried, turned-on, disloyal. She remembered Laurie's words: "Have a good time." They were just dancing; she wasn't getting in bed with him.

"Maybe they'll play flamenco next," Etienne said into her hair. "Are you ready to get up on a table and show us how it's done?"

"You aren't going to let me forget that foolishness, are you?"

"I thoroughly enjoyed watching your flamenco routine, and watching you dance around the house while waiting for the repairman, and watching you play tennis. It's a great pleasure to watch you."

She didn't answer him, but when the song ended she said, "Etienne, all of a sudden the sun and swimming and that tennis punishment you gave me this morning are catching up with me. Would you mind if we went back now?"

"Not at all," he said, smiling. "Let's go."

They didn't talk a lot on the way back, but it was a comfortable silence. They pulled up in front of the barn, and he got out and opened the car door for her. She extended her hand and said, "This was a wonderful evening, Etienne. I really enjoyed it. Thank you."

He took her hand and kissed it. "I, too, enjoyed it. Thank you for going with me. I look forward to dinner tomorrow evening."

....

It was their last day at the gîte. They were leaving tomorrow for two days in Nice and vicinity to take in the Chagall museum and the Picasso museum.

Sylvianne enjoyed her morning in Aron's pottery, continuing her experiments with surface designs. When she was ready to leave, she waited for Aron to be free of customers so she could say good-bye.

"Thank you so much, Aron, for giving me a huge amount of your time. You're a very fine teacher, and you've inspired me to take up pottery. I'll find a place to continue learning when I get home."

"It was my pleasure, Sylvianne. You're a promising potter, and I encourage you to keep at it. I was wondering if you'd like to join me for a farewell dinner this evening."

"Oh, what a nice invitation!" she responded, smiling at him. "I'm sorry, though. I'll have to decline. I already have an engagement. Thanks again, Aron. Good-bye."

He looked surprised and disappointed, but shook hands with her and she left.

After lunch she spent the afternoon going back and forth between reading her book and swimming laps, trying to dispel the butterflies about her coming dinner with Etienne. Guy and Laurie acted as if everything were perfectly normal. They were going out to dinner at a country inn they'd heard good things about.

....

"What is she going to do, do you think?" Guy asked Laurie when Sylvianne had gone in to shower and change. "Etienne is a gentleman, but he's clearly smitten, and I think she's going to have a hard time turning him down. Especially since she seems to be attracted to him too."

"It's like a novel," Laurie said. "Will the heroine stay true to her husband, or fall for the dashing lover? And will she regret whatever decision she makes? I guess we'll find out sooner or later."

"Personally, I think she can stay with Alex and have Etienne too," Guy said. "There's no way she's going to leave Alex. And he doesn't ever need to know if she has a fling with Etienne. We're certainly not going to tell."

"That's what I told her. If she feels their marriage is strong, this is not going to make a difference. But these Americans look at things differently, you know. You're not the standard American, Guy," she said, smiling at her husband. They too went in to get dressed for dinner.

Just before seven, Sylvianne knocked on their bedroom door, seeking reassurance. "Does this look OK? Am I too dressed up, or does this look too 'come hithery'?" she asked. "I saw dozens of dresses like this in the village shops."

They both laughed and said she looked fine, perfectly appropriate. She was wearing a knee-length strapless sheath, made informal by the white cotton fabric and the black-and-white polka-dot sash around the waist. It showed off her tan, her legs, and her shiny dark hair.

....

Etienne was surprised to feel the lurch in his stomach when she met him at the door. He thought feelings like that were long behind him. She was beautiful, and he knew he had an effect on her, and she was his for what he hoped would be a long evening.

Although they conversed easily, he could tell that she was a little tense. He ordered a sparkling wine, and they perused the menu. This was his favorite local restaurant, and he pointed out the dishes that they did particularly well. The wine had its effect, and Sylvianne seemed to relax. As they ate the brie en croute, the trout with sautéed chanterelles, the rack of lamb with risotto, and the cassis gelato, they told each other stories of their childhood, recounted funny and embarrassing incidents, and laughed a lot. He told her about being the black sheep of a well-to-do family, dropping out of college, joining the army, eventually coming to run what was left of the family farm.

....

On his way back from the restroom, Etienne was stopped by Paulette, who had waited on him for many years and was also a friend. She had been watching all this with great interest. "I've never seen you like this with other women. Where's that reserve you're so famous for?" she teased. "The English couple at table two asked me if you were movie stars."

He just smiled and walked back to their table.

They certainly looked it, Sylvianne in her casual chic white dress and Etienne in black slacks and a snowy-white cotton shirt, open at the neck, with sleeves rolled up to the elbows. Both of them were tan and fit and elegant—a handsome couple.

....

"Sylvianne, why are you here without your husband? Are there problems?" Etienne asked.

She was startled, but she smiled. "He has no problems, as far as I know," she said. "But for the past few months I've been feeling . . . something. I don't know what. We're well matched in so many ways. We have what anyone would describe as a very good marriage, and we love each other." She held his eyes and said, "I can't imagine leaving Alex." She looked down and smoothed her napkin. "So the reason I came on this trip was to be away from him for a while, and try to sort out what I was feeling."

"Have you sorted it out?" he asked.

She leaned back in her chair and sighed, her eyes moving around the courtyard as she spoke. "No, not completely.

And I think it will probably take some time after I'm back home before I know what I've learned from being here. You know how it is—sometimes things just whir around in your subconscious, and then one day a thought or insight or understanding pops out. And you get it—things fall into place. At least that's been my experience, and I'm hoping that's what will happen again. I'm trying to force it, in a way, by getting out of my routine, trying new things, like travel and pottery." She glanced at him. He was regarding her intently.

She looked around and noticed that all the tables were empty. "Goodness, it's ten thirty—we should go so our waitress can go home!"

They drove back to the barn with the windows open, enjoying the balmy air. When they got back, he asked her if she'd like to go for a stroll down the road. They walked for a few minutes, enjoying the moon and stars and the noise of the cicadas. Then she tripped in the gravel and his arms were instantly around her. He kissed her, and she couldn't help herself—she kissed him back. One hand around her waist held her tightly to him, and the other moved slowly up her back, across her bare skin to her neck, and tangled her hair. She was breathless.

"Stay with me tonight, Sylvie. I want to make love to you." He kissed her again.

She pulled away a little, took a raggedy breath and said shakily, "I want to Etienne. I want to, but I can't. Let's go back." He reluctantly let her go, and they walked back toward the barn.

He stopped beside the car and pulled her to him again. "Tell me why, Sylvie," he said softly. "Admit there's something special between us. Why can't we have this one night together?"

She kept her face pressed against his shirt so he couldn't kiss her again. He was almost irresistible, and her resolve was in shreds. "Yes, there is something special. I admit it. I can hardly think when you're so close. But I'm married, Etienne. I love my husband, and I'm not going to leave him."

"Your husband doesn't need to know about this. How would he find out? Guy and Laurie would never say anything, and they wouldn't disapprove either. And even if Alex knew, would he think it was so bad that another man made love to you?"

"If Alex were French, probably not. But he's not French. I think he'd feel like he'd failed me somehow if I wanted another man, and that I'd failed him by not sticking to my promise to 'forsake all others.' Even if he never found out, I'd know. I'd know that I'd done something that could hurt him a great deal." She pushed away from him. "Etienne, have you ever been married?"

"Yes."

"What happened?"

A pause and then, "She left me for another man."

Sylvianne knew she'd won the argument.

"I've never felt about another man the way I feel about you, Etienne. I love Alex, but it's different. It's very hard for me to say no to you. With you it wouldn't be just having sex, it would be more like making love. But I have too much to lose."

He continued to hold her, but his arms loosened. After a few minutes, he held her at arm's length. "God, I hate to lose to you!" he said. And then, "Adieu." He kissed her gently and left.

She went to bed and cried herself to sleep.

They were packed and ready to go by ten the next morning. As they were loading the car, Sylvianne found a CD on the backseat. It was a recording made by the group she and Etienne had heard two nights before, including the tunes they had danced to. She held back the tears and tucked it into her suitcase.

She tried her best to enjoy Nice and the museums, but

her heart wasn't in it. Guy and Laurie didn't press her; she knew they felt bad. But there was nothing anyone could do or say.

It was a relief to get on the plane after their hugs and farewells were done. The transfer in London was uneventful, and then she was beginning her nine-hour flight to Seattle.

She went round and round in her head. Why had this happened to her? What had actually happened? Should she tell Alex? What would she tell him? She had no answers. And underneath all these questions was an aching sadness.

....

Alex was waiting for her at the baggage claim carousel. There he was—the blond hair, blue eyes, charming smile, familiar aftershave, father of her sons, the man she had married over twenty years ago. He brought her roses. She put her arms around his neck and rested her face on his shoulder. "How's my contessa?" he asked.

"I'm exhausted. And I'm glad to be back to you. I'll give you a full report when I'm back to normal. Right now I just want to go home," she said with a wan smile, wondering to herself if she would ever be back to "normal" again.

Alex sensed that she was more than exhausted, but also that she wasn't ready to talk about whatever it was. So he provided small talk on the way home. The boys would come over for dinner Friday night to hear about her trip. They were taking finals this week, before summer break.

Sylvianne roused herself to ask about the results of Alex's big meeting, the one that had prevented his coming with her to France. He said it had gone well, the project was moving into the next phase, and the investors were pleased.

When they got home, Alex suggested a little walk. "They say it's good for coping with jet lag." So they went out into the sunny afternoon, hand in hand, and walked a few blocks through the neighborhood. On their return, Sylvianne had a big glass of water and lay down for a nap.

She slept for a few hours, and after they had a light dinner, she unpacked and began her laundry; then she was ready for bed again. She tossed and turned and dozed, and tossed some more, finally getting up at about six in the morning to make coffee. Alex came down an hour later, kissed her, and left for the office.

....

Susannah came in the back door midmorning. "Hello," she called. "Anyone home?"

Sylvianne came up from the laundry room and gave her a big hug.

"How are you, Sylvie? You look pretty tired."

Sylvianne burst into tears, and Susannah enfolded her daughter-in-law in a hug. "Do you just need a hug, or do you want to tell me about it?"

"I think you're the only person I can tell," Sylvianne said between sobs. "I was almost unfaithful to Alex, and I wanted to be."

"I'll make some tea, and we can sit on the couch and talk. I think you'd better tell me the whole story, beginning to end." When they settled down on the couch with their tea, Sylvianne told Susannah about Etienne, her first impression of him, their tennis games, the jazz concert, the dinner, and its outcome. She tried to explain how she felt about him, how he made her feel, why she turned him down, and how unhappy that had made her. Susannah listened intently.

"Do you think I did the right thing?" she asked Susannah tearfully.

"I honestly don't know, Sylvie," she replied. "This was a big decision, and there were lots of pros and cons either way you chose. It's no small thing to give up something like that—my heart goes out to you. But I also know you love Alex, and you made a decision not to do something that could hurt him. Maybe it wouldn't have affected your marriage negatively, but you didn't know that. And if Etienne is a good man, he'll respect you for that."

"Why did this happen, Susannah? I know you can't answer that, but that's what I keep asking myself."

"Ah, one of life's big questions, right? 'Why did this happen?' In my experience it usually takes a while before a person figures it out. Maybe it will take weeks or months or years. But I really think it's important to ask the question, Sylvie. For something this big, you have to keep asking yourself why. Maybe you and Etienne had some karma together, something that needed to be resolved. Maybe in time this experience will bring you and Alex closer together. Maybe you'll be open to life in a way you haven't been before." She patted Sylvie's hand.

"But I don't think you should characterize this experience in terms of wanting to be unfaithful. Acknowledge that you and Etienne were really attracted to each other, that such attractions are beautiful things, that you had something wonderful for a short time. Maybe your life will be the better for it, but it may be awhile before you see how."

"Should I tell Alex?"

"You're the only one who can make that decision, my dear. But you don't have to decide in a hurry. Give yourself some time."

By Friday night when the boys came over for dinner, she had pretty much recovered from her jet lag. She made them pizza from scratch, a perennial favorite, accompanied by green salad and washed down with beer. In between telling their parents about finishing the school year, doing huge loads of laundry, and talk of moving home for the summer, they asked her about her trip. She told them about the place where they stayed and her pottery lessons, and she got out her camera so they could look at the few photos she had taken.

"Guy and Laurie look good," commented Paul. "Looks like a cool place to stay. Hey, Mom, who's this guy?"

Her heart lurched when she looked at the photo. Alex came to look over their shoulders.

"Oh, that's our host, Etienne. I didn't take these pictures. Guy or Laurie must have. I played tennis with him a couple of times. He's pretty good."

"Well, you're pretty good, Mom. Did you win or lose?" asked Drew.

"We tied one match, and he won the other—barely. Would anyone like more pizza, or shall I get out the ice cream?"

As dinner went on, Sylvianne thought Alex was quieter than he usually was when the boys were around. After transferring several loads from the dryer to laundry baskets, the boys went out bowling with some friends.

"Thanks for dinner, Mom. Nobody's pizza is better than yours. Glad you're back safely," said Paul, on his way out the door.

"Yeah, glad you had a good time, Mom. We'll be back late," said Drew, kissing her on the cheek as he followed his brother out.

"I know they love us, but do you think they'll ever think of us as people rather than as roles? What did they used to call us?" Sylvianne asked. "'Parental units'—that was it."

"Is there something I missed?" Alex asked. "Did you really not have a good time?"

"No, no. I had a good time. It's just that sometimes I think they take us for granted. But I'm sure I did the same thing with my parents. Maybe you can't really appreciate parents as people until you're at least into your thirties or forties."

After she and Alex finished cleaning up the dinner dishes, he poured himself another glass of wine and sat down on the living room couch with a magazine. She curled up beside him with the book she hadn't finished on the plane trip home.

"So," he said after a moment, still looking down, "did something happen between you and this Etienne guy?"

She sat for a while, trying to decide what to say. Her fingers ran absently up and down the book. She glanced at his guarded face. "We played tennis, and went to a jazz concert and out to dinner. He wanted me to sleep with him, and I said no."

"So that was it?"

"He kissed me."

"Did you kiss him back?"

"Yes."

"Did you want to go to bed with him?"

"Yes. But I didn't, Alex. Because I love you and I didn't think . . . that would be OK with you."

"Well, you got that right. I'm going for a walk."

....

Their sons moved home for the summer and started their jobs. Paul was lifeguarding, and Drew worked as a laborer for a landscaper. Sylvianne had time for some house projects that she couldn't get to during the school year. Alex was as busy as ever, and unfailingly polite but withdrawn.

One morning before he left for work, Drew said to his mother, "Hey, Mom, is something wrong with Dad? He seems kind of preoccupied or something."

She'd been wondering if the guys would notice, and what she'd say if they brought it up. "I'm not sure," she said, "but I've noticed it too. I'm sure he'll tell us when he's ready, or he'll work it out, whatever it is."

"Yeah, well, it's kind of weird. He gets really involved in work sometimes, but this seems a little different. See you tonight—my shovel is calling."

That night after dinner, Alex asked her to sit on the couch with him and talk. "I guess I need to know more about what happened in France. I'm imagining all kinds of things, and I'm shocked and jealous, and—all over the place."

"Alex, I didn't sleep with anyone else while I was gone. I'm not even sure I fell in love. I was really attracted to

Etienne. I've never been that attracted to a man, except for you." She considered her words carefully. "He wanted to make love to me. I said no, and I will tell you truthfully that it was very hard to say no. But I told him I couldn't do something that might hurt you. I owe you too much, and I love you too much."

He thought about what she'd said and then summarized. "So you gave up something that really mattered to you for me?"

She in turn thought about his question and answered, "Yes, I suppose you could think of it that way. It was for us, really. I didn't want to do something that would jeopardize what we have together." She met his eyes and then looked away. "I'm sorry you found out—even though it was nothing—because it seems like I've hurt your feelings. That's what I was trying to avoid."

"I guess it doesn't seem like 'nothing.'"

"Oh, Alex, for heaven's sake! I've seen you look at other women—don't pretend that you haven't wondered what it would be like to sleep with someone else. The point is, you haven't—at least I assume you haven't, and I trust that you haven't. Isn't that what matters?"

It was a moment before he replied. "I'm not sure that's all that matters," he said.

He left her on the couch, with tears in her eyes.

....

Alex stopped in at Susannah and Will's house on his way home the next evening.

"Oh, hi, Alex," Susannah said. "Come in. What a nice surprise. Do you have a few minutes for a glass of wine?"

"That would be great, Mom." He followed her to the kitchen. "Mom, did Sylvianne talk to you about the guy she met in Provence?"

Susannah got out two glasses and poured some wine. "Yes, she did," she said, handing him his glass. "She wondered if she should tell you about it, and how you'd react. She was very upset about the whole thing. How *are* you reacting?"

"I feel ridiculous. She told me she didn't sleep with him, and I believe her, but why do I feel betrayed and jealous and guilty and angry? I just can't believe something like this happened."

"What do you think happened?"

"My wife fell in love with somebody else!"

"Is that what she said?"

He thought for a moment. "I think what she said was she didn't know if she fell in love." He paused. "And she did say that the reason she didn't sleep with him was because she loved me."

"So whatever she felt for him, she didn't sleep with him and she loves you. So what are you upset about? That another man was attracted to your wife? You must see that all the time—she's beautiful. But you mentioned feeling guilty. What did you mean by that?"

Alex studied his wineglass, then looked up at the ceiling. "I guess maybe I'm feeling guilty that I've taken her for granted, and I'm angry at myself and taking it out on her."

"Well, my son, I think that's pretty insightful. You two are lucky to have each other."

....

After dinner that night, the boys left with friends for a movie, and Alex sat down beside Sylvianne in the living room. "You know what I've decided?" he said.

"What?" she asked warily.

"That I've been taking you for granted. You know I love you, and I know you love me, but I didn't really appreciate how much you mean to me until this Etienne thing came up. While you were gone, I missed being able to tell you about the big meeting and getting your reaction. I realized how much I depend on your insights and judgment.

"And since you've come home, I've been thinking about, if I didn't have you, how much I'd miss your silliness. Like when we play charades. You can be so funny sometimes—you just have everyone in stitches. I'd miss taking you places and watching other men notice you, and feeling so lucky that you're with me. I'd miss how you wear your clothes and your perfume, and your body in bed beside me. I'd miss making love with you. He pulled her up from the couch. "And that's what I want right now! Come to bed with me."

His attention was wholly focused on her; he wasn't half thinking of something else, as sometimes happened when sex had become a little too routine. He was in no hurry as he undressed her, kissed her, and touched her in the ways he knew turned her on. There was a new intensity in his lovemaking.

Later they lay damp and spent and content in each other's arms.

"Sylvie?"

"Mmm . . ."

He brushed the hair off her forehead, kissed her and said, "I love you, and I don't want to lose you. You're the best thing in my life, contessa—you and the boys—and I'll do whatever it takes to keep you happy."

They were quiet, together but immersed in their own thoughts, until they drifted off to sleep.

....

Sylvianne's birthday was two weeks after she returned from France. Alex, their sons, and Susannah and Will took her out to dinner at her favorite Italian restaurant. They ordered, and then Alex produced an envelope and handed it to her. "Happy birthday, darling," he said. She opened it and found a gift certificate for a series of lessons at a highly regarded local pottery.

"I've been wondering how to get started up again—this is perfect! Thanks so much, Alex."

"Drew and I got you twenty-five pounds of clay, but we didn't think we needed to bring it to the restaurant," Paul told her with a grin. "It's hidden on the back porch."

Susannah produced a bookish-looking package, beautifully wrapped. Sylvianne opened it to find a history of ceramics, with full-color photos.

"What a wonderful family I have. Thank you all so much!" She got up and went around the table, kissing each one of them.

The next day Sylvianne stopped at her mother-in-law's. "Susannah, I just wanted you to know that I think Alex and I have gotten through our 'difficulty' or whatever it was. I think we're closer now, and less likely to take each other for granted. So I guess that's one reason the whole thing happened—if the universe sets these things up. Maybe the question isn't 'Why did it happen?' but 'What's the outcome?' And the outcome has certainly been positive, at least for Alex and me."

They talked about other family matters and planned a trip to the art museum the following week. Then Sylvianne left to do her grocery shopping. Without thinking about it, she found herself in front of the French cheeses and then later in front of the French bread. And when she got to the wine, she gravitated toward the Rhône rosés. She pondered these things in her heart.

CHAPTER NINE

The Borders of Reality

It's important to maintain balance, Susannah thought, to live each day fully, not too much in the future—there wasn't much of that left anyway—and just enough in the past to be as clear about it as possible. She walked slowly and carefully into the sunny dining room at the adult family home where she lived. The other four residents were already seated, waiting for Azime to serve. "Good morning, everyone," Susannah said. "Good morning, Azime. What a lovely scarf you're wearing today." She always had a special word for Azime, her favorite of the staff. A shy smile came from Azime, with greetings and mumbles from the other residents, as they were able.

After breakfast, Susannah stopped in the living room. The single-family home in the Leschi neighborhood faced east, catching the morning sun. Most of the rooms enjoyed a view of the lake and the Cascades. She had insisted on finding a living arrangement that would not burden her son and daughter-in-law; Sylvianne had done an exhaustive search to find this place, and everyone in the family was happy with it. The furnishings were tasteful, the food was good, it was always immaculate, and the staff was experienced and kind. Most of these amenities mattered more to the residents' families than to the residents themselves, who were not always capable of appreciating their surroundings. The families' acknowledged and unacknowledged grief, anger, and sense of loss around their loves ones' condition was assuaged by the home's pleasant appearance and high level of caregiving.

Susannah sat in the sunshine in front of the full-length windows and enjoyed the view. A vase of early daffodils stood on the table beside her. She was looking forward to an outing with her eldest grandson, Paul, whom she hadn't seen for several weeks. This afternoon he was going to take her for a walk along Lake Washington Boulevard, and it looked as though they would have a beautiful day.

When Paul arrived, she was ready, bundled up in a heavy wool coat and her ancient fur hat, holding gloves, a scarf, and a lap robe. Paul settled her in the car, buckled her in, and put her lightweight wheelchair in the trunk.

"This is such a treat for me, Paul," Susannah said, laying a hand on his arm. "Thanks for coming. Now tell me about school."

He was doing his PhD in environmental sciences at the University of Washington, and he talked about his teaching assistant duties, progress on his dissertation, and his chance meeting on campus with a high school girlfriend he hadn't seen for years. Susannah thought she detected in his tone a little note of something special about this encounter. They parked at the Mount Baker boathouse. Paul got her settled in her wheelchair, wrapped her robe and scarf around her, and they started off north, toward Mount Baker Beach.

"Paul, tell me what you're going to say at my memorial service."

"Jeez, Grams—you're not dead yet! Why would I want to think about that? You're going to live a lot longer."

"Well, maybe, my dear, but that's not the point. I'm not fishing for compliments. I just want to know what's special to you about our relationship. And I don't want you to have regrets about things you wish you'd told me and didn't, before it's too late. See how controlling your grandmother is?" she added, laughing.

"I don't know about controlling, but I've noticed you usually manage to get what you want, Grams. Anyway, let me think."

He was quiet for a few minutes, pushing her along the lake in the early spring sunshine.

"I'd want to talk about baking cookies with you. The kind you squeeze out of that press thing. We'd make camels and Christmas trees, and I got to shake that sprinkly stuff on them."

"Yes," she laughed. "We had sprinkles all over the kitchen floor."

"And I'd talk about your getting the rabbit for us, without telling Mom and Dad. It was so neat—there he was on the porch one morning in his cage, with his kitty-litter box and food and water bottle. Drew and I were so excited. There was no way Mom and Dad could get out of that! They did tell us that we'd have to help take care of him or they'd give him away, and I think we did OK, for kids our age."

"Well, your father had dogs and gerbils and ducks," Susannah said, "so I thought you should have a pet, even though it was one more thing for them to manage in a busy life."

"Yeah, we loved that rabbit. Good old Lippety," Paul said. He stopped to tuck in the lap robe, which was slipping off her knees. "And I think I would talk about your words of wisdom when I broke up with my first girlfriend in high school. I remember you said you thought I was so upset not just because I was hurt and angry and I missed her, but also because I was maybe afraid that I'd never have a love that strong again. I thought about that a lot. I still missed her, but I didn't feel quite so desperate.

"I could go on and on, but since I just saw Gina, I'll mention one other memory. Remember when you took her shopping for her prom dress, and I got called in to make the final decision? That was a hoot, being the only guy is the dress shop with all those women."

"Thank you, Paul," Susannah said. She turned in her chair to look up at him. "I'll treasure those words along with all the other wonderful memories I have of you."

"I'm going to warn Drew he'd better get busy on his list!"

They had turned around and were almost back to the boathouse, where they could see the kids putting their boats in the water for the after-school rowing program. They stopped to watch. The boys' eight pulled away from the dock and turned, heading north. She pointed out to Paul two of the boys who were slumping and how that would affect their rowing. Then a girls' four left the dock and turned. She explained that, generally, the shorter the boat was, the tippier it was, and that having two oars per person, sculling, was less tippy than one oar per person. The girls had one oar each. "Look at that," Susannah exclaimed. "Straight backs, perfect timing—all four oars going in and out at the same time, no wobbling from side to side. They must be varsity. What a pleasure to watch!"

"How long did you row, Grams?" Paul asked as they neared the car.

"Over twenty-five years, I think. I started when I was fifty, and I was so proud of myself. I'd never done anything physical except hike and ride my bike. No sports. I enjoyed it so much."

Paul helped her into the car, folded up her chair, and put it in the trunk. They stopped at Starbucks, and she treated him to a latte and a brownie. Then he drove her home.

"I'll be your chauffeur on Sunday. I'll pick you up at one," he said after depositing her at her door. "You know, Grams, he said as he kissed her good-bye, "every time I smell Shalimar, I think of you—and I always will."

....

Susannah had asked Alex and Sylvianne to host a birthday party for her at their house—her house for over thirty years. They all knew this might be her last such party. Susannah insisted on its being very simple, to cut down on the effort for them. It was to be just light hors d'oeuvres, cake, and champagne.

    After dinner she went through her closet full of things she no longer wore, and found the bright-blue silk dress she had worn at her stepson's wedding over fifteen years ago. It was dated, of course, but a classic style that would be just fine, and the color was flattering, with her blue-gray eyes. She would ask Azime to look it over and make sure it had no spots.

Susannah's life was peaceful, not boring, but she did look forward to variety now and then. She still meditated two hours a day, though she suspected that she often slept some of that time. She had a simple computer she used for e-mail and for research and writing her stories. *How easily we forget life before search engines,* she mused. She could still type, though her handwriting was rather cryptic. The time from nine to eleven most days was set aside for her writing. One of the staff members took her for a walk every day, weather permitting, and she did her chair exercises and tai chi. She was physically frail, but her mind was still alert.
    The next morning she sat in front of her computer, looking at her hands. There were ropy veins, fine wrinkles, and age spots; the skin was almost transparent. She remembered how she had initially reacted to the early signs of aging: the spider veins on her legs, the belly that would never be flat again, those age spots. It wasn't so much a fear of death as a sense of loss—that she'd never have a lover again, never again experience the erotic part of life. She and Will had been lucky to have that together, so late in their lives. And now she was glad, in a way, for all these markers of old age. *It won't be hard at all to leave this wrinkled, creaky, barely functioning body behind,* she thought. She hugged herself. *Good old body.* "Well done, thou good and faithful servant."
    There was a knock at Susannah's door. It was Bob Stanley, pastor of one of the residents, making his weekly call. They had become acquainted over the course of his visits.

"Hi. May I come in and chat for a few minutes?" he asked. "I've just been to see Iris."

"Please come in, Bob—I'd love to visit. As a matter of fact, I've been thinking about something I'd like to discuss with you. Sit right here." She patted a chair.

"Oh, good! You always bring up such interesting topics, Susannah. What is it today?" he asked, sitting down.

"Well, I've been thinking about how, for most of us, bad or negative things 'weigh' more than positive things. It doesn't matter whether it's thoughts, news, pictures, remarks, whatever. I've heard that it takes five positive comments to make up for one negative comment to your child or spouse. Maybe even to your dog—who knows? Anyway, what's the source of this phenomenon?"

Bob thought awhile and then said, "One thing that comes to mind is that negative things tend to get your attention. They have a sense of urgency. For example, a nightmare may call your attention to something you really need to deal with more directly than ordinary dreams would." He paused, looking out the window.

"Another thought is that most of us construct our sense of self from how others react to us. We depend on others to validate who we are. So something negative feels like invalidation—I'm not good enough, lovable enough, worthwhile enough, et cetera. That's pretty heavy."

"Yes, I see what you mean," Susannah replied. "And if we already feel fearful and fragile—even if it's unconscious—a negative remark seems more real. It matches how we feel about ourselves anyway. And compliments roll off us, no matter how sincere and accurate, because they don't seem to match how we feel deep inside. We don't feel praiseworthy."

"I was reading a book recently by a very highly trained brain researcher who had a massive stroke in her left brain," Bob said. "Fascinating story! Anyway, as I understood it, she said certain events will trigger emotional reactions in our brains and that it takes less than ninety seconds for one of these emotional programs to surge through our bodies chemically and be flushed out of our systems. So if we continue to have the emotion after ninety seconds, it's because we've chosen to let that program run. We could make a decision to let go of the emotion—we're capable of doing that. But most of us don't—we think we don't have any control over emotions." Bob crossed his legs and pulled at his ear.

"Oh, and I heard something else the other day that may be relevant to this topic," he said. "Some research says that eighty-five percent of the language children hear is 'corrective.' Even if not *all* corrective language is what you'd call 'negative,' a lot of it is 'Get your elbows off the table,' 'No, you can't play with Sammy,' 'You have to share your toys,' 'Be quiet,' et cetera. So much for five positives for every negative!"

They sat together, contemplating the "weight" of negativity. "This conversation is reminding me of something my meditation teacher told me long ago," Susannah said. "Something's negative because we define it that way. So it's really important to watch ourselves calling something bad—like something someone does that you don't like. Is the behavior really intrinsically bad, or is it just something you don't like, something that you're hung up about for your own reasons? My teacher said 'negative' things have a certain feel—constricted, tight, hard, weighed down. Whereas 'positive' things—like love, fun, laughter, peace—make you feel light, expansive, free, energetic. So, he reminded us to be aware of our feelings and check to see what we were defining as negative, and ask if it really was." Susannah sighed. "It's certainly depressing to think about a lifetime's worth of critical remarks and negative thoughts."

"You know better than to go down that road, Susannah," Bob said. "What's done is done. I know this sounds like a platitude, and it isn't easy to do, but you have to forgive yourself and others for "negative" thoughts and actions. And

I'll bet you're already doing that. I'll bet you're a lot less critical and negative now than you were when you were younger. Am I right?"

"Yes, I think that's true. I've learned *something* after all these years!"

....

The next day Susannah sat again in the sunny living room after breakfast. Her thoughts turned to her first marriage, which had lasted over thirty years. At the time, she had read a lot of books and articles, trying to understand her relationship and how to deal with marital problems. Her insights and thoughts about the marriage had changed over time, as both she and Dave changed. Sometimes it wasn't that they had changed; it was just that they'd figured out who they were, or how they were—things about themselves and each other that they hadn't known.

About twenty years into their marriage, it had become clear to both of them that they had probably married each other partly for the wrong reasons, reasons that weren't clear to them until later on. But it was also true that there were good reasons they married: They liked and respected each other. They had fun together. Their personalities were complementary. Their important values were similar.

She sifted through her memories of the good times. There was the evening in San Francisco, when he was wooing her. They went to a fancy French restaurant, and she had her first vodka gimlet, followed by coquilles Saint-Jacques, which she hadn't had since her first meal in France four years earlier. After a dinner that could only be described in superlatives, they saw a stunning performance by the Bolshoi Ballet. It was still so vivid in her mind. She was twenty-three.

During grad school when Dave came to visit, they'd go on hikes with her classmates and play Botticelli as they walked, one game sometimes lasting over an hour until the answer was discovered. Exercise, beautiful scenery, and stimulating conversation.

Later there were the camping trips in Eastern Washington with Max and Cathy and the kids. Lots of sun and food and games and waterskiing. On one trip the wind had fanned the campfire to the point that their roasting ears of corn were incinerated—but they ate them anyway. They had joked about it for years.

Dave put up with her when she fell into her "family of origin trance" during visits to her parents. All those years he made sandwiches for her to take to work and was her "blather absorber" when she came home from work still in type-A overdrive. She put up with him when he got depressed every Thanksgiving because of dammed-up grief at his father's death at that time of the year.

The metaphor of marriage as a crucible was a good one, she thought. Something new was formed out of the heat of the relationship—it was a prompt to personal growth and a way of avoiding self-centeredness. On what could they compromise? What was really nonnegotiable? And what could they give up and still keep the meaningful aspects of the relationship?

....

Susannah was savoring the anticipation of the coming party as much as she expected to enjoy the party itself. One of her brothers would be coming, since he lived in the area. Their other brother lived too far away and his health was too precarious to make the journey. They talked on the phone every week. All three of them were very close. She felt it was selfish, but she hoped she died before they did. She'd lost so many dear ones already, and her brothers were among the dearest left. She reminded herself that they wouldn't be totally lost to her; they'd just be together in another dimension. But however one looked at it, there would be some grief for the two of those left after the first one died.

She'd been thinking for a long time about how grief can

be lessened, having experienced her fair share. She believed that grief was natural and should be experienced, but asked herself where the line was between natural grief and suffering. Perhaps it has to do in part with going through the tasks of the dying, she thought. She'd read that before dying, one should forgive and ask forgiveness, say goodbye, and say "I love you" to one's loved ones. If the dying person doesn't do these tasks, the grief of the survivors may be more severe.

Susannah remembered the latter years of her parents' lives. Her mother, especially, seemed to have only a limited ability to appreciate her life, or to change in ways that would make her life more enjoyable. It had been so frustrating to see how unhappy her mother's life had been, when it didn't need to be that way. Susannah had vowed not to burden her family by living that way. She wanted them to be able to say "Grams had a good life, and she enjoyed it." That was one of the best things she could do for those she loved.

She was saying good-bye and "I love you" very consciously these days. The asking for forgiveness was harder. It was too late to ask some people, and she would always have to carry that sadness and regret. Perhaps some things couldn't be forgiven, or wouldn't be until after she was gone. Another measure of sadness and regret.

This melancholy train of thought was interrupted by Azime, who worked the overnight shift. She came around to check on all the residents at about ten at night and again at four in the morning. Most of the residents went to bed early, but Susannah was often awake when Azime did her ten o'clock rounds. They had fallen into a pattern of Susannah asking Azime to stay and chat a few minutes, so Azime put Susannah last on the list of residents to be checked. She sometimes stayed for up to an hour as they talked about many things—Azime's childhood in Turkey, conditions in her country, American customs, her plans for the future.

"Azime, I have something for you," Susannah said one evening after they had chatted for a while. She stood slowly and crossed the room to her jewelry box, removing a pair of delicate silver-and-brass earrings with semiprecious stones. "As you can see, these are from your country. They were a gift from my stepson, Derek. I think you know that he lived in Turkey for about a year while he was traveling and sorting himself out."

"Yes, we've talked about his time in Turkey," Azime said. "It makes me happy to hear how much he enjoyed it."

"It was an important experience. He fell in love with a Turkish girl, but the cultural differences were just too great for them to overcome. Anyway, he brought me these earrings when he came home, and I've enjoyed wearing them for many, many years. I want you to have them."

"I couldn't take these, Ms. Emory," Azime protested. "They are far too valuable and precious!"

"No, I insist, Azime! I have other jewelry to give the women and girls in my family, and Derek and Bridget have traveled to Turkey twice. Bridget has her own earrings from your wonderful country. I particularly wanted you to have these. They're special, and you're special. I appreciate your care for me."

"Thank you so much, Ms. Emory. I will treasure them always." She left the room and quietly closed the door.

....

Back at her customary place in front of the living room windows Friday morning, Susannah thought about the other guests who had been invited to her party: three or four friends from the old neighborhood where she had lived so many years; several of her meditation friends; one or two people she had rowed with long ago; and several lifelong friends. Family included her son and daughter-in-law, two grandsons, her brother, and Derek and his wife and their daughters. Some of them she might never see again. *Well, we'd better have a good time then!*

On Sunday, just after lunch, Paul picked her up, along with Azime.

"Oh, Sylvianne, the house looks so festive," Susannah said when she arrived at their home . "Thank you so much for doing this for me!"

"It is truly my pleasure, Susannah," said Sylvianne, smiling at her affectionately. "Do you have any other requests for your special day?"

"Just one, my dear. May I wear my engagement ring, just for the party?"

Sylvianne took from her finger the diamond ring Alex's father had given Susannah sixty-some years ago. Susannah had given it to Sylvianne when she moved into the adult family home. Susannah held out her left hand, and Sylvianne slipped the ring on next to the simple wedding band Will had given her. "Why don't you keep it, Susannah? With Azime to watch over you, it'll be safe."

"No, I want you to have it. I just wanted to wear it for this special occasion." She held out her hand and looked at the rings. "It's like having them here."

At two o'clock the guests began arriving. Susannah was delighted to see so many old friends and catch up on their lives. The house was filled with the murmur of conversation and the faint fragrance of the lilies Sylvianne had used in the flower arrangements.

Her stepson's willowy wife, Bridget, knelt beside her chair. "Susannah, I just want to tell you, before you're besieged with well-wishers, how much it's meant to me to be welcomed into your family. It's taken me a long time to work through the residue of my parents' . . . um . . . rigidity and disapproval, as you know. Your insights have been so helpful. I really think you're the reason I can still talk to them and care about them. You and Will and Derek—the whole family—have been so supportive." She gave Susannah a shy hug and slipped away through the guests.

About three o'clock Alex asked the guests to assemble in

the living room. Susannah wanted to say a few words. She sat in her unobtrusive wheelchair, in front of the west-facing windows. With her soft white hair and her electric-blue dress, she seemed to glow in the afternoon sunshine.

"Dearly beloved," she began, with a big smile on her face. "Isn't that a wonderful greeting? We should use it for lots more occasions than weddings!

"Anyway, dearly beloved, thank you *so* much for coming to my birthday party. You can imagine how special this is at my time of life. I may never see some of you again, so bear with me for just a few minutes." She got her handkerchief out of her pocket. "They say you have some tasks to perform before you die—"

"Grams, are you going to die?" a small voice said. It was Derek's five-year-old daughter, DeeDee, who was sitting at her feet. The room was very quiet.

Susannah laughed. "Of course I am," she said. "Sooner or later. We all die, DeeDee."

"But what does that mean, Grams?"

"Well, it's when your body stops working—no breath, no heartbeat, it just stops. It's hard to describe what happens next, because we all have different ideas about it. What I think is that it's like being in another place, DeeDee. I think it's a pretty nice place and people I love whose bodies have stopped working are there, but I don't know exactly what it will be like, so it's kind of exciting. But you know, DeeDee, you can't go there until you die, so you won't be able to visit me or anyone else who goes there for a long time. That's kind of sad—we'll miss each other—but it's OK, because you have a long life ahead of you and lots of neat things to do here." She ruffled the child's hair, then turned again to her guests.

"So as I was saying, there are some tasks I'd like to do before I die. One task is to forgive and ask forgiveness. That's best done in private, and I've been working on this painful yet usually rewarding task over the past year or so.

"Another task is to say good-bye. That's partly why I wanted to have this party." Tears were streaming down Azime's face, and Alex put his arm around her shoulders. Handkerchiefs were coming out of pockets and handbags.

"And the most important task—to say I love you. You, dear friends and family, along with many others who are not here, have made my life so rich and full. I love you!" She blew them a big kiss with both hands. "There. I've said my piece, and got through it without breaking down. Thank you for indulging me!" There were smiles, murmurs, and dabbing at eyes.

After a slight pause, her former neighbor, Walt, a sometime poet and master of witty remarks and bons mots, spoke up. "On the occasion of Susannah and Dave's tenth anniversary, I wrote a poem for them, 'Sonnet #10,' and I read it at the party. It was mostly a lighthearted thing, with allusions that no one would understand now. But I thought the last couple of lines might be appropriate for this occasion, with a minor modification:

Her friends know, when life's fair forms become a little fady,

The next-best thing to life eternal is a long alliance with a lovely lady.

We've all enjoyed a long alliance with you, Susannah. Happy birthday!"

Susannah was unable to speak, but she smiled through her tears.

Alex moved behind Susannah's chair and said, "Let's get this lovely lady a glass of champagne and some cake, shall we?"

Agreement and applause followed them to the dining room. The cake was shaped like two packages, a smaller one set askew on top of a larger one, trimmed with frosting ribbons. The top layer was lemon, the bottom chocolate. Susannah cut a ceremonial piece and turned the knife over to Sylvianne.

Susannah was enjoying her champagne and briefly unattended when her stepson Derek came and sat down close to her. "Susannah, not every man is lucky enough to have *two* great sets of parents. You know how much it meant to me to have you and Will in my life after my parents died—and ever since. I love you, and my family loves you." He gave her a big hug.

"Your father wanted the relationship so much, Derek. It was a wonderful part of his life—and mine too. I was so happy for you both when you first got together. And I so much enjoyed watching you two bonding over your absolutely wretched bowling."

He laughed, reminding her of Will. "Yeah, those were pretty funny times, all right."

All too soon the guests were leaving and the last hugs had been given. Her grandsons and Azime were puttering around, gathering up plates and wineglasses from around the house and helping with the dishes. Susannah sat in the breakfast nook, half hearing their conversation. She smiled to herself, remembering sitting here with Peter after the waltz ball, drinking wine and listening to golden oldies.

....

In the living room, Sylvianne and Alex were conferring quietly as they gathered crumpled napkins and dirty dishes. "I think she did really well, don't you, Alex?" Sylvianne asked her husband.

"Yes, she did really well," he said. "But there were a few times when I felt her missing Will so much I was afraid she might break down."

"I felt it too. It reminded me of his memorial service. She seems like such a strong person, and she is in many ways, but I wasn't at all sure she'd get through that service and the wake without collapsing." They returned to the kitchen with their trays of party refuse.

Drew scooted into the breakfast nook next to Susannah. "Paul told me I was supposed to tell you my favorite Grams stories, so I've been thinking about my top picks," he said.

"Oh, good," she said. "I've been looking forward to this."

"I have to start with the story-reading. How many times did you read *Goodnight Moon* and *Kerry the Fire-Engine Dog* to me and Paul? I'll bet you logged thousands of hours reading to us. Then there was playdough. I liked the kind that you made yourself, not the store-bought kind. It smelled like maraschino cherries. I spent a lot of time rolling it out on this very table and cutting out playdough cookies." He made a motion of using a rolling pin.

"And I have to mention Will—he sort of counts as a Grams story because you married him and brought him into our family. I had the best conversations with you and Will when I was a teenager, especially about spiritual things like meditation and the meaning of life. What a gift to have you two—really well-informed but not dogmatic." He kissed her on the cheek. "How's that for a start?"

She gave him a great big smile through her tears.

Alex helped his mother into her coat and took the wheelchair out to the car. Susannah gave each person in the kitchen a big hug. "I love you," she called as she went out the door, followed by Azime.

....

Susannah didn't think of the place she lived as "home." She referred to it as home for convenience. But she really thought of it as a comfortable way station. On the trip back to her way station, Susannah reflected on the party. It wasn't bittersweet, it was sad-sweet. She grieved for her lost loved ones; she missed them, especially Will.

They'd had twenty-three years together when he died two years earlier. Neither of them was afraid of death, and they had talked often about what it meant, what it was about. But she had not been prepared for the shock of his not being there—not seeing him across the table each morning, not having him call her on her sloppy thinking, not putting his arm around her on walks. She wept silently in the backseat, bereft of her most dearly beloved, while Alex and Azime chatted in the front seat.

It was about five o'clock when Alex parked in front of her place and helped her to the door. "You already know this," he said, holding her hands and looking into your eyes," but I want to say it again—you're the world's best mom. Happy birthday!" He gave her a big hug, then waved and called "Love you!" from the car.

More tears. "I think I'll have a little rest," she told Azime. As she took off her shoes, she noticed that along with Will's wedding ring she was still wearing her engagement ring from Dave. She had forgotten to give it back to Sylvianne.

Susannah rummaged through the back of her closet until she found what she was looking for—her long black evening coat. It was more than twenty-five years old now. Though it wasn't voluminous like a cape, it had deep sleeves and a big cowl collar that served as a hood. She thought of it as a cloak—it felt operatic somehow.

Susannah smiled to herself, full of memories. Then she wrapped her cloak about her and lay down to pleasant dreams.

More Susannah Stories

Would you like to hear more stories involving Susannah and Will? My next novel is about Susannah's grandsons and her relationship with them as they come of age. For more information, visit my website: diannshope.com.

Do What Matters

What if your good friend is killed in a car accident that breaks your arm and leg and seriously messes up your face? What if, when you've finally recovered and are leading a big outdoor education program, you find your dad trying to get a drunken chaperone into her tent?

What if a classmate gets drawn into prostitution and in trying to rescue her you get assaulted by her would-be pimp, injuring your hand and jeopardizing your jazz career? What if your girlfriend, Elektra, a fragile dynamo whose family is still suffering from the death of Elektra's younger sister several years earlier, has a bipolar "meltdown" and breaks up with you?

Paul and Drew Emory, a senior and a junior in high school, have a lot to sort out. They have to decide what matters, what's the right thing to do, who they want to be. They have big questions and tough situations to navigate through, even though their classmates think they've got it all–looks, smarts, talent and hot girlfriends.

About the Author

We've lived in Seattle forty-eight years, having moved here shortly after we married. We have pears, raspberries, blueberries and grapes in addition to the usual flora of an urban lot. My husband is a marine surveyor; when he's not surveying, he tends the house and garden and makes grape juice and wine. I make a lot of jam. We're lucky to have our two sons living in Seattle with their families–they eat up a lot of jam. We've traveled in Romania, France, Ireland, Greece and Scotland. And we've been active in supporting Waldorf Education. My degrees are in International Relations, received from Lewis and Clark College in Portland, Oregon, and the University of Denver.